THE B&USINESS DOCTOR

HOW TO TURN
YOUR HEADACHE BUSINESS
INTO A DEBT-FREE
MONEY MACHINE

Arnold S. Goldstein, Ph.D.

GARRETT PUBLISHING, INC.

The Business Doctor
By Arnold S. Goldstein, J.D., LL.M., Ph.D.

Garrett Publishing, Inc.
384 S. Military Trail
Deerfield Beach, FL 33442
Telephone: (305) 480-8543
Facsimile: (305) 698-0057

@ Garrett Publishing, Inc., 1994

This publication is designed to provide accurate and authoritative information in regard to the subject matter covered. It is sold with the understanding that neither the publisher nor the author is engaged in rendering legal, accounting or other professional service. If legal advice or other expert assistance is required, the services of a competent professional should be sought. *From a Declaration of Principles jointly adopted by a committee of the American Bar Association and a committee of publishers.*

Library of Congress Cataloging-in-Publication Data

Goldstein, Arnold S.
        The business doctor: How to turn your headache business into a debt-free money machine! / Arnold S. Goldstein.
        p. cm.
        Includes bibliographical reference and index.
        ISBN 1-880539-25-X : $19.95
        1. Corporate turnarounds--Management.   I. Title.
HD58.8.G626 1994
658.4'063--dc20
                                                        94-14619
                                                        CIP

Printed in the United States of America
10 9 8 7 6 5 4 3 2 1

To my many clients – struggling
entrepreneurs all – who
have taught me that
determination and perseverance
are the true ingredients
for success.

Author's Note…

To preserve confidentiality
and privacy, the names and
locations of individuals and
companies in the cases
portrayed in this book
have been changed.

ABOUT THE AUTHOR

Dr. Arnold S. Goldstein has helped more than 1000 failing companies avoid bankruptcy and is a nationally recognized expert in corporate debt restructuring and asset protection. He is president of the Garrett Group, a national consulting firm for financially troubled companies located in Deerfield Beach, Florida. A partner in the Florida and Massachusetts law firm of Goldstein and Randall, he also is professor *emeritus* at Boston's Northeastern University.

Dr. Arnold S. Goldstein

Dr. Goldstein is a graduate of Northeastern University (B.S. 1961) and Suffolk University (M.B.A. 1966 and LL.M. 1975). He received his law degree from the New England School of Law (J.D. 1964) and a doctorate from Northeastern University (Ph.D. in business and economic policy 1990). He is a member of the Massachusetts and Federal Bar and various professional, academic and civic organizations.

A prolific writer on the subject, Dr. Goldstein has written more than 60 books on insolvency law, business and finance. His titles include: *The Basic Book of Business Agreements, Asset Protection Secrets, Corporate Comeback, How to Save Your Business, 30 Days to a Debt-Free Business, Turnaround Strategies, Commercial Transactions Deskbook, How to Settle with the IRS for Pennies on the Dollar* and *The Small Business Legal Advisor.*

He also has been featured in numerous business and trade journals including: *INC, CFO, Business Week, Entrepreneur, Income, Bottom Line, Success, Forbes,* and *Fortune.*

Dr. Goldstein has appeared on hundreds of radio and TV talk shows. A popular speaker on turnaround strategies and related topics, Dr. Goldstein teaches these subjects at several universities and at his "Business Doctor" seminars.

Dr. Goldstein provides turnaround management, debt reduction and asset protection services to companies and individuals nationwide. He enjoys hearing from his readers so that their experiences can benefit his clients and future readers.

TABLE OF CONTENTS

How This Book Will Help You IX

1 Making That One Big Decision 1

2 Why Good Companies Go Bad..19

3 Who's In Trouble? 37

4 Wake Up The Survivor In You..49

5 SOS: White Knights And The Turnaround Team 59

6 Designing Your Turnaround 77

7 CAT-Scanning Your Business..91

8 26 Ways To Find Quick Cash 105

9 How To Jumpstart Your Employees And Customers.................125

10 How To Turn Your Business Into A Creditor-Proof Fortress......139

11 Workouts And Cramdowns: Tackling Your Problem Loans 155

12 How To Settle With Creditors For Pennies On The Dollar 175

13 Bewitched, Bothered And Bewildered About Bankruptcy?........195

14 Dump-Buybacks: The Fast Track To A Debt-Free Business.......211

15 Making Your Money Machine..225

16 Secrets Of Second-Chance Financing..239

17 On Your Way 253

18 Pssst! Wanna Buy A Business?..265

19 How To Bail Out For A Super-Soft Landing...............................281

Glossary 295

Sources And Resources..299

Index 301

HOW THIS BOOK WILL HELP YOU

Is your business.....

- losing money?
- up to its neck in bills?
- giving you headaches?

If you found yourself nodding yes, then like millions of other business owners you are finally discovering that staying in business is far tougher than getting into business.

The signs of quiet desperation are everywhere. While many struggling entrepreneurs overcome their problems, survive and eventually prosper, too many others fail. In their wake, they leave vanished hopes, lost investments, destroyed aspirations and a heap of unpaid creditors.

Perhaps the real tragedy is that so many of these failed companies could have been saved had their owners applied even a few of the many survival secrets I reveal in this book.

Unless you know these survival strategies, you too may fail. That's why I wrote *The Business Doctor.*

If your business is on the fast track to failure, this book is for you! Don't fail because you don't know essential success strategies. You'll find here the precise, proven and practical ways to rescue your company from the clutches of bankruptcy, the very same survival strategies I have successfully used to help rescue more than 1,000 financially troubled companies during my 30 years as an insolvency lawyer and turnaround consultant. So this book is not based on theory. It is based on proven business-saving strategies that can work for any kind of enterprise, regardless of the situation.

Can these survival strategies work for you? Absolutely. But you must keep three points in mind!

First, salvaging your business will take plenty of hard work, luck, pluck and a bushel basket of determination. There's no quick fix. I don't insult your intelligence by offering quick, easy and simplistic solutions.

Second, no business is beyond redemption. You may believe your business can no longer be saved, but don't give up! I've saved more than my share of businesses about to be auctioned by the bankruptcy court. Your business isn't dead until you bury it. Even then, *The Business Doctor* can show you many ways to capitalize on a dead business.

Third, keep an open mind. You'll see unorthodox strategies not found in other books. I know. I have read every pablum-filled book on the subject of turnarounds. What you need now are real-world tactics. And that's what I intend to give you – brass knuckles and all!

BUCKLE UP YOUR SEAT BELT

What you are now reading will give you all the tools you will need to:

- Decide where you want to go with your business – and your life!

- Uncover whether your business is in trouble – and how much.

- Overcome your cash crunch – quickly and forever!

- Design a surefire blueprint for building big profits.

- End creditor problems for pennies on the dollar, without bankruptcy or borrowing.

- Avoid Chapter 11 and survive if you must file for reorganization.

- Sell your sick business for top dollar.

- Protect yourself and your personal assets from business liabilities ...and much more!

Together, we'll tear your business apart and put it back together again.

I'll guide you through each critical step for fixing your broken business: Cash management, internal controls, personnel, marketing, pricing and selling. We'll even play some head games. Head games? Absolutely. There's an emotional side to business trouble. If you can't think straight, you can't make those all–important decisions or fight as hard as you must to save your business.

Right now you may be consumed with stress, fear and even panic. You may question your ability to save your business. You're afraid of defeat, afraid to lose your paycheck, and afraid you'll lose the family home and your personal assets.

You also are tired from too many lawsuits, too many unpaid suppliers and too many bounced payroll checks. You're frustrated by endlessly operating in a twilight world of no cash, no credit, dwindling sales and mounting bills. You don't know where to go, where you want to go or how to get there. Plain and simple, you hurt. Sure, you hate to go to work in the morning. I know the feeling. I've been there with my own entrepreneurial misadventures. When things go really wrong, it makes you numb, even unwilling to continue the fight.

My goal is not simply to give you business strategies, but to help you through this nerve-wracking maze. Once you see your problems more clearly, with a fresh, positive outlook, you'll bail out your business with new determination and purpose. Make a game of it, and you'll even have some fun doing it!

The Business Doctor won't merely explain turnaround strategies – it will show you these strategies in action. Example after example will illustrate how others, with problems very much like your own, reversed course and turned their headache business into a debt-free money machine.

Now here's what you must do to get maximum value from *The Business Doctor*. As you relive the experiences cited in this book, keep your own business in mind. Imagine yourself in the middle of each situation. Anticipate each action, each development, each outcome. Ask yourself whether some or all of these strategies can work for you, or what modified approaches or alternatives would be better.

By discovering possible solutions to individual problems, you will begin to see the big picture and how to piece together a total turnaround plan. You'll see how to tackle difficult problems and convert those problems into your own unique business-building opportunities. You'll discover how to uncover and exploit your untapped resources and achieve your own peak performance.

You will learn all this and more. But I repeat, it will be no easy task. At best, *The Business Doctor* can do only half the job. While I prescribe to the ailing firm the strategies and every trick of the trade I have learned from three decades as a "Business Doctor," you must take the medicine and apply the therapy.

Flip through the book and you'll see that much of what you're about to learn is truly common sense. They're the ideas that, once pointed out, cause you to slap yourself on the head and say, "Of course," or, "I should have known that." In fact, many of these ideas are so simple and obvious that you'll snicker, "I know that. Everyone know's that!"

But they don't.

And even if some of these strategies seem basic, don't underestimate their worth. They have helped save thousands of failing companies. What I provide in this book is the essence of what works when you're in trouble.

THE BOOK EVERY BUSINESS OWNER MUST READ

No matter what size or type business you own or operate, whether you are a struggling retailer, wholesaler, manufacturer, service business operator or restaurateur, this book is for you.

It's for you whether your business is big or small, old and tired or young with growing pains.

You'll want to read *The Business Doctor* whether your business has just begun its downturn or is now deep in the throes of bankruptcy.

You'll want to read it if you are just starting out in business – or even planning a business – because I give you the smart ways to fortify yourself against future problems.

Whoever you are, whatever the nature of your business, regardless of your troubles, the first thing you must understand is that survival principles are universal to every business!

Remember this always, because the moment you lose sight of it, you'll think your business and its troubles are different, and that the advice I give you doesn't apply.

Rest assured. It does.

So sit back, relax, keep an open mind and discover the simple yet powerful and proven ways to turn your headache business into a debt-free money machine.

Arnold S. Goldstein, Ph.D.

1

MAKING THAT
ONE BIG DECISION

During the past thirty years, more than 1,000 owners of struggling or failing businesses have sat across the desk from me. They ran small retail shops and mid-sized manufacturing plants, gas stations and bowling alleys, software firms and employment agencies. One owned a zoo, another a small commuter airline and yet another a string of massage parlors.

They all told essentially the same story: Too many bills, too little cash, too heavy losses and too few ideas on how to straighten out their mess.

But only later in my career as an insolvency lawyer and turnaround consultant did I begin to realize that my role was not to rescue the sick business. My role was to rescue the owner who happened to be caught up in a financially troubled business. Corporations didn't walk through my office door; people did. These people and their businesses were two very different things. Their interests did not always coincide.

What is best for you is what is important. That may mean saving your business. Then again, it may not.

That's what this chapter is all about. You cannot simply assume you should save your business, any more than you should too hastily decide to sell or shutter it. Your journey begins with you, your objectives, your desires, your capacities.

FIND YOUR TRUE GOALS

If I asked you what you want to do with your problem business, like most owners, you'd probably tell me you want to make it the debt-free profit-maker you've always known it could be.

But would that be an honest answer?

Are these your true goals and objectives? Think carefully. Think objectively. You may find your real objectives are quite unlike what you first thought. You may discover your objectives are best achieved by not saving your business.

Ask Mike, a spunky young guy who hired me to save his small electrical contracting firm which was barely surviving in the hills of North Carolina. Yes, the business gave Mike a healthy income, but if you listened to Mike carefully, you realized he only wanted to save his business to protect his income. That was a darn good reason for saving his business, until a California electronics firm offered Mike twice the salary he could earn from his own struggling company. Suddenly, Mike no longer needed his own business to earn the paycheck he wanted and needed. Does your business only represent a paycheck?

When, after a lengthy consultation, I asked the Claflin brothers why they wanted to save their retail hardware chain, they sputtered, "Because we're stuck on a $200,000 note to the bank. And we'll personally have to pay the bank if our business goes bust." Finally, we were getting somewhere. Listen to the Claflins. What did their business mean to them aside from a troublesome bank note?

Because they were candid, I could now focus on their one big concern. I channeled every last dollar of cash flow to the bank and retired the worrisome note. The Claflins then happily abandoned their business to their creditors.

Is avoiding personal liability for business debts your true reason for staying with your business?

Ann, a novice entrepreneur, sobbed a different tune. "I can't afford to lose the $50,000 I invested in my sinking cosmetic distributorship."

Ann didn't care a hoot about her business; she worried only about the $50,000 she wanted me to save for her. I searched for a few weeks and finally found a competitor anxious to pick up Ann's valuable retail accounts. My deal gave them Ann's inventory at a bargain price. They in turn paid Ann $75,000 for an agreement not to compete with their business. Not only did Ann have her investment back, but she also had a $25,000 profit to boot. You should have seen the smile on her face!

I didn't have to save Ann's business to achieve her one important goal - recovering her investment. Unfortunately, Ann's creditors lost most of the $120,000 that was due them, but Ann had her $75,000 safely and legally tucked in her pocket.

Do you only want to recover your investment? If so, why go through the hassles of trying to rehabilitate your business? There are more direct ways to achieve your goals.

Greg, another confused chap, figured he was over the hill at 52.

Desperately, he tried to save his long-established but failing soft-drink bottling plant in New Jersey. I instinctively knew the business was Greg's security blanket; it had supported his family his entire life, and it was the only business Greg knew.

I was confident I could save Greg's business, but instead I urged Greg to sell to a conglomerate willing to sign Greg to a five-year employment contract at twice the salary he could make as his own boss.

Security: Does it handcuff you to your business?

Money: It's hardly the only reason for saving a business. You may be the type who just can't admit defeat. Saving your business saves your ego.

Paul personifies a great many people who don't easily accept failure. After all, how could he hold his head high at the Rotary Club or Knights of Columbus and symbolize success as president of the local Chamber of Commerce if his debt-ridden appliance store was mired in bankruptcy? How could Paul proudly hobnob at the country club or golf on par with his hugely successful cronies?

Disgrace. Outcast. Failure. Bankrupt! The words haunted Paul. He could not allow his appliance store to fail. So instead, Paul arranged for Mort's Appliance Store to fail.

Mort? Yes, good old Mort, conveniently plucked from the local unemployment office. Mort was overjoyed to pocket $2,000 to "buy" Paul's appliance store. Only two months after Mort hung a bright, new sign announcing his proud ownership of Paul's Appliances, his business went bust.

Paul still cackles to his never-the-wiser friends, "I spent eight years building a healthy, thriving business, and in two short months this jerk Mort ruins it. Some people just don't belong in business."

How true! So what are your true goals and priorities?

- Income?

- Security?

- Saving your investment?

- Avoiding personal liability?

- Ego?

And ask yourself again: Do you really want to save your business?

Why? Which goals are most important to you? How can you otherwise satisfy those goals?

You begin by knowing what you really want. You may have several conflicting goals. You can seldom fully satisfy several goals so you must then prioritize. To do this, you must understand the tradeoffs that will come from achieving some goals and not others.

For example, if you want to save and rebuild your business, you must reinvest in the business every penny it earns. If you want to pay personally guaranteed debts, your cash must go to those creditors. Do you want to recover your investment? You must then legally take from the business whatever cash you can.

Only when you know where you want to go can you set the route. And your path is always right, if it leads you to your true destination.

KEEP YOUR BUSINESS OR LET GO?

How do you know if your business is really for you? You aren't doing yourself a favor by walking away from your business because you let your problems beat you. On the other hand, you may do yourself an even greater disservice by staying with a business you should walk away from. You then have wasted your most precious resources, your own time and talent.

Of course, no one can tell you whether a business is right for you. Only you can decide this. But I can tell you that a business is not for you unless you can:

- **Enjoy** the business.
- **Manage** the business.
- **Earn** what you are worth from the business.

Can you enjoy the business?

A chief reason for business failure is not managerial incompetence but managerial disinterest. Owners often don't perform well because they can't develop the enthusiasm their business needs.

Dennis and his near-defunct drycleaning plant is a case in point. I met Dennis at a social affair. Downing his third highball, he told me his tale of woe. It was a drycleaning plant with the same old problems: Too many creditors and too little cash. Dennis turned his business problems over to me, but I soon discovered his business wasn't the real problem. It was Dennis. Dennis loved computer programming, not drycleaning. I'd talk creditors, and Dennis would talk computer technology.

In our three meetings together, we spent fifteen minutes talking about Dennis's business problems and six hours discussing computers. Dennis just didn't belong in a drycleaning plant. So we sold his business, paid his creditors and gave Dennis the few extra dollars to start a software development firm. Dennis is still struggling, but he'll eventually make it. Smiling entrepreneurs always do. Success requires enthusiasm!

It's foolish to try to save a business you'll never enjoy. It's a tragedy when people wallow in a business they were never cut out for.

Just as people choose the wrong career, they also choose the wrong business. But when they perform poorly on their job, they only get fired. When they perform poorly for their business, they fail.

It's so easy to end up in the wrong business. Dennis ended up in the drycleaning business because it was his father's business, and Dennis had always worked in it as a kid. But Dennis isn't his father. What was right for the father wasn't necessarily right for Dennis. Still, parents too often force their kids into the family business, and kids without strong career goals go along with it. Too few ask whether it is their right career.

Seductive, high-glamour businesses attract novice entrepreneurs like honey attracts bees. Pat, the mechanic that fixed my car, sold his garage to buy a business-brokerage franchise. He despised every minute of it and couldn't wait to get back to his first love, fixing cars. Why then did he give it up to sell businesses?

"Because I was tired of dirty hands and greasy clothes. I wanted a more professional career, where I could wear a nice suit and sit behind a big desk," Pat confessed. Today, Pat's back in the garage business, with dirty hands, greasy clothes, and a very big smile!

I've been in many businesses. Some I thought I'd enjoy and learned to dislike, while others I enjoyed more than I thought I would.

One misadventure of mine was a movie theater. I've been a movie fanatic since I can remember, I can even tell you who won the Academy Awards in 1956! So when I had a few chips to spare and another adventure to conquer, it was only logical that a movie theater would catch my eye. That's when I learned you don't know a business until you're in it. While I thought I'd party with movie stars, I soon discovered it was a headache business. I spent my days hassling film distributors, chasing rowdy kids and working weekends. It cost me $30,000 to find out that you must look before you leap.

Mismatches between entrepreneurs and their businesses doom many a company. Every aspect of a business adds or detracts from your enjoyment. The type of business and nature of the work are only two factors to consider. But, if you are inflexible, even a slight variation from what you are comfortable with can throw you off balance and make you a fish out of water.

For example, a manager of a high-class steak house reasons he can enjoy operating any type of restaurant. But throw him into a pizza parlor and you may as well put him into another business, if not another planet. On the other extreme, some entrepreneurs can happily adapt to a wide range of opportunities inside or outside a particular field. You must discover this about yourself as well.

The structure of the firm is another factor. For instance, countless people hunt for a franchise, but few consider the control they must surrender. A franchise can make a free-wheeling entrepreneur's life miserable, or a less-secure entrepreneur happy for the opportunity to abdicate decision-making to the franchisor. The same can be said about partnerships.

Nor can you overlook business hours or travel demands. Frequently, the opportunity to travel is an attraction when travel is a novelty. But the novelty soon wears off, as many people discover. Spending half your life away from your family can quickly chill enthusiasm.

How about you? Do you really enjoy your business? For the moment, overlook your problems. Pretend your business is a healthy, stable enterprise — the business you hoped it would be. Would it then give you long-term satisfaction, or would you find more fulfillment in a different business or career?

Can you manage your business?

If your poor management contributed to your present business problems, why do you think you can run your business more profitably in the future?

What's that I hear? It wasn't your poor management?

Excuses, excuses. Everyone has an excuse.

I can hear the stories now.

"You can't make a buck with nursing homes. They're over- regulated."

"Variety stores? Dead as yesterday's news. The big boys grab all the business."

"Book stores are all in tough shape. Between chain-store discounting and publishers cutting margins, you can't even make a living."

Name the business. It doesn't matter what it is, when it goes bad, it's the fault of the business. Sit in my office for one day, and see all the "lousy" businesses.

Not everyone blames it on the business. Some are masochists. Everything's their fault. They can do nothing right. Sometimes I wonder whether they sleep on a bed of nails for kicks.

But I remain the poor listener because I know there's no such thing as a bad business or bad management. There is only management that's wrong for the business. These owners simply failed to measure their own management mentality. Their businesses demanded management skills they couldn't or didn't provide. Not all owners see it that way.

In the large corporation, management becomes the sacrificial lamb when trouble arises. The small-enterprise owner is, in contrast, the fixed and unmovable object. The small business must change to accommodate the owner's limitations.

Some examples?

Marty, a fine chap who opened a high-fashion jewelry outlet in my town, didn't invent the word inept, but he did give it added meaning. What a sub-zero management mentality! One look at his jewelry store and you'd agree. Everything was wrong: Out of stock on his best sellers, overloads on the dead merchandise, overdue bills spread all over his desk and two overpaid employees playing poker in the stockroom. But Marty was happy. He loved selling jewelry. Occasionally, he even sold some.

Marty knew what he wanted: A profitable, debt-free jewelry store. Could I give Marty a debt-free business? Hardly a challenge! Could Marty make it profitable? Mission impossible. Why fight to make his business healthy when Marty didn't have the management savvy to keep it off the sick list?

I saw only two possible solutions for Marty: Hire someone who could manage, or put Marty into a business he could handle.

I chose the latter. Marty is still in business selling jewelry as the operator of a concession jewelry department in a giant discount store. Marty buys all his inventory from one jewelry manufacturer, who controls his merchandising. The discount store takes care of most of his paperwork. Marty only has to sell jewelry. That's what Marty does best!

Bill, a young Connecticut entrepreneur, has considerably more managerial talent, but still couldn't quite measure up to the demands of his fast-growing candy business. Bill started his small candy-manufacturing business in the basement of his home. At first, he sold only to local gift shops.

The following year, Bill opened a retail store of his own and was able to open two more within the next two years. A few years later he had eight stores humming along and a franchise network of fifteen stores featuring his delicious candy. Bill could see his business growing but couldn't see it was out of control because of faulty internal systems. Bill, a terrific candymaker and promoter, was in over his head in trying to operate his shaky empire.

As with Marty, I could either bring in people with the necessary management skills or shrink the business to what Bill could manage. The fast-growth potential of the business justified finding Bill a partner with top managerial ability. Today, Bill only owns 60 percent of the business, but what a business it is. It will gross more than $15 million this year!

Sometimes good management is only stifled management. The managerial talent needs a path to break out. That was Al, my closest pal and a bright young pharmacist who took over his father's humdrum corner drugstore. But the challenge wasn't there, and Al's interest quickly withered. I could see it happening.

The pharmacy was rapidly going downhill while Al busily flapped his entrepreneurial wings scouting other business opportunities. Fortunately, Medicare sparked Al's interest. Why not specialize in providing pharmaceuticals to nursing homes? The new Medicare law mandated strict standards on pharmacies providing drugs to nursing-home patients. Day and night, Al worked to build his nursing-home business.

Al's corner drugstore? It's long gone. In its place, Al has nursing home dispensaries throughout the country that gross more than $120 million a year! All it took was a slight twist to make his business exciting.

But usually the solution is to reduce the oversized operation to parallel the owner's more limited managerial ability. Typically, a strong manager will find his own expansion route, but at what point will he grow beyond his capabilities? Al was an exception. Most potential achievers find themselves landlocked in a business with limited potential. Then again, any business can be made more exciting when you are imaginative.

What management mentality does your business need? Plenty. And as the bankruptcy courts can tell you, entrepreneurs don't always use the right yardstick when they measure their management mentality. When you're nursing a sick business back to health, you have no margin for error.

It's not so much a matter of what the entrepreneur can manage, it's a matter of when he or she is ready to manage. It's timing and prior experience rather than capability that are usually the decisive factors.

"And while you're learning, you can be nickeled and dimed to death with 101 small but nevertheless fatal mistakes," adds Bill Portnoy, who confesses to making enough slip-ups in his embryonic Philadelphia restaurant to teach a course in mismanagement at the Harvard Business School.

Just as a business can look like fun to operate, it also can look easy to operate. Illusion on the first point means only less fun. Illusion on the second means failure. And few businesses are as easy to operate as they first appear.

Still, the naive optimists beat their drums and say, "What do you have to know about running a pinball arcade, shoe store or coffee shop?"

I don't know. I have never operated one of these businesses. But why don't you ask someone who has? Take your notebook along and be prepared for a long and hard education. Every business has its tricks.

It amazes me how many people have never worked in a business and know nothing about it, and yet, with a refreshing mixture of chutzpah, enthusiasm, and sheer optimism, throw their life's savings into the venture. What's more amazing is that some people actually make it. They're the fast learners. The slow learners inevitably find their way to my office.

So that brings us back to you. Can you do a good job, given another chance to make a go of your business? If you lack certain management strengths, how can you reshape your business to manage it more effectively? Or how can you gain the added skills you need? Could a partner or key employee make the difference?

Can you earn from your business?

Having fun with your business is only one important consideration. Money is another. If the business can't give you the living you need and deserve, then why stick with it?

Of course, nobody can predict how wealthy your business will make you 10 years from now. That depends on you as well as the business. It's now that counts. That's when the income mismatch (the income you need from the business versus what the business can give you) takes its toll. The answer demands a realistic look at your business!

An entrepreneur, for example, may leave a $40,000-a-year salaried position and start a bootstrap business that can only give him $15,000 a year for the first year or two. For some people, it's not a problem. For the people who need $40,000 a year to support a family, it's a $25,000 problem. Common sense? Perhaps. Yet wild optimists either overestimate what they can earn from their business or somehow think it is possible to live on less.

Rose-colored glasses can distort the short-term income potential of your business. Prepare a cash-flow statement that shows how much you can safely draw from the business. Check it with a jaundiced eye. Underestimate projected income by 20 percent and overestimate expenses by 10 percent. This will usually take you closer to reality.

And don't think you can defy the odds. Several years ago I helped two young partners project their cash flow and the salary they could take home from the tool rental shop they planned to open. Admittedly, a cash-flow statement is at best a "guesstimate" of a business's future performance, but even under the best of circumstances their business couldn't initially afford to pay each partner more than a $10,000-a-year salary.

But that's not how they figured it. Working backwards, they conveniently pumped up the projected sales to produce the bottom line and salaries they were looking for. It's an idiot's game.

Partnerships can produce an even greater strain. A single- owner business usually can juggle personal finances to subsidize what the business can pay. Seldom can two partners perform the same juggling act. The solution is usually a larger business or one partner buying out the other.

Many businesses, of course, are in trouble because the owner drained it for more than the business could afford. Ultimately, the creditors pay the price. If that's your story, the answer isn't to repeat the process. It's to make the business make more money, or take home less money, or get rid of the business and get into something that will give you the income you want.

There are plenty of reasons, aside from personal fulfillment and money, why your business may not be for you.

My neighbor realized that the stress from fighting to save his plumbing business would endanger his weak heart. So Mark closed his shop. Who can argue with wanting to live?

Maybe your business is ruining your marriage. Divorce and business failure often go hand in hand. Believe it or not, a good percentage of my clients with business troubles also suffer marital problems. Do marital problems interfere with the profitable management of a business, or does the tension, stress and lack of money from a failing business destroy the marriage? That's one for the marriage counselors.

But I do know that when you have problems both at home and at work, you can only try your best to separate the two and assess each situation on its own.

Letting go may simply come from being honest with yourself about what will give you the happiest future.

Just the other day, a near-bankrupt luggage manufacturer consulted me about liquidating his business. After glancing at his financials, I asked, "Jon, do you really want to close your business? I can probably make peace with your creditors and save it."

Jon paused for a moment and quietly confessed, "I thought about it, but the business doesn't really mean much to me. I can have more fun doing something else."

I had my answer. Jon wasn't reacting to his financial crisis; he just didn't give a darn about his business. He's now far happier at his old job as an interior decorator.

Some people desperately want their business to survive; others are thrilled to walk away. As I said before, there's no right or wrong answer. You must decide for yourself. Nobody can or should make this decision for you. And it will always be the right decision, if you have the right reasons.

CLEAR THE COBWEBS

To decide where you want to go objectively, you must think clearly. That's no easy task when your business is collapsing. I know that when my business went bad, my thoughts turned to driving a cab in Paris or farming in Montana. You too may want only a dark corner in which to lick your wounds.

Panic and confusion are normal when your business goes bad, but you'll get over your confused thinking more quickly if you learn how to clear your head so you can think straight.

First, avoid negative thinking. That only defeats your ability to think clearly and survive. Negative thinking spawns only emotional decisions, which are always irrational decisions.

Yes, I know what it's like to have creditors on your back, employees jumping ship, competitors sharpshooting your best accounts and customers dumping you in droves. I've been there myself, and I have held the frightened hands of more than 1,000 clients who also have been there.

Do I sound more like a novice psychiatrist than a battle- hardened lawyer? It's not surprising. Head games are what my business is all about. That's why my library includes psychology books as well as business and law books. From necessity, I've played amateur psychologist for years. It comes with the territory. Most turnaround pros do. We don't save businesses! We save people!

But unless you can clear the cobwebs, you'll only have negative, muddled thoughts about your business and your future.

- You won't see what your business could be, given the opportunity.

- You won't see what you've learned from your business experience, or how you can turn events into future success, whether in your present business or another.

- You may be discouraged from every again flapping your entrepreneurial wings. That would be the greatest tragedy of all.

But I know that wrestling with the troubled business is never fun. Throwing in the towel can be a mighty attractive mind-saving alternative. Months or even years of incredible pressure can make a quitter of even the most resolute optimist.

One of Florida's most successful shoe retailers, Carl Shapiro, will tell you, "My failing shoe stores caused me sleepless nights. It got to the point I couldn't stand to go near my business. Another day banging my head against the wall and I thought I'd go insane! When your emotional battery is drained, it's easy to say, 'Get me out.'"

Carl eventually clawed his way back to success. He now has several thriving shoe stores in the Ft. Lauderdale area, with two more on the way! How did Carl successfully change course and recharge his emotional battery? Follow his good advice:

1. Step back from your problems.

Take a short vacation to clear your head and give yourself a fresh start. Carl recalls one particularly stressful day when sixteen employee payroll checks bounced and he had no money for rent or merchandise. Carl nearly mailed his creditors the keys that afternoon. Luckily, he didn't. He instead pocketed the few remaining bucks from the cash register and escaped for a long weekend in New York. It was just the tonic Carl needed. He returned able to look at his situation with a fresh perspective so he could more intelligently and rationally tackle his problems.

Granted, life's important decisions are not always made under the best circumstances. Still, you are now trying to make an objective, critical career decision while neck-high in alligators and shell-shocked from fighting everything and everyone.

The army calls it combat fatigue. Rest and recreation is Uncle Sam's remedy. Make it yours. Get away from your business for awhile. Take a vacation from your problems. Your business will still be standing when you return.

2. Bandage your battered ego

Many people see their business problems as a personal defeat. Whether your problems were caused by managerial blunders or factors beyond your control, what difference does it make?

If factors beyond your control torpedoed your business, why should it shake your self-confidence? And if you blundered, so what?

Mistakes aren't defeats. They're only learning experiences. That's what managerial growing pains are all about. Besides, who doesn't make mistakes?

Ford had 400 bright MBAs from the top business schools give the long-defunct Edsel the green light. Talk about disaster! Pencils have erasers for good reason.

An inspirational pep talk? Sure! But it's therapeutic. Why wallow in self-doubt and slam the door on your entrepreneurial spirit, as almost happened to me once?

I don't forget the days when I was fresh out of college and a buddy and I sought our fortune by starting a discount drugstore chain. Foolishly, we expanded much too quickly from one store to 18. Failure? Well, I know our creditors never called us a stunning success. My drug chain went down the drain, and with it went my self-confidence, entrepreneurial spirit and more money than I can bear to think about. Even today I cringe.

What restored my self-confidence? A candid self-assessment. Grabbing a piece of paper, I commanded myself, "What did you do right and where did you mess up? No cheating!"

My scorecard wasn't bad when I saw my many accomplishments along with my few fatal missteps. It's important to see your failures. After all, you do want to learn. But it's equally important to see your strengths. You'll then see yourself in a different light. I have owned many other businesses since; some were huge successes, others were not. I seldom make the same mistakes — only new ones. We all do. It's part of the game.

Check your scorecard. Don't overplay your mistakes. Think of all you did right. It will work wonders for your self-confidence.

3. Look for the light at the end of the tunnel

You can think neither objectively nor positively when you see only problems, not solutions. When you don't know how your business can be saved, you doubt that it can be saved. You then feel frustrated and powerless. Carl, our now-successful shoe retailer, experienced that problem. I had to find solutions and shape a game plan for Carl before I could turn him into a frenzy of positive action. Big losses, depleted inventory, huge overdrafts and an expired lease with a very unfriendly landlord presented insurmountable problems to Carl. Even a chronic optimist like myself wondered if Carl's Shoes had a future!

Carl hardly tried to save his business and was convinced it couldn't be saved. But Carl was dead wrong. One week later, I found a major shoe manufacturer anxious to convert Carl's tired shoe store into a franchised factory shoe outlet. The bright light at the end of the dark tunnel beamed a $6-million-a-year victory for Carl's Factory Outlet Shoe Stores.

When people tell me their businesses can't be saved, I tell them to call Carl. He can convince anyone that no business is hopeless!

Listen to Carl's story. Keep an open mind. As you turn the pages, you'll find others who once shared your problems and found solutions. You, too, have solutions if you look for them!

Simply coming up with a game plan can do wonders for your state of mind. You will no longer feel like a rudderless ship. My clients usually spring to life when I map an action plan. At last they have a direction. They have a roadmap for going forward. They have very positive and specific steps to take. We may change our game plan a dozen times, but there is still forward movement rather than the helplessness that comes from standing still, not knowing where to go.

4. Probe the bottom of the pit

Do you cling stubbornly to your business because you fear the unknown? The world is a big, dark, scary place. Can you get a job? Who would hire you? Can you start over in another business? Where will you go? Where will you get your next paycheck?

It's part security and part measuring what you will lose by giving up your business. If that's your dilemma, then stand back and objectively explore the opportunities elsewhere. You can then better decide whether to give up your business.

Security is a big issue for people who have owned in their own business for many years. They don't know how they will fit into the employee world. That's why I encourage my clients to job shop even while trying to turn around their businesses. A few good job offers can give an enormous sense of security. As Greg found out once he left his soft-drink bottling plant to knock on a few doors, you may be worth considerably more to another employer than you every dreamed. After all, you now have years of experience running your own show.

TAKE ON A NEW ATTITUDE

How you see your future also will depend on your attitude. Dr. Erwin H. Schell, a highly respected lecturer on leadership, claims, "There is something more than abilities and competence that makes for accomplishment. This linkage factor catalyst is found in one word — attitude. When our attitude is right, our abilities reach a maximum of effectiveness and good results inevitably follow."

Nowhere can Dr. Schell's theory be more clearly seen than in a turnaround. Attitude does make a difference in a turnaround. Owners with the right attitude get good results because they expect good results. Right attitude enables you to see your problems. Right attitude makes you effective in winning cooperation from people.

The best way to check your own attitude is to compare yourself to some of the types I've known in my business.

Most commonly encountered is the "Ostrich." This plentiful species refuses to believe his business is on the fast track to failure and keeps his head buried in the sand until "Louie the Liquidator" padlocks his doors.

The Ostrich is completely oblivious to the danger signals until awakened by failure. By then, he has no nest left to save.

Even more frustrating is the Ostrich who knows he's in trouble but won't admit it. "Ignore it and it will go away!" he chants. Yes, the Ostrich is a mighty tough bird to save. Most only lay more eggs. Ostriches need a special diet of reality, but seldom swallow it.

Throughout the book, I bellow the message: "If you think you're in trouble, get help! Don't put it off. Don't be an Ostrich. It's the one sure way to fail."

Close cousin to the Ostrich in the "Confirmed Optimist." He also knows he's in big trouble, but hopes things will magically improve. "Wait until tomorrow. After all, tomorrow will bring a big sale, a great invention, or the demise of that nasty competitor." Tomorrow will indeed be a brighter day. For the Confirmed Optimist, success is always a day away.

I have no problem with optimism. In fact, optimism is a priceless commodity when your boat is sinking. The trick is to temper optimism with reality. Only then will you accept the fact that you must do something to straighten out your problems and can no longer hope for things to change by themselves. Healthy optimism makes you control events, ever confident you can succeed.

Unlike the Confirmed Optimist, the trademark of the "Perennial Pessimist" is gloom and doom. In his world, everything goes downhill, never uphill. The pessimist probably started his business expecting the worst. If his business can be saved, which he doubts, it will become worse still.

I don't find Perennial Pessimists hard to handle because I never waste time with them. Pessimists lack everything needed for success: Enthusiasm, imagination and hope!

This doesn't suggest that your problem business won't get you down. Wrestling with an unruly business delights few people. Nor does it mean you shouldn't be a hard-nosed pragmatist.

But if you just naturally see the clouds and never the lining, regardless of the situation, then you must take off the dark glasses.

There's no end to the characters who populate the business world. Ever popular is the "Nervous Nellie." This interesting breed can't handle stress. With emotions in high gear, they panic and run from their problems, or remain, only to suffer a nervous breakdown.

I don't ridicule the Nervous Nellie. We each have our own stress threshold. Sometimes the toughest people are least able to cope with their financial pressures. Usually their frail spouses become Marine commandos and successfully battle the business back to health. You never know who will be bravest in the trenches.

I often choose one spouse, partner or even key employee to spearhead the turnaround. It may not be the individual with the best management skills or most knowledge of the business. The ability to cope with pressure is the essential qualification.

Are you more like the "Dreamer," who hides in the clouds? You know the type. He can't be bothered with mundane business problems. And losing somebody else's money is not a big concern. The Dreamer sits busily inventing a better mousetrap and pondering grandiose schemes while the checkbook is a disaster.

Yes, a business needs a Dreamer and a doer who can handle the checkbook. If you're that Dreamer, find yourself a bottom-line manager for those important details that make your business tick.

You can bet the "Buck Passer" will never read this. He never asks the tough questions. He doesn't have to. Nothing is the Buck Passer's fault. He is victimized by everyone else. He is always right.

These birds need a large dose of humility, a feed bag filled with a shopping list of their blunders. Some eventually accept their fallibility, but most Buck Passers remain far happier pointing the finger. I walk away from these creatures. I know it will be my fault if their business goes down the drain.

My all-time favorite? The "Absolute Moralist." He wants to save his business and save his creditors. Tell him its not in the financial cards to do both and he'll quote you the Ten Commandments and Boy Scout Oath. Predictably, most Absolute Moralists lose both their business and even more money for their creditors!

I'm reminded of one holier-than-thou couple who consulted me about their failing San Bernandino food distributorship. I scanned their financials and estimated that it would be necessary to cut their debts from $2 million to about $600,000 as part of their rehabilitation. "What?" they screamed, "And not pay our creditors the other $1.4 million that we owe them?" Suddenly I felt like a leper. You guessed it. Rather than take my advice, they blundered along with their business until they went bankrupt. Their creditors, now owed $2.6 million, received a grand total of $150,000. What price virtue!

Speaking of honesty, we also have the "Pirate," who is anything but honest. His mindset is to rape, pillage and plunder the business and to heck with everyone who gets hurt in the process. Some pirates simply don't know the rules, so I closely guide them to stay on the right side of the line. Others are more than willing to break the law if it lines their pocket. If that's you, then why not rob a few banks instead? You'll make more money with less work and have less chance of getting caught. Could it be that the Absolute Moralist is only the Pirate in disguise?

Does all this sound like I have a jaded view of the human establishment? I hope not. People are people, warts and all. What's important is that you spot yourself in the crowd so you can develop that right attitude!

POSSIBILITY THINKING

Above all, you must marinate your decisionmaking in a large pot of optimism. This year about 600,000 new businesses will be formed. Three years from now, only a small percentage will still be in operation. Most of those that fail will have excuses (the economy, the competition, the government, etc.). The truth is, the rocky road of entrepreneurship breeds defeatism in too many people. And when you think you are beaten, you are beaten. But not until then.

You must believe you can save your business in order to do so. Don't fall into the trap of believing your business can't be saved. Yet untold businesses are collapsed every day by owners who can't see a future.

A business neck-high in trouble never seems to have a future. But as long as it's a business, it can be resuscitated. How healthy it can become is another question. You won't know the answer to this until you have started your business on its turnaround.

The transformation a business, any business, can go through is amazing. Take a peek into some of my files:

■ *A faltering $2-million-a-year Ohio lumberyard grew in eight years to gross $90 million a year from lumberyards located in five states. Its profits this year? $4.5 million.*

■ *A San Francisco ambulance service, pushed into bankruptcy in 1991 by a bank with mortgages on its fleet of ambulances, now has 24 ambulances profitably zooming the streets of Frisco. They went from a $600,000 loss in 1991 to a $2 million profit this year!*

■ *And then there is the Atlanta restaurant that came out of Chapter 11 in 1990 and quickly branched out to operate no* *fewer than 85 canteen trucks, producing a hefty $3-million-a-year profit for the owners of the once-defunct eatery.*

Which of these owners could possibly envision their ultimate success when they were in the depths of despair? Yet each, like yourself, had to assess their business's future when it seemed it had no future.

That's why I say you must never give up hope for your business as long as you know it can give you enjoyment and the income you need — and you can give the business the management it needs.

In business, beliefs become a self-fulfilling prophecy. Owners who think they can save their businesses usually succeed. Those who predict failure usually fail. It's not so much what your business is. It's what you think it can be.

You also must remember that you have a limited perception. You have probably not been involved in a turnaround before, and have never seen the startling revivals that I have seen time and time again. No matter how sick your business may be today, you never know what will happen tomorrow to make all the difference. You just have to believe!

The thrill of the turnaround is that it forces you to do so many creative, imaginative, even daring things to stay alive and turn your loser into a winner. This radical surgery can open the doors to incredible opportunities that stable, complacent businesses never reach for.

So my friend, if you think you have a business worth fighting for, roll up your sleeves. You'll only lose the fight when you give up hope and believe your business can't be saved!

☑CHECKPOINT

1. Do you really want to save your business? Why? Why not? Are you thinking objectively or are your decisions based on fear and worry?

2. Do you enjoy your business? Would you enjoy it if it were problem-free?

3. Can your business foreseeably give you the income you need?

4. Can you effectively manage the business? What can you do so it is properly managed?

5. Can you save your business? If not, how do you know?

2

WHY GOOD COMPANIES
GO BAD

To quote Aristotle: "It is possible to fail in many ways... while to succeed is possible in only one way." Aristotle is at least half right! Look at the many once-proud organizations that are either adrift in a sea of red ink or have vanished altogether. But why do so many businesses manage to plummet from heady success to spectacular failure? The undeniable answer is that every business carries within itself the seeds of failure.

Your company bears its own seeds for self-destruction. The challenge is to find and uproot them before they turn your business into failure!

Business, like apple pie and baseball, is a fundamental part of American life. And so is failing in business. This entrepreneurial heritage goes back to 1606, when shares of stock were sold for $62 in the Jamestown venture, the first permanent settlement in America. Within a decade, the young Jamestown colony was belly-up, leaving behind hordes of angry British investors, one Indian tribe reportedly still awaiting payment for corn and turkey, and a ragtag band of entrepreneurs.

This set the stage for American business – a stage since populated with countless other adventurers, rogues and just plain hard-working folks searching for a better life. Some find it, others don't. But, perhaps like yourself, all soon learn that enthusiasm, energy and euphoria alone won't steer them safely through the treacherous rapids of running a successful business.

Maybe you see failure as a lurking demon ready to grab others, but not you. Beware! The odds aren't with you! The grim reaper is alive and working overtime as the number of business failures peaks higher each year. Companies seemingly indestructible only a few short years ago now are failing with alarming regularity.

It is not whether a business will fail, but when. Eighty percent of all startups succumb within their first five years. Few companies survive beyond a few decades, and those that do are usually unrecognizable. Only two of the top 25 American industrial corporations operating in 1900 are still operating today.

So success and failure are distanced only by time – often a very brief time. Of the ten most profitable U.S. companies in 1983 (based on net worth, profitability and growth), three no longer exist, and four more are floundering after years of dismal earnings.

Corporate casualties abound in stunning numbers within certain industries. Most professional basketball leagues have gone belly-up. But hopes die hard; others are now being formed. More than 90 auto manufacturers failed before the three major automakers emerged victorious. We now are seeing the same shakeout in the computer field. Only a handful of the hundreds of computer companies founded in the late 1960s still survive today. A fresh bumper crop arises every year, only to predictably and quickly disappear like scathed wheat.

No industry is safe from the devastating statistics. Franchised businesses, once considered the safest entrepreneurial path, have had unprecedented casualties in recent years as many major franchise companies vanished. Surprising, too, is the swiftness with which healthy businesses are transformed into debt- ridden cripples.

The vagaries of the marketplace – or that one big disaster – are becoming more commonplace. A.H. Robins once was among the top ten pharmaceutical firms, until its Dalkon-Shield intrauterine contraceptive device spawned thousands of product liability claims, forcing Robins into Chapter 11 reorganization. Manville Corporation fell like Robins, but with asbestos claims. Robins and Manville show how one faulty product can quickly and unexpectedly fell even the strongest companies.

Texaco also shows the thin veneer between corporate success and failure. In 1986, Texaco was one of the world's wealthiest corporations, unconcerned with Pennzoil's nuisance claim that Texaco wrongfully interfered with Pennzoil's agreement to buy Getty Oil. Then, in moments, a feisty Texas moments handed Pennzoil a $10.5-billion victory. Texaco joined the once-proud companies that awake one day to find themselves in bankruptcy. Robins, Manville and Texaco shatter the myth of the indestructible large corporation. The biggies, too, have glass jaws. The fact is, every company has a glass jaw, whether a small business or a large corporation.

FAILURE IS ONLY ANOTHER DIRTY WORD

How can you discuss the failed company when "failure" defies definition? For example, your firm can be a managerial failure, a financial failure or a legal failure. Used interchangeably, these terms, have distinctively different meanings.

Your company may be a managerial failure long before it becomes a financial failure. And it can perpetually linger as a financial failure and never become a legal failure.

Managerial failures do not live up to their potential. The great myth is that management is successful if it turns a profit. How much profit seems unimportant. Conversely, we condemn unprofitable managers even when they side-stepped far greater losses due only to their skilled management. But is the true managerial failure the manager who earns a $1-million profit for a company that could easily have earned $5 million, or the manager who limits losses to $1 million for a company ordained to lose $5 million? The lesson: It is not enough for your business merely to be profitable. It must be the profitmaker it can be. Anything less is managerial failure.

Many companies, large and small, are managerial failures long before they become financial failures. They either lose money or earn so little that their stockholders would do no worse stuffing their investment under the mattress. This prompted Will Rogers to quip, "I'm more concerned about the return of my investment than I am the return on my investment." Stockholders who want something productive done so their money earns more, seek an objective too few managers can achieve. Will Rogers had a quip for this, too: "Executives who do not produce successful results hold on to their jobs only about five years. Those who produce results hang on about half a decade."

We only need to study today's businesses' earning records to spot the managerial failures that will become tomorrow's financial failures. Will your business be one of them?

For every firm that drowns in a sea of red ink, hundreds are merely doused. In 1992, nearly half of the nation's businesses lost money. These firms are striving to be average. Of the profitable firms, two-thirds earned less than what a secure savings account could earn. Only one corporation in seven performed better.

Larger corporations are hardly alone as managerial failures. Most family businesses shuffle along, handing less than a week's pay to their owners. But it's impossible to accurately measure the profitability of the smaller business, which represents two-thirds of the 15 million American companies. Their owners can so easily hide profits, that only they know whether they are making or losing money.

Managerial failure advances into financial failure when your business has chronic and serious losses or becomes insolvent with more liabilities than assets. Troubled companies usually suffer from unprofitability and insolvency, as continuing losses will weaken any organization.

Financial failure, as an indicator of the economic condition of a company, may overlap managerial and legal failure. Financial failure bridges the company that is sub-performing (managerial failure), and the company formally declared a legal failure through bankruptcy.

Legal failure, according to the Bankruptcy Code, occurs when a company's liabilities exceed its assets. Yet companies can operate for years with more debts than assets. They survive thanks to creditor leniency and patience. I have seen many "upside-down" companies eventually turn the corner, produce a profit and brighten their balance sheets, much to the relief of their patient creditors. But few debt-ridden firms survive without both creditor patience and rapidly improved profits.

A company also is a legal failure if it can't punctually pay its debts. Under this archaic test, most American companies are bankrupt. This standard is undoubtedly a throwback to an era when businesspeople paid their bills on time.

Because a business closes its doors doesn't necessarily mean it's a legal failure. Illness, retirement and other personal reasons force many closings. Even when a losing business is closed, it is not a legal failure if it fully pays its debts. And many companies that are financial failures endlessly linger without becoming legal failures. Others file Chapter 11 bankruptcy – an admission of legal failure – but emerge from bankruptcy with a new balance sheet and a new lease on life. No longer legal failures, they stay financial failures until they become profitable – or disappear.

Failure, then, is a relative term, one that exists in the abstract. Your company's performance can be measured against all other businesses, comparable companies within your industry, and its own potential and prior performance. How your company will measure depends on who is wielding the ruler.

UNRAVELING THE BIG MYSTERY

Did you ever wonder why some companies succeed while others with more resources or opportunities fail? The right answer can elude you for four big reasons:

1. Business failure usually has several causes.

Generally, no one problem is the sole culprit. You can't oversimplify the causes of failure or narrowly pinpoint the one problem, nor is there usually a simple solution or a quick fix. Suffering companies have many roots to their problem. Their successful turnaround needs multi-pronged solutions to resolve each problem.

2. The symptoms of failure cannot be distinguished from the causes.

Organizational failure is not unlike organic illness. The symptoms are not always easily distinguished from the disease. Tactical or managerial errors may be confused with the more fundamental weaknesses that precipitated them. Failure is then described and categorized as a clustering of symptoms, when in reality there are a number of underlying reasons.

3. The causes of failure relate to the nature of the firm.

Conglomerates seldom share the problems of simple and small companies. Hi-tech firms seldom face the threats encountered in stable industries. For example, hi-tech firms tend to encounter problems of ill-conceived products or faulty market innovations. Companies in stable industries, conversely, suffer from hardening of the arteries. Larger, highly diversified firms may lose control of their sprawling divisions. The causes of failure usually profile the failed firms.

4. The causes of failure can relate to corporate maturity.

Startup firms face problems unlike those of mature organizations. Many companies cannot easily move from one stage to another. And their problems also are different. The startup company is likely to fail because of a poor business concept, poor financial planning, undercapitalization or poor management. The mature organization typically has too much corporate flab and archaic management policies, leaving the company vulnerable to changes in the marketplace and more progressive and nimble competitors.

So there are no simplistic causes of corporate failure, any more than there are simplistic formulas for success. Organizations, however small, are complex. And what is a weakness for one company may be another's strength. Even Tom Peters was forced to admit in *In Search of Excellence* that "Managers in every field are re-thinking the tried and, as it turns out, not-so-true management principles that have so often served their institutions poorly." Perhaps the one unshakable principle for avoiding failure is to be true to those strategies that work best for your organization.

BEWARE THE NINE DEADLY BUSINESS KILLERS

Companies share common risks. They also share a common managerial snafu: Errors of omission (the failure to act when action is needed) and errors of commission (incorrect actions).

The mistakes even a well-run company can make are staggering. A superbly managed company may make fewer mistakes but fail because it lacks the resources or abilities to correct or overcome its mistakes. Such companies fail not because of their problems, but because they can't afford to solve their problems. Well-heeled companies overcome considerably more serious situations than do weak companies.

But with few exceptions, the failure of the company is the failure of management, a point with which most turnaround consultants agree. So does the Small Business Administration, which estimates nine out of ten business bankruptcies result from poor management.

You may not see your troubles that way. Most struggling business owners blame external factors that deflect blame away from their own bad management. More comfortable is the illusion that they have fallen victim to circumstances beyond their control.

At a business turnaround seminar I conducted at a Boston university, I asked the 80 participants to cite the one big cause of their business problems:

- Forty-one blamed the economy.

- Thirteen held competitors (particularly foreign competitors) responsible.

- Six complained about undercapitalization.

- Eight admitted they had no idea why they were in trouble.

- Only twelve admitted faults with their own management.

While the potential pitfalls are staggering, having handled 1,000 troubled companies, I pinpoint these "Nine Deadly Business Killers" as the death blow to most failed enterprises:

Business Killer #1

FAILURE TO CHANGE

In today's fast-changing world, companies, indeed entire industries, quickly become vulnerable. These changes are not the many minor shifts and advances of everyday business life, but the dramatic and often unexpected events that can strike at the core of your business. Unadaptive businesses then fail.

Government regulations, court decisions, trade tariffs, raw material shortages and changes in technology are only a few of the devastating changes that can tumble even the strongest company.

Events can occur with such suddenness and severity that they could be neither predicted nor protected against. Still, the inability to foresee most events is its own form of mismanagement.

For the adaptive organization, change creates opportunity. Those who stagnate fall victim to competitive, technological, market or economic changes.

Consider the competitive changes your organization faces right now. Competition is in constant flux, whether it's a low-cost foreign producer, a new competitor on the next block or a new spark of an idea within an existing competitor.

I see many troubled firms that stagnated while young upstart companies swept away their markets with new, innovative products, attractive services, or perhaps, just a fresh and more aggressive way of doing business. These troubled firms never had their ear to the ground, and they took their customers for granted. No longer leaders, they became followers, companies forced to react. Companies on the cutting edge of their field may have problems, but it's seldom the sting of a competitor puncturing their soft underbelly. Retail-giant Sears is watching its retail leadership slip away to more aggressive, dynamic and innovative retailers – such as the deep discounters, specialty stores and warehouse clubs that each nibble away a piece of Sears' broad customer base. That's a nasty sting!

Alvin Toffler's best-selling book *Future Shock* warned us of the effect of technological change. The world, as Toffler suggests, is indeed changing at a breakneck pace; too many companies simply cannot keep in step.

While fast-paced technologies spawn hundreds of new industries, they derail others unable to adapt to turbulent change. Consider computers: This fast-moving industry loses 20,000 shakeout companies a year. "New computer companies fasten their signs with Velcro," is now the standing joke in Silicon Valley.

But traditionally stable industries also fall victim to new- age technologies. The printing industry is being squeezed by desktop publishing and larger plants with more efficient, technologically advanced equipment. American automakers, painfully pinched by foreign competition, will fall even further behind their overseas competitors that are a decade ahead in robotic automation. The list of pipe-stack industries futilely straining to compete in the 1990s with the techniques of the 1950s is endless.

Companies victimized by technological change are victims of their own myopia. These companies may see the approaching change but neglect to reinvest in their own future, losing to cutting-edge companies by default.

Companies lose touch with their changing markets. The need for market sensitivity varies greatly among industries. The garment industry quickly dooms those firms lacking a strong market sense. Annually, hundreds of Seventh-Avenue fashion houses bet their bankroll on America's ever-changing perception of style. Many lose the bet!

Companies in other industries serve a less-fickle consumer, but must still adapt to subtle market changes. The marketplace does change for every company as lifestyle, demographics, social attitudes and consumer preferences change. Survivors change with it. Elementary? Sure. Yet even the largest and most sophisticated companies ignore this lesson. American automakers, slow to spot changing preferences in autos, lost much of their domestic market to the more responsive importers. Fast-growth companies, such as Reebok, achieved phenomenal success because they were guided by an exquisite market sense. But for every Reebok in sync with its market, two others tune out to even the most basic industry trends.

A turbulent economy and other economic woes are commonly reported reasons for failure, but the excuse is invariably a cover-up for other management sins. A poorly run company can get away with a great deal when times are good, and sales are strong. But a tight economy magnifies corporate weaknesses. Marginal companies then vanish.

Economics can play havoc with your company. The early 1980s inflationary interest rates of nearly 20 percent devastated companies programmed to pay 10 percent. Predictably, they folded by the thousands.

Tighter credit is one of the hidden but most important causes for business collapse. A credit squeeze, common during inflation when suppliers restrict credit to avoid high-interest borrowing, again tightens when sales are strong, and suppliers are more willing to forfeit their marginal-credit customers.

Economic conditions can't be predicted easily, and management has no claim to a crystal ball. After all, truly clairvoyant managers would be playing the stock market, not running companies. But survivors instinctively position themselves for the bad times as well as the good times. They plan for the worst, confident they can sustain the worst should it come. Survivors never gamble the corporate jewels on events beyond their control.

In today's fast-changing world, every business is vulnerable to the dramatic and often unexpected events that rapidly strike at its core. Change creates opportunity for some, failure for others. The lesson? You must adapt to survive. To spearhead change is to excel.

Business Killer #2

UNDERCAPITALIZATION

Did you start your business with too little capital? Shoestring start-ups can soar to exceptional success, but there would be far fewer failures if more entrepreneurs started with as much capital as enthusiasm.

Undercapitalization results from business naivety and over-optimism. Perhaps throwing too much money into a business can be an even greater mistake, inviting slipshod spending and risking more than is necessary. Well-planned, well-managed companies carefully balance invested equity, borrowed funds and trade credit. The financially-imbalanced firm is a candidate for trouble.

The undercapitalized firm with decent management and a sound business concept usually can survive if it knows how to raise cash quickly to get over the hump. My firm spends much of its time finding financing for poor but promising startups. The answer may be an investor, a timely loan or simply coaxing more credit from suppliers and landlords.

Overexpansion, the cousin of undercapitalization, also spells trouble when you borrow too heavily to finance your growth and your overly rosy projections wilt. Reversing direction and downsizing quickly is the remedy.

Flushed with success, many businesses grow helter-skelter and outstrip both their capital and management. New acquisitions or startups may bleed the company dry.

That was the tale of a small Georgia restaurant chain that hired me in the mid-1980s. The Callahans, owners of four moderately successful fried chicken restaurants, added three more in one year. It was too much for the young, unstable chain. High startup costs, high losses and high construction overruns drained the chain's financial strength. My survival strategy? Liquidate two of the new restaurants, and pay for the blunder by settling more than $300,000 in debts in a Chapter 11 reorganization.

You also can outgrow your management capability. You need different skills to run a large operation than a small business. Entrepreneurs, once running one-man bands must suddenly build complex organizations and delegate responsibilities. Few grow into their jobs gracefully, and their growing enterprise suffers in key operational areas.

But I'm not against expansion. Companies must either grow or shrink. Nothing stays constant. For controlled growth or expansion you can manage, try baby steps, not giant leaps. Grow faster than 20 percent a year, and you can become too big for your own britches!

Business Killer #3

DIVERSIFICATION

Why do so many companies, lost in familiar territory, journey into unfamiliar territory? Diversification has become a corporate buzzword as companies of all sizes and types roam into unrelated areas, whether through expansion or acquisition. This trend is a throwback to the 1960s, when conglomerates discovered that pyramiding companies was the quick way to a fortune. The conglomerate, never fashioned to make money, offered only unique opportunities to manipulate stock prices. But diversification is not only for the big boys:

- *A Boston textbook publisher bought a boating magazine and lost $800,000 in six months.*

- *A successful Texas radio station operator bought a Southern California movie chain and failed after losing $1.3 million.*

- *A 20-year-old Florida eyeglass manufacturer took control of a large Miami Hotel that went bust with $3 million in unpaid bills.*

What was the logic behind these missteps? What sound relationship or synergy existed between their present and new businesses? Why should success in the present business promise success in the new business? You know the answers. That's why in overdiversification cases, I march the owner back to the business he knows and then limit his growth to ventures that provide a logical "fit."

Businesses should diversify to reduce risk. Since sticking to the vagaries of one industry is a common cause of failure, we can't criticize companies with their eggs in several baskets. Yet management gurus like Peter Drucker disagree with diversification as a sound strategy, and suggest, "Complex businesses (conglomerates) have repeatedly evidenced their vulnerability to small but highly concentrated single-market or single-technology businesses. If anything goes wrong, there is a premium for knowing your business."

Owners justify diversification on several grounds. The three most common are inability to expand with existing industries, synergy between the existing and expanded operations, and highly advantageous acquisition opportunities. Each offers a logical reason for diversification – if you have the managerial and financial resources to properly manage your diversified empire.

Both out-of-control growth and diversification can be "sales worship," or the blind pursuit of sales for the sake of sales. Are you just after profits? Sales worship makes you a prime candidate for failure, because you blindly build sales instead of watching your bottomline. Sure, sales are important, but only if they add to your profits. The sales chase may be an ego trip, an attempt to increase cash flow, or you may mistakenly hope more sales will inevitably lead to more profits. Even the smartest managers get into big trouble with this faulty thinking. If that's you, then downsize so profits, not sales, control your planning and decision- making. Your smaller company may lose half its sales, but double its profits!

Business Killer #4
POOR CONTROLS

Without basic controls you can't know where you've been, where you're going or how you're getting there. Financial controls are vital. Good controls must reach into the heart of your business. Yet financial control won't guarantee good operational controls. Many multimillion-dollar companies can't accurately or quickly get a handle on orders, product costs, customer sales or operational break-even. Companies without such basic information at their fingertips get into trouble.

Entire books have been written about controls. Good controls expose discrepancies between a plan and performance. Without controls, you never know when you're off course.

Business experts frequently pinpoint poor financial controls as the major cause of business failure. I disagree. I see poor controls as only another symptom of bad management. An owner who refuses to use solid financial and operational controls will be just as inept in other management areas; poor buying, excess overhead, inadequate inventory controls and faulty pricing are just a few problems that are bound to exist. It all comes down to one fact: You can't run your business by the seat of your pants.

Too much information is nearly as dangerous. In today's computer-driven era, managers become swamped with too much worthless data, which obscures the few important numbers buried in the pile.

You need a management-information system that quickly, accurately and consistently feeds you the facts. Don't have your accountant or MIS people tell you what information you need to measure the corporate pulse. You tell them. The corporate wastelands are blighted with companies whose navigator never really knew what was going on. Don't make your business one of them!

Business Killer #5
OVERDEPENDENCE

When you depend on one key product, customer or supplier, your future is no better than that one product, customer or supplier. Your relationship won't last forever, and you may both be out of business tomorrow.

Companies can downplay their dependency upon another business, or blindly believe their business relationships are permanent. Many of today's highly successful companies may be out of business tomorrow if they rely solely on one or a few customers. Maybe your customer will go out of business. Maybe a long-loyal buyer will be replaced with one less friendly. Maybe your customer will simply decide to drop your product line, or switch to a competitor with a better deal. In business, nothing is permanent.

One long-standing client who owned a fabric-treatment plant counted on one of America's leading dress manufacturers for most of its $10-million-a-year volume. Jack never dreamed his 15-year relationship could end, but it did. When a new assistant manager decided the manufacturer should split the work among several processors, Jack's volume plummeted by 80 percent. No longer able to cover his high fixed overhead, Jack was soon out of business.

If any one customer accounts for more than 20 percent of your business, you are highly vulnerable. It's time to become less dependent so you remain the master of your destiny.

If the customer-dependent company is vulnerable, so, too, is the company that depends on one source of supply. When that source dries up, the company without a backup supplier quickly finds itself out of business. The United States discovered just how treacherous it can be to depend on one source of supply during the Middle-East oil embargo. Hundreds of franchisees suffer the same fears whenever a franchisor closes its doors. The message is clear: No company can afford to be dependent. You need many customers. You need many suppliers. This may mean expanding your products or services (yes, that's diversification), but it can greatly improve your chances for survival in an unpredictable world.

Business Killer#6

POOR LOCATION

Retail businesses frequently wither because of poor location.

Urban decline and population shifts can slowly kill a location, and destroy a business. Every retailer's fortunes are directly tied to the ability to capture high-traffic, high-volume, high-profit locations.

Location is seldom cited as a cause of business failure, yet hundreds of thousands of retailers in secondary locations close each year. Because shopping is increasingly concentrated in chain- dominated malls and shopping centers, independent retailers who remain shackled to poorer locations eventually perish.

Most of my retail clients say poor locations are their primary problem. Their locations, whether originally bad or turned bad, erode sales and profits. These businesses must choose: Aggressively compete for more desirable locations, stagnate in their marginal locations or close.

As locations change, retailers also must change so that they can thrive in their new environment and meet the needs of the changing market. These changes often must be radical. An upscale clothing store can no longer make it in a decayed location with a low-income population. Either the owner merchandises to match the market or abandons the location. Survival means constant adaptation to the changing market, a strategy often uncomfortable for long- entrenched retailers who want a status-quo business.

The retailer's fortunes are almost always directly tied to the ability to capture high-traffic sites. The old Liggett drugstore chain, for example, once the nation's largest drugstore retailer, proved how vulnerable a retailing organization is to aggressive competitors who grab the best locations. While Liggett clung to dying downtown locations, young start-up chains like Rite-Aid, Revco and CVS nimbly monopolized suburban shopping centers, with their growing populations. Liggett finally shriveled to a handful of tired outlets.

Times are changing. Retailing is swinging back to the specialty shops, so independents with a strong specialty focus are again winning choice shopping mall locations. Walk through your local mall. You'll see what I mean.

Business Killer #7

UNPROFITABLE PRICING

"When was the last time you compared your current costs of doing business to last year's operating costs? When did you last calculate your break-even point?"

I asked these questions of more than 300 furniture manufacturers at a management seminar I was invited to give at a furniture-manufacturers convention. Only 30, or one in ten, had done these basic exercises within the past three years. Nine out of ten had no answer. No wonder the room was loaded with manufacturers in big trouble!

Many companies are in trouble today, only because they do not know their costs, and they unprofitably price. Northfield Brick lost its balance on the pricing tightrope. It sold its decorative brick artificial wallcovering for 65 cents when competitive bricks were about 75 cents. But each brick cost Northfield 74 cents to produce, so Northfield was quickly losing its shirt. Remember the businessman who, when asked how he could afford to sell for 10 percent below his cost, innocently replied, "Simple, I make it up in volume." The crew at Northfield didn't laugh when I told them that joke.

Admittedly, identifying increased expenses or pinpointing labor and material costs is far easier than controlling these costs. Inefficient productivity or poor buying at high prices can strangle profits unless these inefficiencies can somehow be passed on to the customer through higher prices – which is seldom possible in today's competitive world. But many companies do sell too cheaply when they can get a higher price. And too many small operators choose to compete on price when they should push service and quality.

That was the all-too-familiar story with a small variety store in my neighborhood. Buy-Rite Superette panicked when a deep- discount supermarket opened around the corner. Buy-Rite quickly dropped prices 10-15 percent in a futile attempt to stay competitive, but it was a ludicrous strategy. To compensate for the lowered margins, sales would have had to jump 40 percent. But Buy- Rite's sales didn't jump; instead, they incurred enormous losses. We turned events around for Buy-Rite by calling in some merchandising pros, who quickly transformed Buy-Rite into an upscale gourmet food emporium. Featured from floor to ceiling were all the fancy high-profit lines the other supermarket chain didn't stock. Margins zoomed.

I can't give you the magical pricing formula for your business, but I can tell you that the difference between a healthy profit and whopping loss may be nothing more than a few pennies added to each widget.

Business Killer #8

GOVERNMENT RED TAPE

Big Brother is rapidly strangling every industry and causing serious business problems locally, where politicians may change zoning or traffic flows, and nationally as well as internationally, where regulation can wipe out entire markets overnight. Each day brings hundreds of new laws and regulations, each indelibly leaving its mark on how business is to be done. More often than not, it means no business, less business or business done less efficiently. You can see the insidious encroachment by government in every aspect of corporate life: Taxation, employment, pollution control, product safety and consumer rights – to name but a few. This country has gone far beyond George Orwell's 1984.

I recently served as a consultant to a bankruptcy trustee who liquidated a nursing home unable to wait nine months for long- overdue Medicaid payments. And I bailed out a construction firm whose projects were delayed 14 months by environmentalists. Wherever I travel to assist business owners, I find a government imposing its stifling bureaucratic ways on companies that can neither function nor flourish in a strangling climate of regulation.

Whether you believe that governmental constraints are necessary or a needless obstruction is, of course, secondary. You must deal with the world as it is. But companies long frustrated by governmental red tape increasingly are throwing in the sponge, if they are not among those forced out of business.

What you can control is whether you go into a heavily regulated industry in the first place. Staying out of such an industry may double your chance for survival.

Business Killer #9

EXCESS OVERHEAD

That's the big killer in about half of my cases. Right down the line are extraordinarily high expenses. Even strong sales can't overcome high operating costs.

Several years ago, I visited a magazine publisher perched in the penthouse of one of Boston's choicest office buildings. The place reeked of success; the financial statements reeked of massive losses. That same publisher now occupies the basement of a suburban supermarket. It's not the plushest accommodation, but the publisher is still in business.

When it's survival time, radical surgery on all unnecessary costs is vital. Survivors cut, cut and cut again. Nothing escapes their scalpels, particularly their own bloated salaries. I'll soon show you how to perform cost-cutting surgery on your business. Read carefully.

MANAGEMENT AND OTHER GREAT MYTHS

These nine managerial blunders show that most companies do not die natural deaths. They are murdered through managerial incompetence.

Running a business is never easy. Still, too many entrepreneurs bravely venture forth without appreciating just how complicated and challenging it can be. They fail because their owners were unwilling, unable or too undisciplined to put in the long hours, cope with the pressures or keep their hands out of the till. This is certainly true with smaller companies, where the business is the owner and the owner is the business. These small businesses also are frequently destroyed through death, sickness or other personal problems.

I frequently see a mismatch between the owner and the business, because people choose a business for all the wrong reasons. They don't ask whether they would enjoy the business and can effectively manage it. They instead look for profits or prestige. So we have become a nation of entrepreneurial misfits who give less thought to the business we should be in than to the car we should be driving. Eventually, these owners must reassess their careers. Small businesses often perform poorly only because their owners lack motivation, a point I made in the first chapter.

Owners who do have an interest in their business may lack essential skills. A plumber may think he has the experience to operate a plumbing-supply firm, but does the plumber realize that managing the supply firm requires more than a plumber's skills? So we see a company out of balance. The owner may have strong sales skills but weak financial know-how. Or the owner may be creative, but a weak implementor.

Larger companies mean larger problems. The larger organization is no longer the sum and substance of its owner. The organization becomes what the owner creates or fails to create – which may be a strong foundation. The management team may be unbalanced, uncoordinated, improperly staffed or poorly structured for its mission. Basic problems within the company may be basic problems in management structure.

Conflict within the management team is another chronic problem, particularly when the company has partners constantly in squabbles or power battles. Partnerships are a leading cause of business failure. Partnerships face the same hazards as other companies, but also require their partners to blend their differences, objectives and styles into a cohesive management team.

Ultimately, the failure of any business is the failure of the individual at the top. Whether it's the owner of a mom-and-pop enterprise or the leader of a major corporation, the top dog must live with the words of Harry Truman, — "The buck stops here" — unless the business is run so badly that the buck doesn't even get there!

You can't personify the ideal manager. While we may catch a glimpse of successful managerial personalities and styles, there is no one ideal manager or management style. For example, we are warned against one-man rule, and yet companies such as McDonald's flourished under the autocratic thumb of Ray Kroc. Conversely, ITT's Harold Geneen performed superbly by delegating authority to his divisional managers, content to make them fully accountable. Observe managers with very different management styles, and you'll see no correlation between style and results. And when you are in business, results are all that count. Style, in this case, is not substance.

Still, even the most sophisticated companies suffer and flounder because of managerial deficiencies. These corporations perform poorly because management is inbred – secure and complacent after too many years on the job. These firms flounder from corporate rigidity – a reluctance to try new ideas, a resistance to change and a low tolerance for independent thinking within the ranks. While these firms may waddle along under their own momentum, they will eventually learn the difference between success and mere survival, and later between mere survival and failure.

The sins of management are endless. For every stagnant enterprise, we see managers who run blindly and impulsively. Power- hoarding executives embark on overambitious strategies, oblivious to the excessive risks. These firms, hell-bent to break past records, take inordinate risks to grow faster than they safely should.

No less intriguing is the headless firm – the company that has neither leadership nor a profit strategy. These firms run themselves on automatic pilot, with no direction from the top. Running on empty, they soon grind to a stop.

Managerial failure, then, is the result of extremes. Too much ambition or too little, too much centralized control or too little, an overly powerful CEO or one who is a benign figurehead.

No business or manager is blemish-free. Some weaknesses are trifling and offset by important strengths. But weaknesses that can lead to failure are weaknesses usually found in the executive suite. It's there that the seeds of destruction are typically sown. It's there that you must begin to troubleshoot your business.

☑CHECKPOINT

1. Is your business a managerial failure, a financial failure or a legal failure?

2. Businesses fail for several reasons. Why is yours in trouble?

3. Which of the nine deadly business killers are destroying your company?

4. Your own bad management may be the number-one culprit. Are you objective enough to see it?

3

WHO'S IN TROUBLE?

Who's in trouble? Not me! That's what they all say two weeks before they flop. Not you, of course. Or is it you? Maybe you're just not sure and need some help evaluating your situation objectively. So what do we see when we take a closer look?

BEYOND YOUR BLINDERS

Did you know that most businesses fail not because they can't solve their problems but because they won't see their problems? It may surprise you, but even the most seasoned business owners prefer blinders to reality when their businesses begin to slide.

Nor will it be easy to convince you to act even when the signals clearly point to future disaster. Like most owners you won't, on your own initiative, accept the facts of your situation for what they are. A troubled company first needs a crisis, and until that crisis comes, they tolerate trouble.

Every turnaround consultant and workout professional I have ever come across shares my frustration with stubborn business owners who refuse to believe their businesses are going broke. It's always much more pleasant to cling to the illusion that your company is simply encountering one of those nasty bumps in the road that all companies experience from time to time.

Owners of troubled businesses often call me when their situation becomes uncomfortable with low cash, slipping morale, tightened credit and pressing creditors. Usually the assets and resources needed to revitalize their company are still intact. For most it is still too soon to get serious about a turnaround. They then disappear for several months, until they can no longer ignore their worsening problems and call again in a panic, but only after their bank has foreclosed, the IRS has padlocked their doors, or another catastrophe has struck. By then, there may be too little to work with! Inventory is depleted, cash and credit are gone, essential employees and customers have abandoned ship or creditors dumped the business into bankruptcy. **Delay destroys businesses!**

As with all progressive illnesses, if you stay alert and respond quickly to your serious and worsening problems, you will greatly improve your odds for recovery. The critical point is when your company starts its downward slide. You then make the decision to act decisively or you play ostrich and squander your assets and your future. Survivors are those who feverishly conserve their cash and assets so they can tackle their turnaround with maximum financial strength and staying power.

What may cause **you** to fight reality? Ego is one big reason. Nobody accepts defeat graciously. A delayed turnaround delays the acknowledgment of defeat. Big executives from big corporations, to keep their paychecks coming, hide the dismal facts from their corporate boards, lenders, creditors and stockholders. They drain the balance sheet until the losses can no longer be absorbed. They fool their bosses. You may fool yourself!

Optimism is another factor. After all, optimism is what fuels all startups and propels their growth. But optimism is only another blinder to mask the early warning signals. You may see your answer in that one business-saving customer, that new product breakthrough, or some other miracle that never happens, at least never in time. Ironically, the very same optimism that encouraged your startup may cause its failure.

You also may be too close to your problems. Your business may be deteriorating so gradually that you don't see the changing picture. Problems then become an accepted way of life rather than warning signals. Inexperienced or oblivious owners never see the gathering storm because they look for the wrong signs in the wrong place at the wrong time – **if** they look at all!

The ability to detect and act quickly to solve problems is the essence of good management. The cardinal management sin is not the error you make but the error you neither see nor cure. Like so many other owners, you too may need to learn that small problems are far simpler to solve than big ones. Poor managers avoid problems. Good managers stand up to trouble only when they run into it. Great managers are on the prowl for trouble. These managers wear no blinders!

Ignoring your problems is only one potential evil. Thinking you are doing something to solve your difficulties when you are only tinkering and twiddling is another. Aspirin won't cure a brain tumor. It's considerably more dangerous medicine when you believe it is your cure and you stop seeking the treatment you need.

A business in deep trouble needs strong medicine. And the medicine may be unpleasant to swallow. Tinkering with your business when it needs tackling is only another form of self-delusion. Don't kid yourself. If you even think you may be in trouble, then take off your blinders. Only then can you see what's really going on and how to fix it.

THE GATHERING STORM

Companies seldom fail without a clear warning. A troubled company throws out numerous operational and financial signals that are weak warnings at first and then grows more frequent and powerful as your company fails.

No two companies generate precisely the same early warnings, because businesses, like ships, never sink in exactly the same way. Some go down at the bow, others stern first. And for every company that suddenly vanishes, others endlessly linger before rolling over. Some giants, such as Rolls Royce and Penn Central, succumbed with little warning. But most companies have a wide window of opportunity to see trouble brewing and have ample opportunity to avert disaster.

Warning signals largely mirror the type of company. Companies have a personality. Some are plodders, the garden-variety, run-of- the-mill enterprises that are the backbone of American business. Others are high-rollers that suddenly reach spectacular heights and as quickly plummet and crash. Then come the dinosaurs, the large, outdated, ponderous corporations, sluggishly out of touch with their markets and dying from hardening of the arteries.

Plodders are led by storekeepers, welders, machinists, printers and other steady-but-less-visible people with personalities in rhythm with their businesses. Characters heading high-roller companies are as colorful as their companies. They are flamboyant, restless dreamers whose ambitions reach to the sky. They build firms on blind ambition if not on absurd concept. These enterprises can capture the imagination of the investing public, fueling the companies to fantastic heights where they attract even more money.

High-roller companies are the most interesting casualties because we have a curious fascination with any company that can appear and disappear like a flash starburst. When headed by luminaries who become household names, the intrigue deepens. High- rollers have obvious warning signals like sharply declining sales as fickle customers lose interest in the fad and switch to newer technology or more intriguing fads. High-rollers live and die by their ability to hold a fickle public.

Dinosaurs, in contrast, see a slow erosion in their sales and profitability. It can take years to kill a well-heeled dinosaur. While the high-roller is like the rose that quickly blossoms and fades, the dinosaur wilts slowly.

But I'm most interested in the plodders who fail for so many different reasons. You cannot predict their early warning signals. That's why you can never rely on certain signals and ignore others. Survivors stay alert to any signs of trouble, knowing the signs may appear when least expected.

SCAN THE FAR HORIZON

Sometimes you must look beyond the horizon to see the first clouds of trouble sweeping in.

Early failure signs may not show up in your financial statements. The first and clearest signs are frequently managerial, not financial, and can and should be seen long before your financials reflect the problems.

Just as the causes of failure depend largely on the size, age and type of business you own, the symptoms of failure also depend on these factors.

For example, hi-tech firms victimized by competition will see their new orders drop long before the financials reflect their decreased sales. Distant problems may be seen even earlier. In fact, a hi-tech firm will find it too late to spot oncoming problems by looking at sales alone. It must instead see what's going on in its labs, know how much it's spending on R&D and decide whether it's ahead or behind its competitors in product development. Today's sales only reflect yesterday's research; tomorrow's income reflects today's inventiveness.

A point I made earlier: The causes and symptoms of failure can be too intertwined to distinguish from one another. Lee Iacocca, for example, considered Chrysler's downfall predictable long before the latter half of the 1970s, when its sales dropped 50 percent. The earliest warnings, Iacocca reasoned, came in 1973: The oil embargo, long lines at the gas pumps and the Detroit automakers stubbornly producing only lumbering gas-guzzlers.

Since the gathering storm has its origins in the causes of failure, your earliest warnings can be:

- New and more formidable competitors.

- A shrinking market or decreased market share.

- New legislation that could hurt profits.

- Technological lag or less-competitive products.

What do you see when you scan the far horizon?

FOUR STAGES TO FAILURE

Companies may fail with varying swiftness, but they almost always move through several stages on their way.

It is in the first stage that faulty management decisions or a failure to respond to change weakens the company's competitive position. The company then loses market share and plateaus or grows more slowly as it lags technologically or slips competitively. In this early stage, you sense a loss of momentum or perhaps your business losing firepower, or that its future is not as bright as it once was.

The second stage brings clearer operational and financial symptoms. Sales slip further as more customers are lost. Advertising, promotion and new-product development are cut. Morale dips. Your money troubles become chronic. This second stage brings a shift from positive, long-term planning to a preoccupation with short-term financial and operational problems.

The third stage is one of total defensiveness, with greater losses, less inventories, no credit and insufficient cash flow. You begin the "bankruptcy spin," a vicious cycle where fewer assets means fewer sales, which means even greater losses, which means still fewer assets, to start the cycle again.

In the fourth and final stage – a point from which few businesses recover – you are sued by creditors and lenders, pressed for long-overdue taxes, operate with too little cash and inventory, and watch key employees and customers abandon ship.

Typically it is in the third or fourth stage that you begin to accept the fact that your company won't turn itself around on its own merits and that it needs a drastic reorganization.

But how do you determine when your company has passed its point of no return, a point beyond which it won't recover without a full-scale turnaround? Like the pilot of the disabled aircraft with one foot out the door who wonders whether his plane might not straggle back to base after all, you, too, may endlessly wonder whether your business could survive without radical surgery.

Here's the answer. Once your company reaches the second stage, it is unlikely that it will correct its own course. You need something more than cosmetically improved operations to make your company straighten out and fly right.

AN EAR TO THE WASHROOM WALL

Your ear may be close to the ground, but you will detect problems more readily if you listen to your employees, customers and suppliers.

Listen most carefully to your employees. Keep an ear to the ground and to the washroom wall. You will then hear all that can possibly be wrong with your business. You will hear about the problems as they develop and you will hear about them loud and clear.

Because your employees are in the firing line, they may best know what is going on. They will share it with you, but only if you learn to communicate with them.

Good communication with employees doesn't just happen. You must cultivate this communication as part of doing business. The key is to let your employees know that bad news is as welcome as good news and is even more valued!

An employee who feels that a problem can only be corrected at the top must believe that his or her message will quickly reach the top and be acted upon. This means an open-door policy for your employees. Of course, it rarely works that way in practice because so many bosses build barriers between themselves and their front- line troops. The barriers? Middle managers who cannot or will not resolve the problems and won't relay bad news to a boss who welcomes and rewards only good news!

My turnarounds start by interviewing employees from the various departments. This gives me a good cross-sample of the corporate condition. I usually encounter frustrated employees who are delighted that they finally have someone to talk to. I become a sounding board for their pent-up frustrations with tale after tale of:

- Unhappy customers who complain about inventory shortages, poor delivery or shoddy product quality.

- Unhappy suppliers who won't ship because of overdue bills.

- Unhappy and demoralized employees whose salary cutbacks or job insecurities prevent them from performing well.

When you let employees tell you the same endless tales of shoddy products, inventory shortages, lost accounts, low morale and countless other ills that befall the stricken company, you may conclude what I suspect: Your employees know more then you do about what is really going on with your company!

A small, informally organized company does not necessarily have an easier time with employee communication. You may be as distant from your one or two employees as is the CEO in his penthouse office from the thousands of employees working on the factory floor or clerking in his retail store.

You can turn your employees into an early warning system with a three-step policy:

1. Let your employees know that you know the company is having problems. When you don't acknowledge and communicate this, your employees think you're either oblivious to the situation or purposely being secretive. Neither makes you stand tall in your employees' eyes.

2. Set up a system for communicating. Tell your employees what information you want reported when and how.

3. Encourage as much direct communication as you can handle. Try to hear about the problems from the front-line employees, because you can't always trust intermediaries who may discourage bad news or not give you the straight scoop.

Check your communications. When your people don't come to you with problems, that doesn't mean you don't have problems. This may be your **biggest** problem!

CREDITORS THROUGH THE LOOKING GLASS

Alice in Wonderland had her looking glass. Your suppliers, creditors, customers and others outside your company have theirs.

A distressed company never keeps its secret, no matter how hard it tries. In fact, your creditors, suppliers and customers may be first to detect problems on the horizon.

You can turn this to your advantage once you learn to look at things as they do. From the outside, things can be appreciably clearer.

Creditors are trouble-sensitive because they have as much at stake with your business as do you. After all, your creditors ultimately foot the bills that you cannot pay.

Growing financial problems mean you will instinctively conceal your troubles from your creditors. You will need credit from unsuspecting suppliers and will want to avoid their scramble to collect your overdue bills.

Keeping your creditors in the dark temporarily may help your cash flow, but it only buys time and never solves the underlying problem. Buying time from unaware creditors also may be counterproductive, as you simultaneously fool yourself and throw in more of your own money before you and your creditors realize a workout is your only possible solution.

On the other hand, early detection of your problems by alert creditors can force you to face your problems, because only creditors have the power to push you and your troubled company into a badly needed turnaround as an alternative to bankruptcy. Creditors also are more cooperative in a workout when they don't feel abused by someone who nonchalantly played with their money. And your creditors (particularly your secured lenders) will probably give you vital support and assistance – if you react quickly to your problems and ally them to your cause.

Creditors can detect problems in many ways. But they are hardly foolproof, as seen by the countless billions of dollars they lose each year in the bankruptcy courts. Alert creditors use visits to the debtor's premises, phone calls, rumors within the trade and a close review of financial statements as a few of the standard detection procedures. And each type of creditor has its own distinct opportunity to spot early signs of financial duress.

Trade creditors will watch carefully for changes in your payment or buying patterns. A company that normally discounts its payables but suddenly pays in 30 days may be in as much financial difficulty as the debtor who consistently pays late. Similarly, customers who buy without resistance or in abnormally large quantities may be anticipating their supplier closing the credit spigot. Trade creditors mostly hear about customer problems through the rumor mills that permeate every industry. Alert credit managers have their information network of customers and other suppliers within the trade all too anxious to spread the bad news of a sick account.

Banks and other secured lenders can't easily tap trade sources and must depend more on financial rather than operational signals. Because troubled companies usually will keep paying their secured loans long after they become delinquent to trade suppliers, lenders cannot rely on payments alone as a good indicator of advancing problems. Lenders, secured by a borrower's accounts receivable and inventory, will review these items on the financials together with shipments, purchase orders, accounts receivable collections and inventory changes.

What do your creditors see when they look at your company?

- Personnel changes, with many of your best people leaving?
- Changes in accounting or other reporting methods?
- Payments coming later and with less consistency?
- Erratic buying seemingly tied to cash flow rather than your inventory needs?
- Shrinking inventories?
- Constant overdrafts and returned checks?
- Unusual returns for credit or demands for other trade concessions that show financial problems?
- Buying from new suppliers who offer more credit?
- Credit reports that show an increase in collection claims and lawsuits?
- Security interests to new lenders, tax liens or other creditor attachments?
- A loss of a key customer?
- A deteriorating physical plant?
- Less advertising and promotion?

Creditors spotting these danger signals become defensive, and they should. They will then want to secure past-due payments and protect themselves on future shipments. These creditor actions are valuable signals that your creditors think you're in trouble, whether or not it is true.

THE VIEW FROM THE OPPOSITE SIDE OF THE COUNTER

Customers also have that sixth sense when all is not well. Most customers simply walk away from you as a crippled supplier who can no longer give them what they want. Your defensive position also can benefit some customers who may try to take advantage of your weak bargaining power and desperation. These customers may withhold payment or demand lower prices or other unreasonable concessions, mindful that you more desperately need their business than do stronger suppliers who can hold firm. Major customers do cannibalize faltering suppliers. The least sign of vulnerability can turn your customers into a feeding frenzy of sharks. Customers with that predatory instinct will look for:

- Unusually low prices or fire sales to raise cash.

- Factored receivables or big discounts for cash payments.

- Chronic inventory shortages.

- Erratic delivery and reduced service.

- Rapid personnel turnover.

- Failure to issue credits, extend customary trade concessions or pay earned rebates.

- Tightened credit.

- Poorer product quality.

Valuable indications? You bet! Saddest is he who cannot see about himself what everyone else can see. Don't let that be you!

GAME PLAYING

The things you suddenly find yourself doing to stay alive also are clues to the health of your business. We each have a "stretch," or capacity to do things in desperate times that we would never otherwise do. I have seen the most honest and ethical business owners quickly become crooks when extremely pressured. Morality isn't the issue. If the things you are doing right now shock you into admitting that you really must be in big-time trouble, then the self-assessment was worthwhile.

Beleaguered business owners do steal from their family, rob banks or even commit murder. You may cut some corners of your own to stay afloat as you:

- Ship defective or substandard products.

- Short-change your customers.

- Pad your invoices.

- Con vendors to ship goods that you will never pay for.

- Misappropriate payroll taxes or other third-party funds.

The list continues, but you see the point. Perhaps you don't do these things because you're too honest, or because you are not that desperate yet! When you catch yourself doing them, you will know you are in very big trouble!

WATCH THE SCORECARD

An eagle's eye for trouble is instinctive. Only your financials can really tell you whether you are in a downturn and how serious it is. All other signals are intuitive. But when your financials bleed, you indeed have serious problems.

Financial warnings usually arise after operational signals. But even when you are aware of developing problems, you may lack the financial controls that can signal approaching danger.

Most failed companies have non-existent or poor financial reporting systems. By this, I mean good accounting information, not just physical data, such as units sold, items in stock, production per hour, or the mounds of operational data most managers rely upon. Your company may lack accurate information in three critical areas: profits, costs and cash position.

Without good budgetary controls, you never know how profitable you are or even if you are operating above or below your break-even point.

Without a good costing system, you won't understand how key activities relate to your bottom-line profits. And without good cash-flow projections, you can never anticipate the next peak demand for cash or how you will meet it.

While responsive financials worsen with approaching insolvency, you won't see the deterioration by casually inspecting your statements. You may resort to creative accounting to disguise poor performance. For years, Rolls Royce deferred millions of dollars in losses simply by capitalizing its enormous research costs. This simple play misled even the most sophisticated London analysts to believe that the badly bleeding Rolls Royce was healthy. You're not Rolls Royce, but your financials may be just as distorted.

Small businesses that operate without audited statements are far more prone to financial distortions, whether intentional or not. Your statements may be nothing more than erroneous information. Small losses may be whoppers. Losses that now panic you may in fact be profits. Allow for a big margin of error if you have a small business with non-certified statements. Have you overestimated inventories, overvalued receivables, capitalized items normally expensed, or committed other accounting distortions to navigate yourself off course?

Your financials can't be built on faulty data. For example, an overestimated inventory will disguise losses, yet many businesses ignore physical inventories and conveniently estimate the current year's inventories at last year's amount. Reduced inventory is easily overlooked when it gradually drops. The most experienced managers may not realize their inventory dropped from $700,000 to $600,000; however, that is a $100,000 loss that must be spotted for the financials to have any value.

On the other hand, you may accurately report assets but inaccurately report liabilities. Good managers watch their liabilities very closely. They set payment schedules to detect instantly when bills remain unpaid longer than usual, which is itself a most important warning signal. A record of prompt payments can quickly become a stack of dunning notices. But a surprising number of small-business owners have no idea what they owe. An owner may initially guess $500,000, which grows to $900,000 with a prepared, updated list of unpaid accounts. How accurate are your financials?

Even when you have accurate financials, they are worthless unless you know what they say. You may have ignored your financial statements because you never mastered them as management tools. Few small business owners can properly interpret their financials. This is a recurring theme! Business people everywhere cannot tell you whether they are making or losing money. Their books and records do not exist or lay in shambles or are buried away. As one accountant who handles a number of small companies once confided, "Financial statements may be the closest thing to a precise guess."

If you can't make sense of your financials, then make sure your accountant will toll the warning bell. Because many accountants are only tax preparers, they don't offer their clients close financial guidance. I can tell you story after story of companies that came to me deeply in debt and after years of big losses – without one warning from their accountants. Still, I don't indict the accounting profession. Many accountants are on the ball and yell loudly at the first sign of trouble. I have seen many others drag their confused, sometimes screaming clients to professionals like myself. Still others defend their lack of navigational involvement by reporting, "The client didn't want my help. He paid me only to do the taxes, nothing more." And they're right! You need more than a tax preparer. Make your accountant your financial navigator!

I check the accuracy of the company's financial reporting systems as my first role in the case. I reconstruct the financials if I doubt their reliability. To determine the speed and gravity of the downturn, I ask:

- How much money is the company losing, and for how long?

- What are the debts compared to the assets?

The answers to these questions give a very good idea of "who's in trouble!"

On the bright side: You may discover that you're really not in big trouble after all. Your financials may show you are making money and still have a reasonably sound balance sheet, but you have failure symptoms and a tight cash-flow because you managed your assets poorly. Plenty of businesses make loads of money but still strangle to death on a negative cash flow. They typically build inventory or receivables too rapidly or take on more financing than they can service.

The solution? Prioritize cash flow and halt growth. It will slow progress but it will give you a self-correcting situation without the need to restructure debts or seek new profit strategies.

HEED YOUR GUT FEELING

Even mountains of financial reports won't tell you what is instinctively in your gut. If you have been in business for sometime, you know intuitively when things are abnormally bad. Sometimes your intuition helps you figure out what you must do to correct your problem. Precise formulas or rigid rules aren't the only way to tell when a business turns bad. Check your gut!

☑CHECKPOINT

1. Are you problem oriented or do you still wear blinders?

2. Do you think your business is in serious trouble? Why? How much trouble?

3. Do you encourage your employees to come to you with problems?

4. How would your creditors and customers view your business? What symptoms of serious problems do they see?

5. What do your financial statements tell you about your business? Are your statements reliable? Do you know how to use them to navigate?

6. What's your gut feeling about your business?

4

WAKE UP THE SURVIVOR IN YOU

$\mathbf{G}$ood things don't just happen. You must make them happen.

Turning around a failing business has little to do with balance sheets or business plans. It's much more basic. A successful workout is the product of a helmsman with those special qualities and knows how to salvage a sinking ship. Whoever they are, whatever their business, no matter how desperate their circumstances, these stalwart souls stand ready to do what they must to take their businesses from where they are to where they must go, while overcoming every nasty obstacle along the way. Successful workouts have more than good managers. They have survivors.

SHARPEN YOUR SURVIVAL INSTINCT

What makes a survivor?

First, you must think like a survivor. Begin by breaking away from textbook management practices that work only for healthy enterprises. Failing companies must rely upon unconventional strategies that go contrary to Management 101 principles. You can't think mostly about profits, as do well-heeled managers. Cash flow is your game. You hire and fire not according to the "safe" rules but by what leaves you the people you most need to survive. You must have different priorities when in trouble. And you achieve your objectives differently. You don't dare think long-term. Your goal is to make it to next week.

Running a crisis company is in so many ways so unlike guiding the stable enterprise. Unless you have been there before, you must de-program yourself from how you have done things in the past, or it will cloud your thinking on how to do things now. More than survival instinct, you must develop that survivor mentality!

It's more than strategy. The stripes of a survivor are earned with managerial qualities custodial managers don't have. Custodial managers are content to keep their companies on a straight line, buoyed by occasional small gains in their fortunes. They can afford to run their businesses by the book because they have the resources to play a conventional game. They stay safe as long as they can avoid serious blunders. Good custodial managers are adequate caretakers of the corporate fortunes in good times, but how good are they in bad times?

So who are these survivors I speak about? Survivors are "blood-and-guts" managers. They take big risks because they are unavoidable. They kick butts, snub their noses, and fight everyone both inside and outside the company who blocks their way. Above all, they know exactly what their businesses need. A survivor reluctantly but necessarily becomes an S.O.B because a survivor understands that popular decisions are seldom the right decisions. Survivors are the General George Pattons of the business world – unlovable but most effective.

"Dyed-in-the-wool" custodial managers can't easily be converted into survivors. It's part personality and part style. Prior training and experience also shape how they handle things.

So managers and survivors are very dissimilar creatures. While a survivor must manage, a manager seldom needs sharp survival instincts. And surviving is your one important goal in a workout.

Unfortunately, survival skills aren't taught in college. America's 600 business schools churn out 150,000 budding executives every year. One innovative institution now offers their MBA program on New York's commuter trains. Their program might more usefully be offered on the subway leading to the bankruptcy court. Yet business schools naively continue to turn out textbook managers who quickly become disoriented when things go wrong, all because business schools ignore the nasty subject of turnarounds.

I recall my own business school days. Our cases always involved the lofty problems of plush Fortune 500 corporations. I never realized so many companies could lose so much money until I graduated out of "B" school and into business. That's when my education really started!

And you can't rely on others when you lack the survival instinct to save yourself! Professionals may offer strong support, and good employees may bolster your managerial deficiencies, but when your survival instinct fails, your business inevitably fails.

Still, if you aren't that survivor, you have options. Take on a partner? Sell the business? Liquidate? Hire a workout consultant to fully reorganize your company? They are all possibilities. The "rent-a-boss" idea may be your smartest answer if you can believe an outsider can run your business as well as you. You may think your presence is doubly important in troubled times, but your involvement may destroy whatever chance your company has for survival, particularly if you are not that survivor and stand in the way of someone who is!

Most small- to mid-sized businesses must center their workouts around their owners. If that's you, your workout strategy must be what you can tolerate and achieve, even if it is not the best possible strategy for your company. For example, if you lack the stamina for a grueling and prolonged Chapter 11 reorganization, you need a simpler solution. Each survivor has his or her own parameters. You alone must decide how badly you want to survive. You alone must decide what you will endure to survive. You alone must decide what survival capabilities you can bring to the workout.

A SURVIVOR IS AN ARCHITECT FOR CHANGE

First and foremost, survivors reshape their businesses from what they are to what they must become. They are architects of change.

As chief architect, you must quickly, clearly and objectively assess your company's present condition, realistically visualize its future, and develop and implement a workable game plan to get it there. Even with entrepreneurial talent and broad business experience, you need a certain creativity and ability to see things as they can be, not as they are.

Creativity is far more important to a workout than is business know-how. Experience may, in fact, entrench your way of thinking so that you lose creativity. Imagination dulls, and you ignore or reject new ideas or concepts. But even highly creative people tire in a turnaround, becoming uncreative and unadaptive. It's difficult to be creative when you're hit on the head a thousand times a day by angry creditors and must cope with thousands of other problems.

Fortunately, opportunists can be found who are willing, even eager, to breathe fresh ideas into tired companies. Sometimes a more objective outsider can spot opportunity where none was seen before. The key is to think positively, not negatively.

Did you hear the long-enduring tale of the two market researchers independently dispatched by a shoe manufacturer to an undeveloped country? Two telegrams soon arrived at corporate headquarters. One dismally read, "No market here. Nobody wears shoes." The other happily promised, "Great market here, nobody has shoes." Survivors are opportunity-oriented, not problem-focused. You, too, must be opportunity-oriented if you are to be an effective architect for change.

How do you change your business into a money machine? We both know that no serious book can tell you. I offer no magic formula for making money. It is you who must decide whether to upscale or downsize, to add or drop a product, to raise or lower prices, or whether or not a sizzling new marketing program can turn the tide.

I can tell you that radical change, not minor alterations, most often turns loser into winners. Unless you visualize a radical transformation, you may forfeit your fortunes while you tinker.

Look at your business through new eyes. Abandon old ways of doing business. But be guided by the numbers. Where are you making or losing money? What more can you do to make money? What must you do to turn losses into profits?

Talk to people: Your employees, your suppliers, your customers. Their ideas may be right on target. Fresh ideas are for the taking – if you listen!

Be inquisitive. What new and exciting things are happening in your industry? What do your more successful competitors do that you could do? Why do prospective customers shop your competitors and not you?

Basic questions? Of course. But architects of change answer these questions so they can design a profitable business.

However, vision is not enough. You also must implement change. The doing is tougher than the dreaming! Ten managers can foresee their companies future. But maybe only three can make it happen. These are the survivors.

SURVIVORS CREATE A CLIMATE FOR SUCCESS

Survivors expect success! Survivors demand success! Survivors let everyone know their loser is about to become a winner. And they unshakably believe it. You can hear it in their voices when they sell the proposition. When you are confident of success, it becomes a self-fulfilling prophecy. The same can be said of failure.

As one of their first tasks, survivors reinstate a sense of purpose within their businesses. Your own employees, customers, suppliers, stockholders and creditors are disenchanted with you and your company. When you're in trouble, you have very few believers.

Somehow you must change how people think about you and your business. Those involved with you and your company must no longer see failure on the horizon, but success. Make everyone involved in your business your partners in this self-fulfilling prophecy. If they truly believe you will come out of your tailspin, they will help you make it happen. But only then. People won't perform futile gestures.

You must have what it takes to convert those slumbering spirits. Become an evangelist! Paint a smile on your face so others will smile too. Your people want to believe. Make them believe! And when you do, you can slink home, down a stiff drink and privately drown in your own doubts.

Old-timers like myself remember how President Franklin Roosevelt navigated the country through the Great Depression, history's largest workout. Long after his social and economic programs have become blurred in history, Roosevelt is still well- remembered for his inspiring "fireside chats." Americans knew things would indeed change for the better once they heard Roosevelt's sincere, convincing words.

Demoralized employees and financially troubled companies go hand in hand. Why shouldn't employees be down? They may soon be fired, or their pay cut. Your people work in the same bad conditions and nagging pressures as you do. You can't erase employee worries when you mope around with your own unhappy face.

So smile and throw back your shoulders. Make a game of it. Convince your people you will succeed. Convince your employees you need their help to succeed. Motivate everyone connected with your business with special incentives and rewards as a special thanks for their support through the hard times.

Yes, all this is easy to say and very difficult to do when you're weary, depressed and overloaded with business problems. But you must inspire even when you don't feel inspired. Either develop that spirit, or step aside, and let that spirit flow from somebody else.

If your people are scared, let them see your self-confidence. Roosevelt had his fireside chats; Churchill flashed his famous victory sign, even when London smoldered in ruins. What did these two great leaders really think? Who knows? The world only knew they would succeed.

SURVIVORS ACTIVATE AND ENERGIZE

Survivors aren't afraid to give their organization a strong kick because they know that can be the quickest way to shake the doldrums.

A complacent business needs a good jolt before it pays attention. Your people must see that things are finally happening. You may make some wrong moves, but at least you're moving, and that's what counts. Even small actions show forward movement.

Survivors do a variety of things to get adrenalin pumping. They fire long-entrenched laggards, scrap favorite but costly projects and dump big but unprofitable customers. For positive energizers, they unwrap a new marketing campaign, an exciting product, a new and better way to do an important job or win that new and profitable customer!

How do you motivate your organization? You must get your troops to think about things other than problems. The kick-in-the- pants carries a vital message: You intend to stay in business, and you have what it takes to stay in business.

Action alone is not enough. Accompany it with the necessary fanfare so the word is spread that you are moving again. Use both symbolic and substantive shock to shake your company. Circulate bulletins. Call your employees together. Giving your organization a swift kick announces to your troops that a survivor has finally arrived. Are you that survivor?

SURVIVORS COMMUNICATE

Survivors communicate, communicate and communicate. Survivors continuously flow information to everyone connected with the business, inside and outside the organization. Survivors know that effective communication wins support, while keeping people in the dark builds resentment.

Communication also helps you motivate. Open, sincere two-way communication is as vital to a workout as it is to selling. Workouts suffer when there's poor communication between management and employees, creditors, lenders and customers. When these groups hear nothing, they imagine the worst.

Because your workout needs the cooperation and continued confidence of these groups, you must keep them thoroughly informed and actively involved. Constantly communicate meaningful, accurate information. And survivors demand a constant flow of information in return, to help them monitor performance during the workout. Survivors keep their fingers on the pulse by communicating.

Communication is more than a device to send or receive information. Communication mends relationships easily strained during a workout. Spend a day or two each week talking to your suppliers, creditors, customers and lenders. Don't hide. Take a major customer or supplier to lunch. This builds confidence, and without confidence you won't see your next order or shipment. Good communicators are a businesses' goodwill ambassadors, particularly in the bad times.

You need no brilliant strategies to become a good communicator. Start with monthly progress reports to your suppliers, creditors, lenders and employees. Newsletters or bulletins to your customers may instill the positive tone needed for them to stand by you. However you do it, when you communicate sincerely and frequently to the people whose help you need, they won't easily turn their backs on you! Be a nuisance; Overly communicate.

In successful turnarounds, good, strong communication is the glue that holds the various groups together. But honest, open communication during a workout is never easy, even for naturally good communicators. If you are a poor communicator in the good times, recognize that you will be reluctant to communicate bad news that risks losing support.

Managing a troubled company usually means dodging those who are hostile, which is, of course, virtually everyone involved with your company. But true survivors take the heat in face-to-face confrontations with angry employees, hostile creditors and skeptical stockholders.

Survivors understand that when you need people to rebuild, you win their support by communicating – even when the message is painful!

SURVIVORS ARE S.O.B.s

Survivors don't win popularity contests. They don't try to. To keep your company alive, you can't be a sheep in sheep's clothing.

Survivors become S.O.B.s because it's the unpopular and tough decisions that keep their businesses going. They roll up their sleeves and fire long-loyal workers, cut salaries, scrap pet projects, withhold payments to desperate suppliers and say no to a hundred people who beg for a yes. Saying no is a very unpleasant but essential part of saving a business.

Survivors become tough-minded and thick-skinned because so many of their decisions are painful. What else can they be when they must, for instance, fire loyal employees of 25 years who can no longer pull their weight? And if only an S.O.B. can withhold payment to a small, struggling supplier who needs that check, you become that S.O.B. Every day, survivors make hard but very necessary decisions. Survivors spread blood and guts because sacrifice is one very unpleasant but necessary part of survival.

Can you orchestrate a massacre? Most people can't. Most of my clients are kind, sensitive people who desperately want to succeed while "doing right by everyone." But that's not how you survive. You must choose between being a nice guy and giving away the shop, or becoming a grizzled S.O.B. who stays in business. Survivors understand there's no middle ground.

That hardly makes survivors insensitive. Hard-nosed survivors are as sensitive as benevolent failures. Survivors simply make their decisions with the painful awareness that they are necessary decisions. Look at it from a different perspective. An S.O.B. who fires a longstanding but incompetent employee is being kind to other employees, who now have a better chance of holding onto their own jobs. S.O.B.s don't always just benefit themselves. An unpopular decision benefits everyone when it helps the business survive. That's why tough decisions are usually the fairest, and S.O.B.s are usually the fairest turnaround leaders.

Sure, I feel like Attila the Hun when committing mayhem to rescue a business. But when I must save a business, I go on the premise that nice guys don't finish last. Nice guys don't even finish.

Okay, Mr. Nice Guy, how do you become that S.O.B.? You can train yourself to do many things, but becoming an S.O.B. is not everybody's cup of tea. That's why the more sensitive souls hire me to be their resident S.O.B. It's my role as a turnaround consultant, and one I accept. The meek may inherit the earth, but we S.O.B.s keep it in business! So either become an S.O.B. or hire one for those dirty but necessary deeds.

SURVIVORS GIVE AND TAKE

A workout is negotiation. Yin and yang. Give and take. You must divide a few corporate resources among players who each want more.

Survivors negotiate deals so everyone wins — or thinks they win. But without dealmaking there's no business.

Lenders, suppliers, creditors, employees, prospective partners, investors and financiers all test your negotiating skills. Because you're on the defensive, they assume you have the least negotiating power. You want to keep your business alive and you need them to do it. That's what they think. Only when you level the playing field can you negotiate the deals that spell survival.

Lee Iacocca's negotiating ability saved Chrysler. Iacocca masterfully negotiated essential loan guarantees from the government, major wage concessions from United Auto Workers, and significant profit cuts from his own dealers. Iacocca's "equality of sacrifice" pitch didn't save Chrysler. His ability to sell the pitch saved it.

Your business may not be Chrysler, but your role as masterful negotiator is no less important. Consider how very different the interests and objectives are of each group involved with your company and how your company's survival needs each group's support. Uniting these divided and often hostile groups to approve your workout plan won't be easy. I'm a veteran of the negotiation wringer and I can tell you that it's like magic to pull a deal together. It takes Henry Kissinger's tact and Will Rogers' wit to get a creditor to accept ten cents on the dollar, and shake your hand. Your ability to persuade is even more keenly tested with employees who are asked to produce more while earning less.

Only through your negotiating power can you pull together the people, resources and money needed to reshape your troubled company into a winner.

If negotiating isn't your strong suit, it's one more skill you can hire. Your consultant and lawyer may have plenty of experience in the yin and yang of a business workout. Unless you enjoy a good game of poker, let them cut your deals.

SURVIVORS INNOVATE

Merchandise on the shelf and cash in the till spell successful companies. Survivors innovate.

Survivors have the consistent ability to make something from nothing which is perhaps their most intriguing quality. But to survive they must innovate, because nothing is usually all they have.

Innovation creates new policies and procedures, produces new ways of doing business, and teaches people new jobs. Innovation is much more than change. Even healthy companies change. Innovation is the art of improvising and juggling to compensate for chronic shortages everywhere. Survivors innovate because innovation is borne of desperation.

Survivors unshackle themselves from traditional procedures when traditional procedures no longer work. Innovation makes your business work with the resources you have today. Companies fail when they can't adapt to poverty. Those too accustomed to fixed ways of conducting business don't easily replace cash with creativity.

Talk to Chuck Collins about innovation. When the electric company cut the power to his floundering Toledo meat-processing plant, he hooked up a rented generator to keep it operating. Genius? No. But it is innovation, and this one innovative maneuver, along with a 1,001 other small tricks, helped save Chuck's business. The Chucks of this world survive because they innovate!

Innovation is critical in a turnaround because no workout goes according to plan; they zig, zag and bump against unexpected obstacles. And the smallest obstacle can stop the largest corporation unless it's an organization blessed with an innovative leader who knows how to navigate.

SURVIVORS BUST BUTTS

They start by busting their own butts. Survivors bring that critical ingredient to their sick company: Plenty of hard work.

Trying to survive is never glamorous. You must possess endless problem-solving techniques, the ability to work against intense pressures from every direction, and a willingness to slave sixteen hours a day, seven days a week. This "sweat-on-the-brow" commitment to your survival is often the difference between failure and success.

A workout can consume twice the effort needed to run a stable enterprise. Without the enthusiasm for endless hours in a pressure- cooker world, you'll inevitably quit. Scores of clients say essentially the same thing: "It's not so much the long hours, but what you have to put up with that gets to you."

And they're right! Ten hours on the job feels like thirty when you spend all your time dodging bullets. So how do you cope and bust your butt when things are at their darkest? Believe things will soon improve, and that your business will be worth the effort you gave it.

A stint with a troubled business is like a stint in Marine boot camp. You not only work harder than ever before but you reach an endurance level never before reached. As so many survivors report, once they've reached this peak performance, they never again want to slide back to mediocrity.

SURVIVORS PERSEVERE

Survivors don't quit.

Perseverance is essential. All other talents and strengths are meaningless if you quit or throw in the towel when things go wrong – as they invariably will. Survivors are optimists and perpetual believers because they often have nothing to trade on but their hopes and expectations. When this optimism gives out, there's nothing left to that word "survivor." There's only a quitter.

A dramatic lesson on the value of perseverance came my way about five years ago when I started to work with a brilliant, young Chicago semi-conductor engineer. Carl, a frustrated engineer, developed a series of microchips that represented a substantial technological advance, but because of serious production problems his young company was soon floundering in Chapter 11. His company languished in bankruptcy court for nearly three years while Carl ran into virtually every obstacle imaginable. I can't recall another case when so many things went wrong and so few things went right. Sure, Carl was down in the dumps. You bet! But there's a difference between disappointment and quitting. Survivors know how to get through their disappointments. Carl, after endless efforts, worked out his problems, and his company, now publicly traded, grosses about $150 million a year. Most people I know would have quit years earlier.

Perseverance is a remarkable strength, but one that must be tempered with reality. After all, there can be a time to call it quits. So balance perseverance and objectivity. Knowing when to give up can be as virtuous as perseverance if you surrender for all the right reasons, at the right time and in the right way.

Survivors sometimes survive best by not surviving at all. Think about it!

☑CHECKPOINT

1. Can you create the change your company needs to survive?

2. Can you build a climate of success for your organization?

3. Can you shake your organization out of its doldrums?

4. Can you talk about your problems and your progress with employees, suppliers, customers, lenders and creditors?

5. Can you make those tough decisions?

6. Can you negotiate effectively?

7. Can you innovate and make something from nothing?

8. Can you work your tail off to survive?

9. Can you persevere and stick it out...and can you call it quits when that's the right decision?

5

SOS: WHITE KNIGHTS AND THE TURNAROUND TEAM

Turnarounds are seldom one-person shows. Most well-orchestrated corporate comebacks team skilled workout and insolvency professionals with the best talent from within the company. This blend achieves optimum results.

Misery loves company! And company can be a mighty valuable commodity when your business hits the skids, particularly if you pick the right company to help piece your broken business together again.

Ask Ted Kaplan, whose Seventh Avenue Kaplan's Fashions sales plunged deeper than the daring necklines on its dresses. Its beleaguered owner had no answers and knew it was time to call in someone who did.

Nor is Ted ashamed to admit it. "We walked around in circles," he says. "Our stockroom bulged with unsold inventory. Our desks were buried under an avalanche of unpaid bills. And our competitors were hustling our best accounts. Disaster! My wisest investment was a twenty-five cent phone call to our attorney."

Kaplan's attorney quickly called in a top insolvency lawyer, who threw Kaplan's into a Chapter 11 reorganization to freeze creditor lawsuits and buy time to regroup and reshape the troubled manufacturer. Next, a sharp accountant came on board to control Kaplan's finances with a strict, no-nonsense budget. To raise fast cash, they hired a liquidation consultant. Kaplan's excess inventory was soon unloaded to several discount outlets. A more aggressive advertising campaign breathed new life into Kaplan's tired image. Soon Kaplan's showroom bustled with buyers from Macy's, Filene's, Bloomingdale's and Nieman Marcus. Kaplan couldn't produce his stylish dresses fast enough to fill the orders. You should have seen the smile on his boyish face.

If you ask him what magic saved his business, Ted laughs. "No magic. We were just a little too close to our business to see our problems, much less find the solutions. You sometimes need more objective and hard-nosed professionals to see what you can't see!"

CALL NOW, CALL COLLECT

You can't be too proud to accept your own limitations and call for help from the growing cadre of consultants, lawyers, accountants and other workout specialists who each offer essential skills and resources you need to save your business.

Timing is critical. When you ignore your problems, you also prolong seeking professional help. When you finally seek help, your business may be beyond the point of no return and no longer salvageable.

Why would you hesitate to call for professional help? You may see it as admitting failure or as an inability to solve your own problems. We turnaround consultants often play psychiatrists to convince struggling business owners that there is no shame when you lean on stronger shoulders. You are not infallible, nor are your business problems a loathsome disease. Every business eventually gets into trouble; the smartest business people use every resource at their disposal to survive and build a better business.

Money is always a factor when you can't even meet your payroll. You hardly welcome a $200-an-hour consultant or lawyer. At that point, professionals are seen not as a vital investment but as an unaffordable cost. One reluctant client once told me, "I don't need a high-priced consultant to tell me I'm running out of money." But he did! More importantly, he needed someone objective, forceful and skilled to show him how not to run out of money. A few dollars in professional fees can save you more money and save your business. Reverse your thinking. Think about investment, not costs.

If you own a small- to mid-size business, you are probably less familiar and hence less comfortable with outside professionals than are corporate executives. You may not fully understand the many ways professionals can help you. The idea of a consultant can be scary. Perhaps you envision a mystery man in a three-piece suit drowning you in complicated reports, charts and hieroglyphic graphs. It happens. But not if you choose the right professionals. Success or failure often depends on you finding the right professional talent. But you must find them! Keep one point in mind: You got your business into trouble. Why would you think you can get out of trouble on your own?

Technical skill is only part of what a consultant, attorney or accountant can offer. More important is how these professionals think. As difficult as it is to navigate the thriving business, a complex turnaround demands unique skills and strange techniques that defy conventional management practices. Pros who understand how to put together broken companies play by rules only others within the insolvency field understand.

While their managerial and professional skills are invaluable, their professional objectivity is critical. Like Ted Kaplan, you may get too close to your problems to see them clearly. Your situation blurs when you are deeply involved emotionally and financially. And independent professionals are not tainted by existing biases. They enter the picture with the fresh ability to look at things as they are, not as how you see them or want them to be.

You can have the right answers and correct solutions to your problems and still need outside professionals as a sounding board to confirm that your solutions are right. Your intuition about what must be done will usually be correct, but unless you have been through a turnaround or two, you may lack confidence in your own game plan. When a pro ratifies your decision, you can more confidently follow through and more forcefully press your decisions into action.

Outside professionals do for you what you cannot do for yourself. They tackle the dirty work of firing people or standing up to creditors, jobs you have no stomach for. Dirty work becomes my job when my client's company doesn't have a bastard on board.

Then there are the resources your advisors can provide. Insolvency consultants, attorneys and accountants form a small, closely knit professional network and can help you locate other star players for your team. My Garrett Group offers a nationwide roster of hundreds of other consulting firms and law firms, each outstanding in its specialty. We routinely match difficult-to-find professionals with financially troubled business owners. Most professional advisors similarly maintain close affiliations with banks, lenders, liquidators, business brokers and the many other specialists who serve troubled firms.

Of course, no two troubled companies need precisely the same professional aid. If you are unprofitable but still solvent, you need a consultant who can help you regain profitability. An insolvency attorney is of no value at this point. If you suffer from poor financial controls or a weak marketing strategy, your professionals must have those specialized operational skills; broad turnaround experience may not be enough. So your one most important decision is determining precisely the assistance you need from:

- Turnaround consultants

- Business or operations consultants

- Insolvency attorneys

- Auditors and accountants

- Key personnel

WHITE KNIGHTS TO THE RESCUE

Turnaround consultants, or "white knights," as they like to be called, are always ready to ride to the rescue of the company in distress. For a fee, of course!

Turnaround consulting is one of the fastest-growing specialties within the broader field of management consulting. However, there are still relatively few good turnaround consultants, far too few for the many distressed companies that need their help. In fact, only a handful of America's management consultants (fewer than one percent) do turnarounds. Despite skyrocketing business bankruptcies, "corporate fixer-uppers" are so rare a breed that their craft lacks a universal name. I call myself an R&R expert — in the "repair-and-rebuild" business.

Turnaround consulting is a highly segmented field; you won't easily find the right consultant. They excel in different situations, seldom work the same territory and operate in narrow niches. Some turnaround consultants, for example, handle only certain types of businesses like manufacturing, wholesaling or retailing. Others work specific industries such as textiles, real estate or nursing homes. Consultants also can characterize their practice by the size of their clients' businesses. Few consultants handle small businesses because small businesses can least afford the staggering fees. So the more skilled consultants seek the challenging and financially rewarding opportunities only a big company with big problems and a still bigger bankroll can provide.

Turnaround consultants also offer very different skills — but no one consultant is an expert in every phase of the workout. Don't let one who claims to be fool you. Forget the turnaround consultant's aura of mystique. They still put their pants on one leg at a time, just like the rest of us mortals. And a consultant waving impeccable credentials can easily con the unwary.

There are plenty of guys and gals running around with degrees from Harvard and Stanford who have never talked to a creditor or knows what to do when your checks start bouncing. And a stint at Booz-Hamilton or Arthur Anderson doesn't necessarily produce a pro who knows the 101 dirty little tricks you must resort to when the going gets rough.

The turnaround consultant's strengths and weaknesses are based on his or her own training, experience, aptitudes and interests. A consultant who can brilliantly stem losses may be helpless with your creditors. My Garrett Group has a nationwide reputation for restructuring corporate debt; we don't become deeply involved in operational problems. Many turnaround consultants handle only one or two stages of the turnaround. I frequently work with one busy Chicago consultant who only stabilizes cash flow for companies in deep financial crisis. Once stabilized, the business is turned over to other consultants, who continue the rehabilitation by tackling the debts and making the company profitable.

Consider your company's condition when you shop for your consultant. Not all turnaround consultants are good crisis managers. Some prefer companies in the early stages of the downturn rather than the challenge of a company on the edge. And yet others thrive in the pressure-cooker climate of a firm a half-step away from bankruptcy. The stress-induced exhilaration is, for many in my kind of work, its own reward.

Turnaround consultants also work in different ways. Some rescue floundering companies by completely taking over their management until it is fully revitalized. Such "fixer-uppers" rely heavily on teamwork and bring in their own turnaround people to chart the course and implement the plan. They bet on themselves. When they win, as they nearly always do, they rake in big fees. In contrast, small-firm consultants are usually part-time advisors who simultaneously service many clients on a per-diem or hourly basis.

Most turnaround consultants don't work for the troubled company. That may surprise you. They represent banks, other lenders and creditor groups. Their job then is to recoup what they can from the stricken debtor. Commercial lenders routinely employ workout consultants to breathe new life into a dying borrower with hopes that prolonged life will produce prolonged payments.

Caution: Never mistake a lenders workout consultant for someone who will look out for your interests. The chicken should never look to the fox for comfort. In a workout, you and your creditors have adversarial interests. You need an independent consultant with no allegiance to creditors.

Turnaround consultants, whatever their differences, usually share an accidental career born when their own company fell onto hard times. Virtually all turnaround consultants I know, including myself, can recollect the days when they wrestled the very same problems they now wrestle for clients. From this experience, they discovered that the challenge becomes even more enjoyable when they save someone else's sick company!

How do you find a capable turnaround specialist? The *Turnaround Management Association, Society for the Advancement of Management* and the *American Society of Consulting Engineers* are three national organizations with turnaround consultants as members, although consultants in these organizations usually handle only larger companies. Court-appointed bankruptcy trustees are frequently skilled at rehabilitating financially troubled companies. Ask the clerk at your local bankruptcy court for some references. Trustees appointed by the court to operate Chapter 11 companies are who you want, not trustees who oversee Chapter 7 (liquidating bankruptcy) cases.

Credit associations, banks and lenders are other good sources if they can recommend conflict-free consultants. This is an important point. Your consultant must be doggedly on your side as a debtor, and consultants who consistently represent creditors don't always switch gears easily.

The Small Business Administration's SCORE (Service Corps of Retired Executives) program also can provide workout consultants. You need not be an SBA borrower to qualify for this valuable free aid. One drawback is that SCORE consultants are part-time volunteers, so you may not get the firepower you need. Look around. If you still can't find a good consultant, give me a call. Because I work with consultants throughout the country, I can probably recommend a good consultant in your area.

Talk to several consultants before you hire one. Probe their ideas. Beware consultants who paint too optimistic a picture or guarantee results. The field is full of phonies who trade on false hopes. Listen carefully to your prospective consultant's ideas and how thoroughly he or she approaches your situation. Fast answers and glib solutions are not what you need. The consultant's questions will reveal more about the consultant than will his answers.

Scrutinize references! Investigate your prospect's track record in similar situations and for comparable companies. A good consultant will gladly refer you to former clients. While professional skills are important, you also must develop a comfortable and compatible relationship with your consultant, so personalities are equally important.

Selecting the right consultant is only half the battle. Unless you effectively use your consultant, you will accomplish nothing worthwhile. A poor working relationship between you and your consultant can do more harm than no relationship.

Having run your own business, you may find it difficult to suddenly accept direction from a newcomer, even one with impeccable credentials. We all naturally resent outsiders. And you will certainly resist a consultant who is forced on you by lenders or creditor groups who have lost confidence in your ability to rescue your business.

Even if you welcome your consultant, your employees may not. Employees typically view consultants with disdain, because they see the consultant as a threat to their jobs and authority.

On the other extreme, you may be only too glad to abdicate complete managerial responsibility and decision-making to your consultant. You may be too weary to continue the battle, or foolishly believe your consultant has magical managerial powers. Turnaround consultants may better understand the turnaround process, but you are best qualified to coordinate turnaround decisions with everyday business operations. After all, you best know your own field! Consultants who dominate decision-making will make serious mistakes without your continuous input. If you relinquish all control to a consultant, you may harbor unrealistic expectations about what your consultant can accomplish, and you'll be disappointed when those results are not achieved.

For an effective working relationship, you and your consultant must each understand your respective roles in the workout. You must then clearly communicate the consultant's authority and functions to the key people within your company. Establish a clear chain of command. You start by deciding whether your consultant will have direct decision-making authority or will only serve as an advisor and report to you.

Your consultant's role must not only be clearly defined within your company, but also within the turnaround team. Only then can the consultant develop a good working relationship with your attorneys, accountants and other advisors. Consultants can overstep their managerial roles just as lawyers offer business advice and accountants practice law. Good professional teamwork starts with mutual respect for the respective professional roles.

Conflict between turnaround consultant and attorney is common, as each sees themselves as captain of the team. Lawyers have traditionally headed the team, but this is only because they can so easily intimidate. Then too, turnarounds usually are steeped in legal proceedings.

As a turnaround consultant and insolvency attorney, my view is that the turnaround consultant should head the team. A turnaround consultant has a better grasp of the overall situation and can emphasize practical business solutions rather than legal solutions. Lawyers are too pigeon-holed in the law to be good turnaround leaders.

Your consultant can only be fully accepted if presented correctly. Employees who might view your consultant as a sign of your managerial inadequacy must instead see the consultant as bolstering your capabilities. Creditors who believe the consultant's fees may drain cash best used to pay their bills must instead see the consultant as their best hope for recovering even more of their money. Everyone concerned with the company's future must see the consultant as a source of credibility – a voice to say exactly what is – when you can no longer be taken at your word. An effective consultant knows that to repair a faltering business, he or she must communicate credibly to employees, suppliers, lenders, creditors and stockholders. That means an ability to anticipate and satisfy their respective concerns.

What about fees? Good consultants are worth whatever the asking price, because they alone spell the difference between success and failure. Because you will find plenty of incompetents and frauds who will hit you for a big retainer and never give you the help you need, pay your consultant as your case proceeds. Refuse big retainers. Let the consultant generate his or her own fees by producing more cash flow. Nor should you dig into your personal pocket to pay the consultant. If the consultant isn't clever enough to figure out how to extract fees from your business, he shouldn't be your consultant.

All in all, the turnaround consultant's life is far from easy. You may unrealistically expect too rapid or smooth a turnaround, and others involved with your company also may expect miracles. You may see a consultant as a substitute for bad management. But that's wrong! A consultant can only help a good manager straighten out a bad business.

BUSINESS CONSULTANTS:
Back to Basics

Business consultants are a breed apart from turnaround consultants, but are equally critical for most turnarounds. While the turnaround consultant cures the effects of corporate ills, business consultants attack their root causes. One example: A six- month turnaround of a near-bankrupt Texas kitchen cabinet manufacturer. I successfully stabilized their cash flow and restructured over $1,200,000 in liabilities. But why did the company get into trouble originally? Inefficient production and poor marketing were the two big reasons. The company is rapidly becoming a big profit-maker because I found a production engineer who improved productivity 200 percent. And a top-notch Fort Worth advertising agency soon will roll out a hard-hitting marketing program. I know this will dramatically boost their sales and profits. Troubled companies are sometimes victimized by very basic production, merchandising, marketing, distribution or similar operational problems that are best solved by consultants with specialized operational skills or industry experience.

Turnaround consultants may see obvious problems within a troubled company, yet not know the tricks of that particular trade. But those tricks can make the difference between a failed, mediocre, or highly successful turnaround. That's why we summoned a five-star Boston restaurateur to help a struggling Cape Cod restaurant break away from three years of big losses. Profits came with a new menu, stricter portion control, smarter buying and a vastly improved waste-prevention program. Only a hands-on restaurant pro could deliver this valuable know-how. A turnaround may only involve correcting one or two very basic problems solved by someone with good industry experience.

To find your business consultant, look for someone with a track record from within your industry. You don't need inexperienced business consultants in the operational areas where you need help. Seek practical, nuts-and-bolts answers. Identify your operational weaknesses. Who in your field excels in merchandising, promotion, inventory control and buying? Your industry has its heavy hitters who don't compete with you. Do you need a restaurant consultant? Why not approach a highly successful restaurant owner outside your trading area?

Ask prospective consultants what they can do for you and how long it will take. Remember, few consultants can take much time from their own businesses, but they may improve your business significantly with only a few hours of valuable tips.

Most of the best "consultants" never consulted before, but work full-time in their own businesses. I look for retired businesspeople who were highly successful in their industries. They offer more time and more experience. I find these people are flattered when you ask for their help because you are acknowledging their business skills and success.

Give your consultant a free hand to thoroughly review your entire operation. If you define the problem, you lose the opportunity to have your consultant detect other problems. This can be his or her most important function.

But do set guidelines. Ask your consultant to outline your major problems. Rank each by priority and decide how each may be best solved.

You may need more than one consultant if your business needs help in different operational areas. But too much reliance on outside consultants can be overkill for the smaller business.

Still, no business is too small to seek outside help. And the smaller the business, the more help it may need. When Zisson's Bakery began to lose customers, I called on Harry Winston, Boston's bakery king. Harry gladly appeared in his colored apron, which served as his trademark, sampled a few cookies and, within two minutes, rendered his diagnosis: "Too much salt."

Harry's prescription? A new recipe, an advertising campaign and higher prices. Harry even threw in recipes for a few of his famous ethnic delicacies guaranteed to attract every sweet tooth within ten miles. Zisson's sales climbed steadily from $350,000 to more than $1 million a year. Harry, always delighted to help a fellow baker, boasts, "Why not? I'm still king! Why not kiss a few toads if I can turn them into princes." The Harry Winstons of your field mean business! Plenty of business!

And I have had plenty of similar cases. Higgins Motors couldn't sell enough new cars to stay afloat until a high-powered dealer from a nearby state showed the Higgins brothers all the proven tricks to sell more cars. All it took was a small fee. Higgins Motors now ranks first in Mercury dealership regional sales.

Save-On Foods was victimized by its own poor merchandising until a retired buyer from a large supermarket chain loaded Save-On's shelves with precisely the right merchandise at the right price. Sales doubled.

Salvatori's Italian Foods, neighborhood pizza and beer favorite with the college crowd, never made any money. Mary Salvatori couldn't see her problem, but a more successful Italian restaurateur did. Following her consultant's advice, Mary upgraded her restaurant and dropped the pizza and beer from the menu. Higher-priced Italian cuisine boosted sales and profits dramatically, as the big spenders replaced the college kids on tiny budgets.

Why did White Cross Drug lose money when it looked like it was flourishing? Another successful pharmacy owner found the answer. Poor buying. The consultant made one phone call to an out-of-state supplier with lower prices and saved White Cross about $40,000 a year. It wasn't a fortune, but it was enough to turn a loser into a winner!

Your business has only your talent, experience and capabilities to rely upon. When you lack certain know-how on these countless decisions that affect your bottom line, you often guess wrong (it is invariably a guess). If you stumble on a few big decisions, or too many small ones, your profits quickly become losses. To correct the situation, you must detach yourself from your business long enough to stick your head out the front door and yell for help.

Too few troubled firms follow my advice. Perhaps you never thought about a consultant to show you how to run a better business. Without this help, your turnaround will suffer from the same day-to-day errors that originally caused your losses. So give top priority to a consultant who can give you objective, expert advice on how to make your business a money-maker. It's smart business. The winners within your industry will put you on the fast track to profitability if you ask for their help!

LAWYERS RIDING SHOTGUN

Consultants and workout specialists are invaluable in a turnaround. Good legal advice is vital. As much as we all want to avoid lawyers and big legal fees, a turnaround always involves legal issues and problems, even when bankruptcy is unnecessary. You too will invariably need an attorney, even if it's to forestall and defend creditor suits and to threaten your creditors with bankruptcy if a more pleasant and cooperative workout is unsuccessful.

Yet after nearly thirty years as a bankruptcy attorney, I confess that too many troubled small- to mid-sized businesses are lost each year because of poor legal advice. These firms, trying to struggle through their problems without a consultant, rely too heavily on their attorneys for guidance. This can be a fatal mistake because few attorneys are skilled in rehabilitating troubled companies. Real estate, criminal and probate lawyers, who wouldn't know a balance sheet from a cash-flow statement, too frequently get involved in complex business and insolvency cases. Since law is as specialized as medicine, forget Uncle Joe the lawyer. He drafted your superb will, but what does he really know about business insolvency, bankruptcy and turnarounds?

Hire an attorney well-experienced in saving troubled companies. You need a legal gunslinger who knows every trick and strategy to defend you and your beleaguered company from your numerous foes. A rare breed? You bet. There are fewer attorneys who can legitimately claim competence in this field than there are bona fide turnaround consultants. Many lawyers routinely handle Chapter 7 business and personal bankruptcy cases, but these liquidating bankruptcies are relatively simple and require far less skill than do complex corporate turnarounds and reorganizations.

Salvageable businesses are liquidated every day because their attorneys didn't know how to save them. If your attorney can't recommend a workable rescue strategy, find one who can. Whatever you do, do not liquidate or throw your business into bankruptcy without a second opinion from a seasoned turnaround consultant. I offer this advice because too many lawyers don't see solutions other than liquidation or bankruptcy. A turnaround consultant, on the other hand, seeks ways to avoid liquidation and bankruptcy to keep a business alive.

The right lawyer knows not only the right legal strategies, but how to maneuver within the insolvency system. She or he has battled creditors' lawyers many times before and knows what to expect. Creditors' and debtors' counsel meet on many cases and necessarily forge a smooth, if adversarial, working relationship. Having handled scores of Chapter 11 cases, I can tell you it's easier to negotiate a plan of reorganization with an attorney for the creditors' committee when you are on a first-name basis. This same familiarity also benefits you in the courtroom. A bankruptcy judge may give the benefit to a lawyer who regularly appears before him. This judicial leeway can decide the outcome of your case.

Insolvency attorneys, like turnaround consultants, have a network of resources to help a business survive. They know which banks lend to troubled companies. They deal with accountants who can untangle your numbers. Consultants? Your insolvency attorney is probably your best referral source.

Your regular lawyer probably can refer you to a good bankruptcy lawyer. Don't be reluctant to ask for a reference. Few lawyers resent referring a client to a specialist in another area of practice. Or ask the clerk of the bankruptcy court for the names of local practitioners. State and local bar associations also list qualified bankruptcy attorneys, and some states even provide certification to bankruptcy specialists who have passed rigid competency exams. In these states, this probably is the best place to start.

Stay away from a large, silk-stocking law firm unless yours is a larger company. Blue-chip law firms are too expensive for the smaller business. I also don't recommend them because they are too conservative and stick to traditional textbook remedies, such as Chapter 11, when a more creative zig-and-zag strategy may be your answer. Nor do larger firms guarantee you better service for their bigger fees. Small, less important clients end up with overpriced junior associates, not the more seasoned partners. The best bet in almost any city are the small, aggressive law firms, or even sole practitioners.

Legal representation is a necessary evil. The lawyer is necessary, the fee is evil. But here are four money-saving tips:

Tip #1. Don't avoid legal help because you don't have the money.

A good insolvency lawyer, like a seasoned turnaround pro, knows how to squeeze fees from the business. No small-business owner ever walked into my office with a large retainer. Few insolvency lawyers expect it. If you had plenty of money, you wouldn't be there.

Tip #2. You and your counsel should plan what your business can afford to pay and when.

Your attorney will, of course, want reasonable progress payments, while you instinctively will fight for every dime to help keep your business afloat. But you can't expect lawyers or consultants to bill you at the end of your case any more than they should insist upon a large, unaffordable retainer.

Tip #3. Don't negotiate a fixed fee arrangement.

It's impossible to predict how may hours will be required to properly handle your case, as unexpected problems may arise. But do ask for a fee range.

Tip #4. Your workout options will depend on what you can afford.

Attorneys, for example, cannot profitably handle even a small Chapter 11 reorganization for less than $15,000, a fee well beyond the reach of a tiny corner store whose solution must fit its pocketbook.

Remember, when you retain an attorney (or other professional) you do not spend your money. You spend your creditors' money. Creditors, for all practical purposes, own the insolvent company, and it is they who eventually and indirectly pay your bill for professional services.

Plenty of my colleagues agree with me when I say that lawyers are counterproductive to a turnaround because they think narrowly in terms of legal solutions. They don't understand business, which must, after all, be the foundation of the turnaround. But the lawyer does have a role in a turnaround. Lawyers shouldn't drive the stagecoach, but they are great for riding shotgun.

THE NUMBER CRUNCHERS

I fire accountants who don't help our mutual clients to financially manage their business. We regain credibility and creditor confidence only when new accountants take the financial controls. Replacing accountants is absolutely essential when your accountants helped conceal your poor corporate condition through manipulative accounting. Fire your accountants if they were too slow to alert you to your declining financial condition. Accountants who only prepare neat balance sheets, but won't tell you how untidy those numbers really are, do not belong on your turnaround team.

Every company needs basic financial controls to stay on course, but accurate, detailed and timely financial data is absolutely critical for the crisis company. Your accountants must understand your business if they are to know how to plug in the important controls quickly. One highly successful certified public accountant in my area specializes in workouts for financially troubled nonprofit schools. To bolster his effectiveness, he designed a remarkably efficient financial-information system that has proven invaluable in navigating troubled schools back to health. This level of specialized expertise is uncommon, yet it shows that accounting nurtures its own brand of specialists. Even the once-stodgy Big Seven accounting firms are now organizing boutique-turnaround consulting divisions.

For those important numbers, your accountant must thrive in a world of cash flows, cost analysis, break-even projections, forecasting and budgeting. Your accountant must answer critical questions: Where are you making or losing money? What is your new break-even point if you drop a product or shut a plant? What is your forecasted cash position in the next 60 days? Bring on board a first-rate financial navigator!

The right financial navigator will skillfully analyze your operation. He or she is a rare breed; a blend of comptroller, visionary, and magician who coordinates the numbers to guide you toward a positive cash flow and ultimate profitability.

I consider the financial function so important to a successful workout that I frequently hire a comptroller for even small firms that ordinarily would operate without this level of financial support. Larger firms may have number crunchers, but not necessarily the right ones. So we then search for new financial talent.

Larger firms usually have their financials audited by the creditors' accountants. Auditors for lenders and trade creditors also may check for fraud, embezzlement, creditor preferences as well as monitoring the company's financial controls. This includes the cash flow and profit projections creditors must rely upon for credit and settlement decisions.

Most accounting firms are eager for turnaround work. However, not all accounting firms can commit the time and personnel. Complex workouts demand considerable accounting work, particularly in the early stages. A major bankruptcy reorganization can consume thousands of accounting hours.

The financial function is considered so important to a turnaround that some turnaround consultants employ their own accountants to ensure they get the support they need. Even a company with good accounting systems may have its consultant's accounting staff monitor accuracy. Because turnaround companies can over optimistically forecast, I continuously challenge the assumptions upon which they base their rosy future. Only then do I see things as they really are. Your accountant's most important function is to see things as they really are, not as you would like them to be!

What type of accounting firm should you look for? A new professional designation, CMA (Certified Management Accountant), is now awarded to accountants expert in managerial accounting (as opposed to auditing, taxation and statement compilation, the CPA's bread and butter). CMA's are ideal to navigate your turnaround. But titles are unimportant. Bookkeepers guided some of my most successful cases, and they performed exceptionally once we told them the numbers we wanted.

Bankruptcy courts frequently appoint accountants as trustees for Chapter 11 reorganizations. These accountants are usually in private practices and can be an excellent addition to your team. They possess the right financial skills because they have handled many other financially distressed businesses. Considering the importance of accountants' reports to both the courts and creditors, employing an accountant they know and trust can be a very smart move.

TALENT FROM WITHIN

Your turnaround also will need all the help it can get from key employees who can work closely with your outside advisors as valuable members of your turnaround team. The employees you select will, of course, depend on the size and nature of your company, its organization and the quality and capabilities of your staff. Include no more than four insiders, as larger groups become too unmanageable.

Select employees with the broadest operational responsibilities. This will give you a more balanced input and a more accurate assessment of how the turnaround decisions will affect general business operations. Line managers best understand the practicalities of turnaround decisions, and since they must implement those decisions, it is best to have them participate in their formulation.

Encourage employees on your turnaround committee to express their own views and to freely disagree with you and your professional advisors. You don't need followers or "yes men." Also choose key managers ready to initiate and carry out the changes. In fact, populate your team with employees most anxious for change. Avoid long-entrenched employees who will resist change when it discredits their prior actions or threatens their authority. Otherwise-excellent employees impede progress when they fight change. And they seldom work well on a turnaround committee whose goal is to bring change. Look deep within your organization for those mavericks. Pick people who can enthusiastically put your company on a more profitable path.

To pick the right people for your turnaround team you must know your people. And you only know your people when you plan with them, work with them and encourage them to communicate openly with you. Are they results-oriented? Can they work well in a crisis? Can they carry out difficult orders? Can they implement and improvise without essential resources? Can they motivate their subordinates? Do they possess the unique skills and strengths your turnaround needs? A rising star glows most in a moment of need. Many of today's corporate leaders won their stripes in the combat of a turnaround. Few return to the boring luxury of working in normal companies that simply make money.

I always invest time talking to the key employees of a troubled business. It's a good investment, because they usually see the problems and solutions most clearly. They offer objective and sensible advice, because they have watched the company deteriorate daily. I test their interest and measure the added responsibilities they can assume. I ignore complex organizational charts. I simply assign individual tasks to those who can best handle them. When it comes to getting your business out of trouble, you must accept the reality that you cannot do everything yourself. And you must know which of your employees can perform various functions better than you can. That's why I routinely delegate creditor problems to a tough-skinned employee. I know employees usually can run interference and field the time-consuming creditor threats more easily than the owner. Tough-skinned employees make invaluable turnaround-team players.

A key and trusted employee also can be a godsend when you're tired and beaten. A key employee may be your perfect takeover candidate. Dyson Lumber's owner Dick Dyson will tell you he was only hours away from a nervous breakdown when his assistant manager grabbed the reigns. He had sound ideas for curing the ailing multi- million dollar lumberyard, and he had the energy and ability to convert those ideas into reality. Dick's up-and-coming assistant was quickly appointed captain of the turnaround team and worked with me night and day to save the business. Thanks to his help, today it operates six highly successful lumberyards in eastern Pennsylvania.

The turnaround process also includes detecting and curing staff deficiencies. If your people won't support you, change your people, not your game plan. If Dick Dyson's aggressive assistant manager hadn't been around to spearhead the turnaround, I would have found that person. I knew Dick Dyson couldn't handle it, but the job had to be done. Surviving means plugging the holes in your team. Key employees adequate for the solvent enterprise are not always the answer for the troubled company.

To motivate employees on your turnaround team, you must effectively use their talent. They then feel involved because they are making good things happen. These key employees can create an infectious enthusiasm that inspires other employees.

Sometimes you need a crisis to get the best from your employees. When Star Electronics, a $6-million-a-year St. Louis transistor firm, over-expanded, our turnaround team included the sales manager and production manager. These two employees had a bushel of terrific ideas for expanding sales and production. Why didn't these ideas surface before? The owner never asked them for their opinions, and seemed uninterested in their views. The turnaround team was their open forum.

We encouraged Star's sales manager to pursue institutional accounts. The production manager was invited to act on his recommendation to dump their old and inefficient typesetting equipment for a leased state-of-the-art computerized printer. The turnaround team carefully analyzed their ideas before flashing the green light. The sales manager and his staff of twelve salespeople became balls of fire. The production department also came alive. Positive things were happening, and these two employees kept it no secret.

Your key people may not be of this caliber. Your support may be from someone outside your company. Is a partner your answer? Conglomerates merge for managerial synergy. It can make even more sense for the small business owner with neither the inclination nor the talent to whip a company back into shape.

It was the answer for Carlos, the once-proud owner of New York's Skyway Stereo Centers, whose $3.2 million-a-year business was mired in bankruptcy. Poor Carlos just couldn't cope. And Carlos had no employees capable of taking control. I developed the turnaround strategies, and Carlos's accountant ran the numbers. But who would implement our plans?

We were convinced the business could succeed, but who could turn it into a reality? Certainly not Carlos, busily putting away his sorrows on the golf course. With Carlos no longer on the turnaround team, we searched for a designated hitter. To the rescue came Barbara, who had masterfully converted a nearby Radio Shack store into the pride of the Tandy chain. Barbara soon became Carlos's partner, acquiring her share in the business from her share of future profits. Carlos and his golf course are now inseparable. That's OK. Carlos can afford 18 holes every day because his business now earns him over $600,000 a year!

Your starting lineup may or may not be your best team, but without a good captain there's no team! The owner still is the best leader for any turnaround team. An owner can delegate substantial responsibility to employees, but turnaround success usually needs an owner who cares as only an owner can. Leadership, for what it's worth, is most prized when it comes from the top.

☑CHECKPOINT

1. Do you need professional help? Why?

2. What type of professional assistance do you need?

3. Have you considered hiring a turnaround consultant?

4. What operational problems do you need assistance with?

5. Is your lawyer qualified to handle your financially troubled business?

6. Has your accountant financially navigated your business well in the past? Can he effectively guide you throughout the workout?

7. What key employees would be valuable members of the turnaround team?

8. Are you ready to assume your role as leader of the turnaround team?

6

DESIGNING YOUR TURNAROUND

Any troubled business can find success if it chooses that one correct strategy. Your business is no exception. Most strategies follow what any good manager does to survive and improve profits: Change products or services, undertake new marketing, improve efficiency and productivity, make organizational changes and reduce costs.

You must consider these same options. But when your losses are large, you may need to combine these strategies, because your goal is not simply to improve profits, but to transform a poorly performing operation.

So not all turnaround strategies are basic management manipulations. While some do correct fundamental operational weaknesses — such as introducing stricter financial controls, others exploit new markets, products or services far afield of what they offered before.

Turnaround strategies must reshape organizations on a speed and scale unknown to the stable, well-performing firm. Most turnaround companies drastically downsize, but others may grow rapidly through acquisition to become profitmakers. Nearly all turnarounds restructure their debt.

All successful turnarounds share the goal of creating a financially stable, profitable and solvent company. Those must be your objectives. Accomplish less, and you have a failed turnaround.

KEY RECOVERY STRATEGIES

There is no one way to bail out of trouble. Yet from working with hundreds of troubled firms, I have found significant differences in how successful and unsuccessful firms attempt recovery.

Successful recoveries nearly always improved their financial controls. Failed companies usually tried to improve their financial controls but usually didn't use their financial data intelligently.

Successful recoveries prioritized cash-generation tactics throughout the workout. Cash generation was sporadic, weak and a technique largely ignored among failures.

Both successful and unsuccessful companies tried to improve marketing, but successful firms made fundamental changes in their products, services and prices. Failures were generally status-quo marketers.

Cost reduction is attempted by nearly all troubled firms, but failures relied on it as their primary strategy. Cost-cutting, while always important, is only one of many strategies survivors employ.

Selling profitable parts of the business to raise cash is common among successful turnarounds. Failures more slowly shed their winners.

Improved communication and decentralization characterize surviving companies. Failing firms usually are autocratic, uncommunicative and centralized.

Larger firms that succeeded usually bring in new management to spearhead their turnarounds; failing firms generally didn't.

Most importantly, survivors use many turnaround strategies. Failed firms rely upon few or solitary survival tactics.

Interestingly, this is true of all industries; from manufacturers to service firms, these basic survival tactics are universal.

If strategy is important, so is how well you implement your strategies. A good job on one or two central strategies beats dabbling with a dozen. Yet all successful turnarounds must do enough important things well!

FIVE KEYS TO A SUCCESSFUL TURNAROUND STRATEGY

Which turnaround strategies are for you? The answer is partially intuitive and often beyond your control. But to the extent you can intelligently plan, you will be guided by five key factors:

1. the severity of your problems

2. your resources

3. the reasons for your troubles

4. your type of business

5. the attitude of those involved with your company

#1 Severity of the problem

If your business has been steadily losing money, it needs a turnaround, although you may not yet have a crisis. A crisis (whether you are making or losing money) occurs when you run out of money, or creditors try to close you down.

A serious cash crisis requires that cash-raising strategies take priority over all else. Instant stability, not long-term profitability or solvency, is the essence of your turnaround. Cash- raising must be immediate. Defer tactics that will improve cash flow later, or that may produce cash. Do what you know will produce cash.

Non-crisis firms also may be unprofitable and insolvent, but they have less need to raise fast cash. These firms can more leisurely assess their problems, options and opportunities. They can tinker more with organizational and operational adjustments than can crisis firms. When you're out of money, urgency is your only strategy.

#2 The available resources

Virtually any business can be saved if you throw enough money at it. But what if you don't want to throw more money, or have no more money to throw?

What you can do to pull your business out of trouble obviously, depends heavily on your resources; resources within the business, as well as your own, and what you can borrow.

An ailing company with modest assets may have enough strength to withstand an always-draining Chapter 11, but more anemic firms may be limited to a faster and less costly dump-buyback, as described in Chapter 14.

You need common sense in a turnaround. You also must innovate to keep your doors open, hold creditors at bay and find those long- lost profits using the resources available to you.

Being resource-rich is not always good. Companies losing money but that still have healthy balance sheets may remain too comfortable to develop a survival instinct. The most spectacular turnarounds are usually firms without two pennies to rub together.

#3 Why you're in trouble

To discover how to get out of trouble, you may need to discover how you got into trouble. An oversimplification perhaps, but a good starting place nevertheless. Poor financial controls require good financial controls. Excessive costs require cost reductions. Still, your overall survival strategy may include sub-strategies. For example, a non-competitive firm plagued by price predators may try cost reductions, product changes or new marketing tactics as sub-strategies. Turnarounds must tackle the root causes of their problem as well as all other problems.

#4 The type of business

The industry or the specific service or product sold influences the turnaround strategy. For instance, undifferentiated products are overly price sensitive. This eliminates price increases as a feasible turnaround strategy, while product-focusing works on highly segmented markets with identifiable customer preferences.

Firms within fragmented industries also are more likely to survive than are those in monopolistic industries controlled by several key players. Industries with only a few major customers create equally poor turnaround environments, because the troubled firm too easily falls victim to its customers' strong bargaining position.

Rapidly changing high-growth industries offer a more hospitable turnaround environment for several reasons: First, they can more readily regain the competitive edge through new technology. Second, more alluring companies more easily attract capital. Third, mergers and takeovers within these industries create more opportunities to hitch a straggler to a star.

#5 Attitude

How a company wiggles out of trouble – or whether it can wiggle its way clear – rests chiefly on the attitude and desires of its managers, employees, shareholders, creditors and customers.

In a downturn, problems at first are internalized. Outsiders remain unaffected. Decision-making is left to managers. Only as the corporate fortunes erode do shareholders become more vocal. Non- performing loans put lender pressure on the organization. Employee terminations create proactive labor union which influence the fate of the company. Soon all play tug-o-war with the company as they each try to protect their respective interests.

Lenders and creditors may see liquidation as the best way to recover their money. Managers or labor unions may want the business and the paychecks to continue. Shareholders may want liquidation or continuity — depending on how they see the business's future.

Even with shared, broad objectives, there may be conflict with individual strategies. One group may prefer to reduce debts through Chapter 11, others through an informal workout. To improve profits, one group will support downsizing, another acquisitions.

One advantage of the family-owned business: It's less political. "Mom and Pop" decide what happens with the business. Attitude is still all-important because the turnaround strategy must match what they can comfortably handle. A winning strategy fits the business and its people. Your attitude, skills and how you react to your situation are important considerations when selecting your right remedy,

My most successful cases have turnaround plans the owner could handle. Failures were usually mismatches. I may have correctly analyzed the business, but not the owner. As one bankruptcy specialist aptly stated: "Designing the right turnaround plan is like buying clothes. You need a suit that fits."

TYPES OF TURNAROUNDS

Every turnaround company also faces a wide range of possible outcomes – from complete and immediate failure, to short-term survival, to a sustained but unexciting future, to phenomenal success.

Unsuccessful turnarounds are either "no-hopers" or the temporary survivors.

The no-hopers can't even survive short term. They usually are woefully insolvent and slowly bleed cash with no prospects of ever making money. No-hopers have no *raison d'etre* and cannot justify the time, money or effort for a turnaround. No-hopers, whether a tired, beaten corner store or a Fortune 500 company, are dinosaurs or companies without futures.

Temporary survivors may linger for years. To the untrained eye, they may appear to have achieved a successful turnaround.

One reason these firms ultimately go bust is that they may have artificially survived, buoyed by a cash transfusion from their owners, or credit from a new round of lenders. What short-term profits they may have made never lasted. Most temporary survivors voluntarily close once their owners realize that despite their best efforts, the business will never meet their goals.

Long-term survivors can be similarly classified. First are the drifters who endlessly cling to life, if only by their thumbnails. Drifters usually lack the resources, skills or opportunities to become formidable players in the marketplace; still, drifters may produce enough profits to keep their owners happy and, as long as they do, they continue their unremarkable existence.

Achievers are the true turnaround successes. They emerge from their workouts to consistently earn above-average profits, or even to become industry superstars. Few survivors become achievers because most turnarounds continue to suffer serious weaknesses, whether in management or business concept. But any firm will stand a better chance of becoming an achiever if it tackles its problems sooner, not later.

Regardless of how turnarounds are classified, no company is static. Today's drifter may sparkle tomorrow, while today's achievers go bankrupt.

STAGES OF RECOVERY

Businesses fail in stages. They also recover in phases:

■ The evaluation phase

■ The stabilization phase

- The reorganization phase
- The growth phase

The evaluation phase:

During the evaluation stage, identify the causes of your problems, detect the most immediate threats and select short-term survival strategies. Start a long-term strategic plan to restructure your company's debts and become profitable.

The stabilization phase:

This phase begins almost simultaneously with the evaluation stage, but lasts longer. The stabilization stage centers on staying afloat through cost-cutting, cash-raising and revenue-generating strategies. Building a positive cash flow and tightening financial controls become priorities that shape organizational and operational changes: Terminating excess employees, closing plants, selling idle assets and reducing surplus inventories. To bolster cash reserves, seek short-term financing or asset-based loans. Stabilization usually lasts three months to a year or more, depending upon the size and complexity of your company and its losses. Most failures occur during the stabilization phase.

The reorganization phase:

Two important events characterize the reorganization phase. First, through strategic repositioning, your business begins to make money as you realize you must do business quite differently than before.

Profitability is only one goal. You still cannot ignore cash flow, improved controls and operational efficiency, all necessary for continued stability. Within the reorganization phase, you also begin to restructure your debts as you clean up your balance sheet.

Whether you're trying to regaining profitability or restructure debt, the primary objective depends on the company. Some companies are both unprofitable and insolvent. These firms, obviously, must become both solvent and profitable. But even consistent profitmakers, for a variety of reasons, can become insolvent. Once they become financially stable they need only contend with their creditors. Unprofitable companies with a healthy balance sheet must, in turn, concentrate on how to become profitable. These companies are rare because few businesses get serious about their problems until either they run out of money or creditors seriously threaten.

More companies survive the reorganization phase than the stabilization phase. Companies that stay financially stable have excellent survival odds. They may never earn big profits, but they can squeak by as long as their owners don't mind a mere squeak.

The growth phase:

A company's problems are largely behind it when it reaches the growth phase. The business is financially stable. The balance sheet is clean. It's making money or about to. It is again in a position to grow, whether through new products, improved marketing or through acquisitions. Growth may be modest, but at least the business is no longer going downhill. Many turnaround firms find that staying level is its own form of growth.

IMPLEMENTING YOUR TURNAROUND PLAN

When do you begin your turnaround? In a sense, you already have! Seeking survival strategies is the most important step toward recovery. But you probably have taken many other steps, which pinpoints a conscious attempt toward corporate recovery.

You can't precisely chart a turnaround course, because what you must do in a turnaround, and in what order, depends on several factors previously discussed. Speed is the only common characteristic.

While your initial plan may lack detail, it nevertheless will need a framework and action steps that lets you:

- ■ Visualize where your company should be.

- ■ Develop the strategies to get there.

- ■ Implement change.

- ■ Measure your progress.

Action Step #1: Set turnaround objectives

Clear and achievable objectives are to your business what a rudder is to a ship. Companies flounder without clear objectives and achievable goals. There's truth to the old axiom, "To get there, you must know where you want to go."

To create and communicate a new direction for your company, begin with a mission statement of what you expect your business to become within a fixed time. Turnaround leaders who mastermind brilliant comebacks to transform failing companies into dynamic entities are captains who knew exactly where they wanted their ships to go.

General Electric, a once-stodgy pipe-stack company with old-fashioned products and old-fashioned ways of doing business, became an industry pacemaker and trend-setter for a wide variety of consumer products. Jack Welch, GE's leader, had a precise vision for GE.

RCA, unlike GE (which later acquired RCA), envisioned a different future. It downsized back to the more familiar consumer electronics while shedding the unrelated companies that dragged RCA down. Like GE, RCA also knew exactly where it wanted to go.

General Electric and RCA are different companies with very different problems, that turned themselves around in completely different ways. They shared a vision of what they must become to succeed. Companies seldom stumble into a better future.

Corporate transformations aren't always radical. Nor should they be stated too broadly. Minor modifications may do. Good turnaround objectives are often mundane. For example, a stagnant New Hampshire wood-burning stove manufacturer carefully grouped five objectives into a clear, three-year mission for his young firm:

- Double sales in the midwestern states from $2 million to $4 million a year.

- Finance growth only from profits.

- Increase plant utilization from 70 to 90 percent.

- Reduce payroll from 12 to 9 percent of sales.

- Go from break-even this year to 6 percent profit next year and 8 percent in year three.

This entrepreneur knew exactly where he wanted to take his company. Notice how marketing, financial, operational and cost- reduction objectives can be neatly rolled into one coordinated blueprint for success!

Make your corporate objectives a target that you and your employees can shoot for. Turnaround targets must be singular and specific, not platitudes or generalizations. You want a specific result to be achieved so make your objectives measurable, with deadlines for achievement.

Above all, good turnaround objectives are simple. Complex, ponderous objectives seldom work. Too many MBAs author 300-page strategic plans that few understand and even fewer can implement. Your turnaround objectives are too complicated if your key employees can't immediately understand them.

Unrealistic turnaround objectives also are worthless. You need optimism in a turnaround, but optimism is neither fantasies nor delusions about what your company can soon become. Your objectives must be both financially and operationally achievable, considering your company's rocky track record and limited resources. Too ambitious turnaround objectives fail.

Prioritize your objectives. A company that loses money and is insolvent must improve profitability and become solvent. But which objective is more important? Which should you tackle first?

As your circumstances change, reshape your objectives. Because the interests of everyone involved in your business compete and clash, your nervous system will go through the wringer as you try to mesh your respective objectives. You must define your objectives, but they can't be set in a vacuum. When those involved in your company are a factor, diplomacy may force you to publicize one agenda and secretly work your own.

To reduce conflict, set long-term objectives first. You can easily work your way back to short-term objectives. Interchange, feedback and fine-tuning will keep your objectives on target and in sync with those involved in your workout.

Top managers don't easily see the forest for the trees, and are more likely to set unworkable and ill-conceived objectives, while employees may more accurately assess the corporate condition and more closely see its future. If owners are visionaries, employees are pragmatists. Good objectives need both.

Your objectives must be your own, but you must still sell your plan to lenders and creditors who have different objectives. Weak managers have their turnaround objectives set by lenders, creditors, suppliers, distributors and customers. They each add a piece to the jigsaw puzzle, but you invariably must piece together a total and often very different picture.

Action Step #2: Plan the right strategies

How will you achieve your objectives and turn your business into a debt-free money machine?

- Shutter losing activities?

- Cut costly programs?

- Undertake new marketing?

- Develop new procedures?

- Merge with another company?

- Grow by acquiring new companies?

- Shrink operations?

Strategies, like objectives, will change as your company navigates its way through the turnaround. During the emergency stage, you must improve cash flow and cut costs. Once stabilized, you plan for profits and restructure debts. You consider new acquisitions, new products or more aggressive marketing. These are strategies of opportunity, not the earlier strategies for survival.

You must overcome three obstacles to good strategic planning: First, sound strategies demand accurate short- and long-term financial forecasts, which may be unavailable. Without dependable financials, strategic plans can't be monitored. Incorrect strategies are usually the product of faulty financial assumptions.

Second, your strategies may be too rigid. You must quickly adapt to a rapidly changing corporate condition. Sound turnaround strategies are flexible, adaptive and reactive. Stay loose. You never can anticipate every unexpected bend in the road.

Third, strategies, like objectives, may be unrealistic. While objectives tell you where you want to go, strategies tell you how to get there. Coordinate the two. For instance, a goal to double the company's size is useless without a strategy to raise the necessary money.

Objectives and strategies also must match what you can afford. Distressed companies don't generate cash quickly or copiously. A strategic plan that depends on lots of cash carries a presumption of faulty thinking.

Strategies also mirror personalities. Some troubled companies are run by daredevils anxious to risk the corporate jewels on one bold turnaround gamble. Such adventurers "atomize and synthesize." Others are "fix-'em, close-'em or sell-'em" strategists. The turnaround style becomes the style of its leader. You have your own style and risk level. Your strategic moves make you comfortable. Stay loyal to your inner feelings.

Bold and assertive strategic plans can still offer a fall-back position. Good strategists have their escape hatch. Murphy's Law says if something can go wrong, it will! You must know when to abort one plan for another.

Don't expect to achieve all your goals or to accomplish them on schedule. Turnarounds don't travel straight roads or proceed without annoying pauses and spurts. Be prepared for what is, not for what was supposed to be.

Planning becomes bedraggled when you have misplaced faith in the infallibility of planning for planning's sake. The fallacy is that business problems can be completely and objectively recognized, defined, analyzed and solved. Human brains don't function quite so neatly.

Still, you must somehow define and arrange strategies. Keep it simple. Those around you will make decisions at different levels, at different times and each from a different perspective.

It was Napoleon who said, "Unhappy is the general who comes on the field of battle with a system." Napoleon knew the importance of keeping open strategic options.

Action Step #3: Implement change correctly

To implement your turnaround plan, keep your eye on four points:

1. What will be done?

2. Who will do what?

3. How will it be accomplished?

4. When will it be completed?

Organize your company for the task. Large corporations have squads orchestrate their turnarounds. Platoon systems need close coordination if turnaround decisions are to mesh well with everyday operations. Everybody must know his or her job. Turnarounds stumble when employees neither know the overall game plan or their own roles in the workout.

Implementation requires strong management control. Employees don't always know how to transform broad goals into practice, particularly when they must go against routine procedures, an all- too-common event. The old ways may have been the wrong ways. New procedures may be necessary to overcome obstacles and limited resources.

Good communication make your implementation program understandable, credible and appealing to your employees. Their commitment to your corporate objectives builds when you clearly explain the process and the purpose behind each action. Your employees will then more quickly and enthusiastically adopt new methods.

Pinpoint responsibility. Who is responsible for every turnaround activity? You and your employees must know the expected results and review whether those results are achieved. More than ever before, you must know who does and does not pull his or her weight!

For strict accountability, set quantifiable standards to measure your employees' performance and your own. Delegating is always good management particularly in a turnaround, where responsibilities shift and authorities blur. Without strict accountability, planning and implementation are only gestures in the right direction.

Avoid sweeping changes if your company is not prepared for them. Move slowly but deliberately. To implement your turnaround, take small steps, not quantum leaps.

Employees won't understand what you expect of them unless you communicate. You then will see any potential problems they may foresee and possible alternatives. Building a house needs an architect, a builder and a carpenter working from the same blueprint. You and your employees must talk.

Your employees also need the resources to get the job done, whether it's people, equipment or money. But passive or hostile employees may try to sabotage your turnaround by demanding unessential or unobtainable resources. Discuss needs and what you can and cannot deliver.

The resources your turnaround requires largely depend on your employees' attitudes. Enthusiastic, motivated employees innovate — particularly if you innovate! Apathetic employees find excuses and reasons to justify poor performance. Change these employees. But you still must control this change if your firm is to go from here to there. "Here" is one set of operating circumstances. "There" is another set of circumstances. This is how you make good things happen to a bad company.

Implementation takes commitment. Don't become sidetracked from your mission. This easily happens when:

- You don't have enough time to do everything and ignore the critical tasks.

- You get buried in day-to-day problems and lose sight of your overall agenda.

- Your priorities and problems constantly change and your plan loses substance.

To avoid these problems, focus first on what most affects cash flow – then move on.

1. Identify every turnaround task you must implement.

2. Determine the relative importance of each task.

3. Develop workable action plans for each task. (Plan carefully, because there may be more than one way to do the job.)

4. Commit everyone to completion dates on their specific assignments.

Action Step #4: Monitor the plan

Workouts are change-sensitive. Only constant and detailed feedback alerts you to new threats and new opportunities. Carefully monitor your progress, and move swiftly and decisively to modify plans when you are steered in the wrong direction.

Quantify turnaround objectives whenever possible. Numbers provide greater control, because you can then objectively compare actual performance against expected results. A turnaround plan is worse than useless when you can't accurately track performance and recovery.

Start with weekly reports on sales, cash flow, major controllable expenses and purchases. I frequently obtain daily reports, even hourly reports, from clients in deep crisis.

Don't get bogged down with too much information. Focus on the few essential indicators. Avoid detail. For instance, a manufacturing firm has a good handle on its situation if it knows its break-even point as well as orders shipped and in process.

Successful turnaround pros who track corporate progress on the back of an envelope find simplicity a virtue.

Don't measure performance and progress only by your financials. Physical measures, such as units of sale, orders received and units produced, can more quickly and accurately highlight the corporate condition.

Set realistic benchmarks. Track your recovery against crude but predetermined goals so you can make adjustments when your plan goes astray. While you may modify your goals, you must know what you expect from your business next week, next month and next year.

☑CHECKPOINT

1. What factors will most influence your turnaround strategy?

2. Do you have the resources needed to get your business out of trouble?

3. What are your turnaround objectives?

4. How can you best implement a turnaround plan for your organization?

7

CAT-SCANNING YOUR BUSINESS

The stories of great corporate comebacks abound with legendary turnaround leaders who measure the corporate pulse even before they walk in the door. In short order, they grasp the problems, magically produce solutions to seemingly hopeless situations and just as magically leave in their wake a thriving enterprise. The legend is legend. Still, for turnaround veterans, evaluating a business is largely instinctive. Experienced corporate doctors who have walked through the doors of hundreds of troubled companies can as instinctively tell what a bad company is all about as a physician can assess a wound. You need instinct, because time counts when your company is badly hemorrhaging.

To know where to go, you must know where you now stand. And you must find this out quickly. A company in crisis can't stall the evaluation. Larger, more stable companies may allow months of detailed analysis to ferret out their problems and opportunities, but even these crippled corporations can seldom afford to linger over endless reports. Companies die on the operating table while their surgeons ponder the X-rays.

You do not survey your business only at the beginning of the turnaround. It must be continuous. How severe is your crisis? Is your company heading for cardiac arrest or recovery? Within hours, I can guess with reasonable accuracy whether or not a company has the makings for a successful turnaround, how the debt can be restructured and what the balance sheet will look like at the end of the turnaround. What takes time is figuring how to make your business profitable. Most businesses never find the answer. Nor is it necessary to concentrate on profits early in the turnaround, when your objectives are mainly to stay afloat and to stabilize your business.

There is no one correct way to survey a sick business. The survey largely depends on who is examining the business and why. You are interested in your business's long-term prospects. Your creditors want to know whether your company can pay its debts. Your secured lenders are most concerned with the value of their collateral. Your suppliers want to know whether or not you can and will pay future bills. Your employees question whether you will downsize and cut jobs and salaries. Your stockholders worry about getting their investment back.

Because each group has different objectives and perspectives, you can expect different conclusions about what can and should be done with your company. Perhaps their one common objective, even though they all have different reasons, is to see that your company survives.

FACT FINDING

To survey your business you must gather the essential information. What information you need depends on the size and nature of your business, the cause and gravity of your problems and the apparent condition of your company. The right information gives you the pieces to the overall puzzle. Your job is to put the pieces of the puzzle together. You will probably produce data never before compiled and implement controls you never thought possible or even necessary. It may give you your first real look at your own business.

The right information is more important than lots of information. You can get a quick fix on any company with remarkably little information. Detailed, sophisticated information needed to make your business a moneymaker can come later.

The quick fix starts with basic financial information: Your balance sheet and profit-and-loss statements for the past two or three years. Changes in financial position also are extremely useful. Most important is a detailed monthly cash flow statement for the year ahead.

You may need more information concerning your business operations as well as pending or threatened lawsuits. Again, this depends on your situation. But even scant financial and operating information must be current and accurate, and forecasts and projections must be realistic, not overly optimistic.

Key managers, employees, suppliers, creditors and customers are frequently tapped sources of information. Each contributes his or her own perspective of your company's strengths and weaknesses, and can usually offer valuable insights beyond what financial statements and operating data tell you.

Beyond the numbers and the people is the actual tangible business. I always inspect the condition of inventory, fixtures, equipment and general housekeeping to get a "feel" for the situation. No company can be accurately measured by sitting in an office. Good turnaround leaders kick tires!

SURVEY YOUR STAYING POWER

Your information must quickly reveal the extent and urgency of your crisis and how rapidly and forcefully you must act to financially stabilize the business.

The two most serious threats are: **1)** Inadequate cash to continue operations, and **2)** Creditor actions that threaten to shut down the company. Finding these problems rarely require much detective work. Most companies only tackle their problems when creditors push them into bankruptcy, a lender forecloses or a tax agency padlocks the business. Then the only way the company can regain control of its assets is through Chapter 11 or another form of creditor workout.

While the fast-stepping troubled company can ordinarily block creditors, serious cash-flow problems are less easily solved. You must answer three vital questions: **1)** What is your company's present cash position? **2)** When will your company run out of money? **3)** How can you raise money quickly to stay afloat?

Chapter 8 reveals the many often-overlooked ways to raise cash, but the threshold question is, can your company become sufficiently stable to rebuild, solve its creditor problems and become profitable. You must make this quick prognosis before you can decide whether you should even attempt a recovery.

The answers to these questions are always based on assumptions that may or may not be correct. You assume certain sales for next month. But to what extent can you rely on those sales? All planning and forecasting has an element of "blue sky." Planning ahead, even a few months, is mostly blue sky, although banks and other creditors routinely demand five year projections that are not worth the paper they are written on.

When you only manage for profits, it takes a reorientation to manage for cash flow. But when you're in trouble, you go for cash flow even if it means less profits or no profits. And you will need an alarm system to alert you to any forthcoming cash-flow crisis. This will, at the least, include a weekly or bi-weekly cash plan and daily reports against the plans.

Can your business stay afloat? Even when the situation looks bleak, plan ahead. Once you are in the turnaround, you will find many opportunities to ease the cash crunch.

SURVEY YOUR VEIN OF GOLD

Stabilizing your business is protecting its "vein of gold" – those core assets and activities that are your profit generators. Your vein of gold is the foundation upon which you rebuild your company; your winners as distinguished from your losers. Identify your vein of gold, and you reciprocally identify what drains your company and what you must shed to downsize from what you are to what you must become.

Quickly identifying your core business, or vein of gold, is critical. The goal of both short- and long-term planning is to preserve your vein of gold, which may be the smallest, least significant and perhaps least interesting part of your business. For example, Dart Industries suffered sizable losses from its retail-drug (Rexall), real-estate and cosmetic divisions. Yet its relatively tiny Tupperware division threw off enormous cash. So the Tupperware division rebuilt Dart. Similarly, Penn Central, long synonymous with railroads, turned to the net worth and stability of its valuable Manhattan properties to rescue itself from its long- ailing railroad business. In a different fashion, Continental Airlines' rescue came from rapidly identifying and preserving its most profitable air routes. In each case, survival starts with identifying and protecting the vein of gold.

Your vein of gold may be hidden. You may scour heaps of detailed financial and operating data before you fully understand what produces your profits and losses.

You may be without a vein of gold. Many companies lack even that one definable business unit, product or activity that can stand apart as a future moneymaker. Small retail stores and service companies, for example, are simple, unified organizations that cannot easily divide themselves into winner and loser parts.

Or you may have once had a vein of gold that you forever destroyed by allowing it to wither. Whatever the case, a company without that vein of gold has no potential. There is nothing worth saving. Still, the search is always valuable. You never truly understand your company as a whole unless you understand the strengths and weaknesses of each part. When you find the strengths, preserve them come hell or high water. Figure out how to do so sooner, not later!

SURVEY YOUR FINANCIALS

Numbers, numbers, numbers. Numbers are concrete, unemotional and detached. Numbers let you navigate accurately and objectively. Crunch some numbers!

Start with your profit-and-loss statements for the past three years:

■ What is your current break-even point?

■ How far below or above break-even are you operating?

■ What can your break-even point be reduced to? How quickly?

■ What are your overall sales trends? By product? Line? Division?

- What are your margin trends? expense trends?

- What factors most contribute to your losses?

- What is the profit contribution (sales less variable costs) per product? Line? Division?

- Who are your highest-volume customers?

Don't spend too much time with your profit-and-loss statement during the emergency stage. Roughly identify where you are losing and how much you are losing when you begin the analysis. You do this to shut down the major cash drains. Fine tune the income statement when the company is completely stabilized and you can afford to think in terms of profits, not survival. But separating your winners from your losers will demand precise and accurate income statements broken down by company, division, product line or plant (as makes most sense in your case). Like most companies, you may be in trouble because you never knew where you were making or losing money. You may have tolerated poor management information systems in the past, but if you want an intelligently planned workout, you will change that. Of course, when there's one easily identifiable cause for your losses, you need no complex strategic plan. You simply fix what's broken.

The multiproblem company cannot initially accomplish much more with its profit-and-loss statement than to find significant opportunities to reduce expenses. Even here you must consider whether expense cuts will seriously affect the business. Continuous and substantial losses force you to examine your income statement for telltale relationships between costs, volume and profits. Computerized financial models can help you project what your bottom line would look like under various scenarios, and it's a worthwhile exercise. These income-statement manipulations are just another example of back-to-basics management as you continue your search for the key to making money from your business.

Balance-sheet trends for the past three years reveal your financial strength from a different perspective:

- Are fixed assets valued accurately?

- Are accounts receivable verified and accurate?

- Do accounts receivable collections depend upon contract completions or continued business operations?

- Is the inventory accurate?

- Are the inventories salable, obsolete or slow moving?

- Are there valuable patents, trademarks, copyrights or other intangible assets?

- What assets are leased or financed?

- What equipment can be sold?

- What other assets are unessential and can be sold?

- What is the amount, nature and aging of each trade obligation?

- Will slow-payment or non-payment of trade obligations affect continued supply?

- Are trade obligations so excessive or unmanageable that they need restructuring?

- How are overdue payables handled?

- What are the past-due tax obligations?

- What tax collections are threatened?

- What personal liability do officers and others have for unpaid taxes?

- Are secured debts and leases current or in default?

- Is foreclosure or repossession threatened on any secured or leased equipment?

- Are monies owed to pension plans?

- How insolvent is the firm?

- How illiquid is the firm?

Once you uncover your dirty financial linen, your balance sheet may show that you are considerably poorer than you first estimated. The right numbers may reveal overvalued assets, obsolete inventories or capitalized expenses improperly valued to cover up larger losses. The liability side may include understated payables and unlisted contingent or disputed liabilities. Don't fool yourself! Make your balance sheet tell the real story!

Grasp your company's overall financial condition during the crisis stage so you can determine whether yours is primarily a profitability problem (requiring a strategic restructuring), an insolvency problem (requiring a debt restructuring), or both. Most troubled companies have both.

Your short-term concern should be your liquidity. Build the highest cash reserve possible. Closely examine receivables, inventory and equipment. How can they be transformed into cash or other liquid assets needed to keep operating?

Examining hard assets is a high priority for manufacturers and other businesses with considerable capital tied up in plant and equipment. The objective is to turn unproductive capital assets into cash to finance future operations. You do this by investigating five points:

1. What is your present plant capacity?

2. What is your present and projected utilization of plant and equipment?

3. What plant or equipment can you sell without hurting present or future sales or profits?

4. What improvements or upgrades can produce greater efficiency and productivity?

5. What plant or equipment wastes overhead?

Even a casual glance at your balance sheet should tell you whether or not debt-restructuring is needed. Yet a business with liabilities two or three times its assets may be in no immediate danger if its creditors are patient. So you must always look beyond the numbers to foresee immediate dangers and threats to your company.

More critical is the level of your current assets: Cash, receivables and inventory. You must have sufficient current assets to maintain a reasonable sales level and positive cash flow. Excess debt can always be reduced. But you can't always rebuild your assets to a critical mass.

Your balance sheet examination must focus on that one question — how can you revamp your assets and liabilities so you have the current assets you need to stay afloat? That's what counts!

Countless books available at any library can show you how to analyze a company financially. There are many more ratios, comparisons and tests to help you fine tune your analysis. But you should get a reasonably good handle on where you are and where you're going within five minutes, if you know what to look for! Inexperienced with financial statements? Hire a good accountant or turnaround consultant to help you make sense of the numbers.

While your P&L statement and balance sheet are important, your cash-flow statement is the key. Only a detailed and realistic cash-flow projection can forecast whether you will have the operating funds you need for short-term survival. You can lose money and survive. You can be insolvent and survive. You can't run out of money and survive.

- Do you project a cash surplus or deficit in the next month? Next quarter? Next six months? Next year?

- What can you do to increase cash income?

- What can you do to reduce expenditures?

The cash-flow analysis is central to your financial analysis because it answers the one central question on which any workout depends: Does your company have the financial strength and stability to survive a workout?

SURVEY YOUR ORGANIZATION

Once you have crunched the numbers, cat-scanning the business begins at the top. A basic organizational survey answers these points:

- What is the organizational chart? What organizational changes have occurred in the past three years?

- What is the detailed job description for each executive?

- What is the composition of the board? How often does it meet? How active is it in managing the company?

- What are the staffing levels in each department?

- What are the line and staff relationships within the organization?

- Is management centralized or decentralized?

- What changes in the organization are necessary to carry out the turnaround?

Your people must be good for your organization to perform well. Many turnarounds only turn around employees, who now produce more.

Start with yourself. Chapter 4 profiled a turnaround leader. If you don't measure up, then for the good of your turnaround, step aside so your organization can be guided by more capable hands. The one most important question in the entire evaluation is one you must ask yourself: Can I really turn this company around?

If you cannot honestly and objectively evaluate your own capabilities and performance, how can you evaluate your subordinates and employees? Even when you understand your own shortcomings, you may fail to evaluate your employees against what the turnaround demands. Don't consider merely whether your employees can do their jobs. Ask whether they can perform significantly better. You must strive to improve results, a goal that is never easy when you operate within the rigors of the workout.

Outsiders can more objectively assess your employees. But employees can be judged too harshly, only because they came from the tainted regime that tumbled the company into trouble. Replacements then pop up in a remarkably arbitrary style. But good or bad, junk the "yes men." Say something stupid to them, and they always agree. You can't afford these people, you need free thinkers.

You need open, candid, face-to-face meetings to evaluate your key managers and employees. Deep-rooted employee problems within your organization take the form of:

- high employee turnover

- recruiting problems

- employee theft

- employee protests or grievances

- poor morale

- reduced productivity

In an age when many employers must think twice before axing people, your evaluation must assess not only each employee, but also whether or not your company can freely make changes. Your important questions are then:

- Will firings bring unfair dismissal or discrimination suits?

- Is there a union? Will the union cooperate or be hostile?

- What employment contracts are outstanding?

- What employees possess special knowledge, relationships or unique skills critical to the workout effort?

My assessment of employees is global. When I come into a case, I meet with as many key employees as possible. My goal is to answer one question: Are there enough good people on board to put the business back together again? A few really good employees is better than a bunch of mediocre ones.

A successful turnaround needs a certain infrastructure. You don't always have the time to hire and train new people. You may be too tired or stressed to build a new team, and you need people you can lean on rather than people who must lean on you to learn their jobs. The difficulty, of course, is that people aren't numbers on a financial statement. A quick judgment is not always accurate.

A demoralized crew may spring to life with new leadership or be invigorated by a turnaround. And I have had my share of disappointments — employees who looked strong but fell down on the job miserably. Quite a few hung on to take advantage of the situation. A workout requires competent and trustworthy employees. It's tough to find both attributes in one individual. And unless you are an extremely good judge of people, you too will be in for your share of disappointments.

SURVEY YOUR COMPETITIVENESS

Evaluate your company's competitive position. You then know where your company is now, and where it is likely to go. Here you face the moment of truth: Whether or not your company has a future.

Younger companies that never left the ground must decide if their business concept will work. For most, it is a very bitter point, the end of a lifelong dream, particularly for the small entrepreneurial firm built around a new, unique product or service.

Still, just because a young company never made money doesn't mean it can't. Many small, young startups have sound, even exciting and brilliant business concepts, but suffer the same problems other young companies face: A good business idea entangled within a badly designed or poorly managed business. Don't throw your baby out with the bath water. Evaluate not just your company but each product and service you sell.

The mature company encountering hard times has no less of a challenge. There are many reasons for marketing slips but countless, too, are the possible strategies to regain competitiveness, if you know the starting points:

- Does your company have a well-defined market niche?

- Has your company followed industry trends?

- Can your company easily change and adapt?

- Who are the key customers?

- How profitable is each key customer?

- Are relationships solid with key accounts?

- Do others within your industry share your problems?

- Why are sales or market share shrinking?

- What products or lines are declining?

- What products perform well?

- Who are your key competitors, and what are their advantages?

- Can you regain the competitive edge? How?

To discover why your business is performing poorly, you must carefully analyze each product, channel of distribution, end-user customer group and market area. Your evaluation may show dismal innovation in new products, markets, promotions and other strategies, which explains your poor overall performance.

Understanding your company's market position is not sufficient. You also must examine your company's marketing.

- Do you have a marketing strategy? Does it include marketing analysis, planning, implementation and control?

- Do you measure your marketing results, and do you try to improve those results?

A thorough product analysis not only examines what you now sell but determines what you should sell. The two can be worlds apart. Scrub sluggish products or services that probably never pulled their weight in the first place. Downsizing through product elimination is common in a workout, because you must concentrate on what produces fast cash, not what makes money. Companies with uncontrolled product proliferation get into big trouble because they lose track of their vein of gold.

- Which products or services produce your largest profits?

- Which products or services have the greatest growth potential?

- Which ones only tie up capital or lose money?

SURVEY YOUR LEGAL POSITION

Most turnarounds create a legal maze that must be untangled early.

- Is your business one or multiple entities?

- Can you protect your healthy entities from the sick entities?

- What litigation now disrupts the business? Is attachment, foreclosure, seizure or repossession of key assets an immediate threat?

- Is there current or potential litigation from shareholders, franchisees, customers or the government?

- Does the company have major claims against others? Can these claims be resolved quickly to help raise cash and rehabilitate the company?

- What contracts or affiliations dictate the workout strategy?

- How will outstanding warranties and service contracts be handled in a turnaround?

- What regulations or laws limit the turnaround options?

- What other legal factors influence the workout strategy (such as whether Chapter 11 or a non-bankruptcy workout will work best)?

Your lawyer must consider these legal factors, without allowing them to dominate your decisions, which happens when a lawyer controls a turnaround. Consider legal issues as one small piece in a huge puzzle.

The legal analysis must focus closely on the legal relationship of each class of creditors with the others. This must be done early in the turnaround so you understand your short-term defensive position and how best to deal with each creditor throughout the turnaround. The creditor-analysis checklist includes:

- Who are the major or essential suppliers?

- What debts are in dispute?

- Are secured debts duly perfected and binding as secured obligations?

- What payments have been made within the past 90 days that may be recovered in bankruptcy as preferences?

- What debt has the company guaranteed? Have all parties or affiliated companies guaranteed the company's debts?

- What setoffs can be applied against debts owed creditors?

- What are the loan renewal or expiration dates?

- What credit remains available?

- What loans are in default?

- Has a lender engaged in any acts that may constitute lender liability and be a defense to the lender's claim?

Tax obligations require special analysis, as troubled businesses often become delinquent in their tax obligations (i.e. withholding tax, unemployment tax, sales tax, meal or room tax, etc.). These taxes could be owed the IRS, the state or the local taxing authorities. Here the analysis considers:

- Can the tax arrears be rapidly paid from the cash flow of the business?

- Are there existing or threatened tax liens that may impede the reorganization options?

- Are there threatened seizures of the business by any tax agencies?

- Can any tax agencies cancel a trading license or otherwise close the business down through seizure?

A survey of leases and other existing contracts also is important.

■ What is the original date and remaining length of each lease?

■ How important is each lease to the business? Which can or should be terminated?

■ What important leases are in default, and how can they be cured?

Related to the legal issues are the political considerations.

Politics can influence the outcome of a turnaround. Corporate survival goes beyond management or resources. Every business has a place within the community. Some are strongly supported because the community needs them and will go to bat for them. Others, less favored, are encouraged to close shop. Chrysler's workout was politics in action. Tens of thousands of less-known firms play the same political game. Is your company a small but vital defense contractor? Is it minority-owned? Does it heavily owe the government? Test your political clout:

■ Is your company a major employer within the area?

■ Does your company supply important goods or services to the government?

■ Would the public, community, industry or government suffer if your company closed?

■ Do business groups or government agencies have good reason to support your workout?

ANSWERING THE FIVE BIG QUESTIONS

Answering five big questions gives you a solid starting point for diagnosing both your problems and your opportunities.

Then, you must synthesize the various surveys in this chapter into an overall assessment of your company's position. But before you can shape objectives and strategies, resolve these key issues:

1. How serious is the situation? Is your company critically ill or still stable and in fair health?

2. What is the gravity of the downturn? If your company is heading downhill, how rapidly and forcefully must you start the turnaround?

3. What caused the downturn? Do the problems continue? If there is more than one cause, which one is most significant?

4. Does your company most need a strategic turnaround (profit improvement) or financial restructuring (debt reduction)? If you need both, which should you tackle first?

5. What are the major weaknesses and strengths of your firm? Is it strong enough to go through a turnaround? What weaknesses may jeopardize the turnaround?

Tough questions? You bet! That's because you are finally in the corporate cockpit, with one eye on your tailspin and one eye anxiously scanning the cockpit instruments. But if you have been staying alert before, you should already have your bearings.

A more thorough and objective evaluation of your firm, goes beyond the answers to questions in this chapter. Ask follow-up questions. Be skeptical. Never accept things at face value. Listen to Harold Geneen, former ITT chairman: "Getting the facts – the unshakable facts – is one of the hardest parts of the turnaround." I only partly agree with Geneen. It's always a bit harder to figure out what to do with the facts.

☑CHECKPOINT

1. How seriously ill is your business?

2. How rapidly and steadily is it failing?

3. What vein of gold must you protect?

4. What do your financials tell you about your business?

5. Are your employees an asset or liability?

6. How strong or weak is your competitive position? Can you effectively compete considering your handicaps?

7. What are your winning products or services? What are your losers?

8. What legal and political factors can you capitalize on? Which factors threaten you?

9. Can you spearhead the turnaround, or must someone else lead the charge?

8

26 WAYS
TO FIND QUICK CASH

"Happiness is a positive cash flow" shouts a small sign on my desk. But it's more. Cash is your business's lifeblood. To save your business, you must first stabilize it by stopping the cash drain and building cash reserves. Only with cash can you replenish inventory, advertise, promote and turn profitable sales. Only with cash can you bail out your debts. Only cash gives you a future. Cash is king, whether in a workout or a healthy company!

Your business, like so many others, may fail not because you can't become solvent or profitable, but because you can't stay afloat long enough. When more cash goes out than comes in, you bleed to death before your survival strategies take hold.

To survive you must reverse events. From this moment, more cash must come into your business than goes out! You can't run on empty. Survivors know how to fill their tanks before they run dry.

Troubled businesses that are forced to operate without cash become defensive. You no longer operate your business as you want, but as everyone else wants you to. Preoccupied with protecting yourself, you can't make money. You must fight back when:

- Suppliers tighten or eliminate credit, which drains cash reserves.

- Suppliers/creditors demand override payments and charge higher prices, or take away valuable trade concessions.

- Lenders boost their interest rates and shorten their terms.

- Creditors and lenders push for faster payments.

You can see why cash-poor businesses become even poorer. Begin right now to turn your cash situation around by answering three questions:

1. What can you do right now to immediately and significantly increase your cash flow?

2. Which cash-raising actions will least hurt your business?

3. Which cash-raising actions can you most readily achieve?

This chapter will give you tips on how to raise fast cash and close the cash spigot so you quickly build your bank balance. Pay close attention and watch it zoom!

Cash-Raiser Tip #1
COLLECT RECEIVABLES

Your business has buried cash. But you must know where to find it. You can squeeze cash from even the poorest business.

Where do you look first? Begin with your accounts receivable, because they can produce the fastest cash. What customers are playing with your money? Pursue them with a no-nonsense and aggressive collection policy. Antagonizing slow-paying customers is of less concern than getting the money they owe you. But try positive motivators first. Will a two-percent discount bring faster payment? Will five percent? Talk to your customers. What reasonable deal will get them to write you a check? But don't appear too desperate or your customers will withhold payment, hoping to settle more favorably after you go bankrupt. Involve your entire crew. Make collecting overdue accounts everyone's responsibility, particularly your sales staff and reps who know your customers best.

If a generous discount doesn't succeed, then immediately pursue collection. Forget collection agencies. Retain an aggressive collection lawyer who will quickly sue and not waste time writing collection letters.

Cash-Raiser Tip #2
SELL RECEIVABLES

You can sell or factor your current receivables for quick cash. Cash-poor companies often have a wealth of receivables a factor will buy. Factoring is high on the cash-raising list when you have unencumbered receivables owed you from solid business accounts.

The factoring fee of six to eight percent is a necessary expense when you need money. I routinely factor my clients' receivables. For example, I turned $800,000 in receivables due a dress manufacturer into a fast $750,000 check. The $50,000 factor's fee was a big bargain, because his $750,000 rescued the dressmaker from certain bankruptcy.

You can factor receivables easier and faster than you can get an accounts receivable loan, because your financial condition is unimportant to a factor. Factors are only concerned with the collectability of your receivables.

Many factoring firms will buy your receivables in exchange for a business-saving check. Although most factors prefer long-term arrangements, you can nevertheless find one-time factors. Call the Commercial Finance Association in New York for names, or I can refer you to factors who routinely buy receivables from troubled companies.

Cash-Raiser Tip #3

TIGHTEN CREDIT

Coax your customers to buy for cash. Offer a small discount for cash, or tighten your credit terms!

You can't afford consumer charges. MasterCard, Visa and Amex avoids waiting for your money. Commercial accounts may expect credit, but you can induce even commercial accounts to buy C.O.D. for a better price. Ask your few key accounts. You'll be surprised how many will snap up C.O.D. terms in exchange for a one- or two-percent discount.

Evaluate the credit you extend every customer. Is the customer worthy of tying up money on their receivables? How profitable are they? How quickly do they pay? What are their long-term prospects as customers? How can you get them to pay faster or buy for cash?

Your credit policy must balance sales and cash flow objectives, but unless you are a well-heeled company able to comfortably finance your receivables, give cash flow top billing.

Cash-Raiser Tip #4

TRIM INVENTORY

Companies that mismanage their inventory get into trouble. How well do you control your inventory? You know the answer if your cash flow sits on your shelf or warehouse floor. You may have bought too heavily for those attractive extra discounts and bigger gross profits, and ignored turnover and cash flow. Sound familiar? Slashing inventory is your answer.

Actually, reducing inventory to free up cash is only half the answer. Poor buying practices will keep you cash-starved unless you correct the cause of your problem. Strict budgeting and rigid inventory controls are what you need to stay lean and mean!

Sanborn Drug nearly collapsed under its uncontrolled inventory. Sanborn's financials reported $80,000 in inventory, but I knew their financials lied because merchandise was piled everywhere.

I waved a dusty bottle of vitamins in front of Sanborn's owner and asked, "Jim, what's this?" "A bottle of vitamins," he sheepishly replied. "No, Jim, it's $12 that should be in your checking account." Jim began to see what you must see – merchandise is money, so treat it as money!

Within days, Jim had a half-price clearance sale underway. Overstocked merchandise poured out, and $68,000 poured in. Jim's cash vault had been right under his feet, and he couldn't see it. Can you see yours?

Move fast if you are strangled with excess inventory. Quickly sell it in the ordinary course of business. Or dump it on a liquidator, where you will get fewer but faster dollars. Wherever you are, you are only a phone call away from liquidators who buy merchandise of every type. Their cash is priceless when you must sell fast and can't wait for those bigger but slower dollars.

Cash-Raiser Tip #5

DUMP IDLE EQUIPMENT

What idle equipment, machinery or real estate can you sell for quick cash?

Perhaps your cash is buried in fancy office furniture, fancy equipment or fancy cars. It happens. One insolvent publisher of children's books wove her tale of woe from behind her lavish $8,000 marble desk. Today, her desk and her designer lamps, oriental rugs and more than $200,000 in other nonsense trimmings are history. The publisher now sits behind a battered $50 metal desk – but she has money in the bank. She's lucky to still have a desk.

Dumping unessentials may be your key to survival. From ceiling to floor, make your assets work double-time or sell them.

Essential equipment and real estate can produce fast dollars in a sale-leaseback. Investors buy and lease back business assets for the tax benefits. One cash-starved plumbing-supply firm raised $165,000 through a sale-leaseback of its trucks. The $165,000 financed them out of Chapter 11.

A growing but undercapitalized advertising firm unloaded little-used furniture for $80,000 and, for only $600 a month, rented back those few items they needed. The $80,000 paid their pressing bills and gave them enough extra money to open two profitable branch offices. The young, creative founders, who assumed super-plush surroundings would guarantee their success, soon discovered that money in the bank spells success much more convincingly!

Stroll through your business. What do you see? Computers? Manufacturing equipment? Cash registers? Airplanes? Bulldozers? School buses? What you don't absolutely need you can turn into fast cash.

Cash-Raiser Tip #6
REFINANCE

What equity or borrowing power is left in your assets? Refinance to the hilt. Turn that idle equity into hard-working cash.

Additional financing is one of the first things I investigate when cash is tight. A hosiery manufacturer had equipment worth $500,000 and commercial receivables worth another $500,000. The $1 million in assets was pledged to secure a bank's $250,000 loan. The equipment alone had a loan value of $300,000 or more and I knew countless banks would lend 70 percent against the receivables. Refinancing could raise another $400,000. With $650,000 in real borrowing power, we could put another $400,000 into the checking account if we simply shopped a few more lenders.

Refinance before your financial troubles destroy your lending relationships and credit ratings. Conservative lenders will consider credit and financial stability as well as your collateral's value. Even with severe financial problems, you may squeeze more money from your assets – although at higher interest.

Refinancing offers a big benefit aside from more money. Fully encumber the equity in your assets, and you gain a stronger bargaining position with your general creditors and taxing agencies, which then have little or no equity to seize.

Cash-Raiser Tip #7
EXPLOIT HIDDEN ASSETS

Your most valuable assets may be assets you cannot see: Interesting product ideas, exciting technology or unique business methods you can turn into cash.

Can you sell or license your name? What about marketing rights to your products? Plenty of companies seek innovative products or services for new, untapped markets. If you know how to exploit what you have, a cash cow made of heavy up-front cash and ongoing license fees and royalties awaits you.

One clever Silicon Valley software firm ingeniously escaped bankruptcy by licensing its popular sales-tracking software to a British software publisher, aiming at the untapped United Kingdom market. Their $400,000 advance paid their entire $300,000 debt, plus the company expects $150,000 in annual royalties for years to come!

Exploiting hidden assets similarly saved an Indiana burglar- alarm company that licensed its patented alarm system to an Arizona dealer for $70,000. Now licensing nationwide, the company receives $850,000 a year in royalties from 32 licensees. Desperation bolsters imagination and opens your mind and pocketbook to similar opportunities!

Hidden assets spell big opportunity. Time and time again, I have seen struggling, creative entrepreneurs turn intangible assets into great fortunes. Put your proprietary assets, those with the greatest value, to their highest and best use, and watch your cash flow take off!

Cash-Raiser Tip #8

TAP PENSION PLANS

Employee pension plans have cash reserves, money you can legally borrow to get your business through the hard times. America's leading companies routinely borrow from their pension funds. But move carefully!.Borrowing from your employees' pension accounts jeopardizes your employees' financial security if your business fails and you can't repay the fund. Borrowing from pension accounts is not something you should do without considering your responsibility to your long-loyal employees. You should have unshakable confidence in your ability to repay the fund. Before borrowing from pension funds, consult with your attorney and plan administrator. Pension law is complex, so you will need good legal guidance.

Cash-Raiser Tip #9

RECOUP PREPAID EXPENSES

What prepaid premiums can you reclaim if you cancel your insurance today? It may be unwise to cancel all of your insurance, but smart to cancel unessential insurance.

I later highlight insurance you might cancel, but the point here is that canceling wasteful insurance can get you a sizeable refund on prepaid, unused premiums.

Insurance is only one cancelable prepaid expense that can get you a big refund check. For instance, I canceled the country-club membership for a faltering commuter airline that couldn't afford to fuel its planes. The three-year, $15,000 prepaid membership had two remaining years, so a $10,000 refund was soon back in the checking account.

What expenses have you prepaid that are not absolutely essential? What refunds could you claim? What money would be back in your pocket?

Cash-Raiser Tip #10

RENT IDLE SPACE

Do you have idle space? What is your idle space worth? A downsizing furniture manufacturer found his answer when he sublet 8,000 square feet of spare warehouse space for $80,000 a year. That's big money when you scrounge for pennies.

And a cash-tight supermarket concessioned a tiny block of high-traffic, upfront space in their supermarket to a branch bank for $100,000 in advance rent. The space rents for far more than they ever earned from selling groceries – and swarms of banking customers now shop the supermarket. This same savvy supermarket operator rented his vacant basement space to a local newspaper printer for another $40,000 a year.

Idle space is everywhere! A Boston restaurateur shrewdly leased his high-visibility rooftop to a billboard company for $25,000 a year.

These cash-raising opportunities are tough to spot when you're in trouble, but unused or underutilized space is a potential cash- raiser.

Turning idle space into cash works for many troubled companies that downsize products, employees, overhead and space!

For fast cash, offer prospective tenants a 20-percent discount if they fully prepay the first year's rent. This has worked for me for many deals, and put thousands of dollars into my clients' empty coffers the day they sublet their idle space.

Cash-Raiser Tip #11

COAX CASH FROM CUSTOMERS

Is it possible your customers will hand you cash to keep you afloat? Customers can be a terrific source of fast cash but you must know how to coax cash from them.

A struggling health club in my town advertised a half-price annual membership fee if paid in advance. To save $300 a year on the club's regular $600 fee, two hundred new members quickly added $60,000 to the club's bank account.

In today's high-pressure business climate, coaxing customers to prepay is acceptable and smart marketing. And customers will happily prepay if they see a big benefit for themselves.

Customer advances and pre-payments prime the cash pump for many industries. Is your product or service offered on an annual or an installment basis such as a club membership, warranty or subscription? Why not offer a big discount to renew or prepay today? If you collect after you render the service or sell the product, re-engineer your thinking so you collect first.

- A three-lawyer Philadelphia law firm's prepaid legal services raised them more than $265,000.

- An enterprising Chattanooga druggist's customers earned a 30-percent discount on their prescriptions by joining the Golden Key Discount Prescription Program. This sharp idea put $38,000 in the bank and boosted prescription sales 40 percent.

- A Seattle movie theater peddled more than $165,000 in movie tickets through a "one-free-with-10" special. No- frills airlines hawk their tickets the same way.

Cash-Raiser Tip #12

RAISE PRICES

Increase prices? Did I get your attention? You've probably cut prices, hoping to generate more business! But for most businesses, that's the wrong way to go.

You can raise prices faster than you can implement most other cash-raising strategies, whether you raise list prices or reduce discounts.

Increasing list price is the safest route, because distributors will resist lowered trade discounts more than customers resist higher prices. Which of your products or services are least price-sensitive? When did you last increase prices?

If you need a big price increase to survive, then go for it. You may need higher prices to make the game worthwhile. Let your instincts and the economics of your situation – rather than what your competitors charge – dictate your prices. Competitors aren't always right.

Camouflage price increases. Or give your products or services greater perceived value than the competition's products.

Can you charge for extra services, extended warranties or other tack-on charges? Push the frills before you hike product prices.

If you increase list price for consumers, give bigger trade discounts to dealers and distributors to encourage wider product distribution and to maximize sales potential. The higher list price should offset greater trade discounts.

Cash-Raiser Tip #13

SELL SOMETHING

Selling brings in the fastest money. Troubled companies are often companies that can't sell. The turnaround is their last opportunity to become that super-energized selling organization.

Concentrate your sales efforts on your most profitable products and largest customers. Limited time and resources force you to prioritize your sales effort on what will produce the fastest dollars.

Motivate your salespeople with incentives that tie performance to rewards. Pay incentive commissions on additional sales.

Reprogram your sales force. Sales reps who call on old and familiar accounts must be pushed to land new, less friendly prospects.

Replace salespeople and redefine territories so your best sales people sell your most important accounts.

You can sell more. Consider: What related products or services can you sell? What upgrades would your customers buy? Can your sales reps carry complementary but non-competitive lines? Can you lock in your customers with special prices so you're guaranteed their next order? What about a special deal if they buy more right now? Give selling 10 percent more effort, and you'll have 10 percent more income. What would that do for your cash flow?

PENNY-ANTE MANAGEMENT

Hunting cash is one way to green your bank account. Cutting costs is another.

Every type and size business – whether a shoestring home-based venture or a corporate giant – can slim down to shape up.

How you spend money is critical to your cash flow. You cannot control your income, but you can control expenditures. Cost-cutting is your surest, fastest route to financial stability.

Companies usually slenderize only when their corporate flab becomes too noticeable in their bottom line. For smart organizations, cost-cutting is not a knee-jerk reaction to poor profits but a way of life. They know that watching costs only when business is bad is a recipe for bankruptcy.

Cost-cutting can permanently and dramatically change how you do business. Nevertheless, when you need profits and cash, you must lower your break-even point. Improving productivity, buying smarter, traveling more frugally and operating with fewer people are all roads leading in the same direction. Cutting costs means getting more for your money – whether in accounting fees or copying costs.

Turnaround businesses cut costs by downsizing so there are lower overall expenses, and then belt-tightening the expenses they do have.

Cost-cutting forces change, so expect resistance and opposition. You change how you do business, your resources and perhaps even your corporate mission.

Sudden, tight-fisted policies are traumatic in a traditionally lax company and, unless handled correctly, cause less productivity and destroy employee morale.

You can largely counteract these potential problems by getting your employees involved. Explain why cost-cutting is vital, and define your new priorities. You won't totally salve wounds from scrapped projects or fired employees, but your people will understand your reasons. Again, communicate frequently and persuasively. Sell the message like you've never sold before, and you will win the cooperation you need for cost reduction.

Every good cost-cutting program follows five steps:

1. Set specific cost-cutting goals (i.e. 20 percent). Set goals by department and for the entire organization.

2. Challenge every expenditure. Never assume you can't squeeze more savings.

3. Identify all areas in which you can cut costs.

4. Implement cost-cutting immediately. Don't procrastinate!

5. Follow up continuously on each cost-cutting measure to assess impact upon your business. Cost-cutting must be continual.

Cost reduction fails when you're weak-fisted. Become very tight-fisted. It's not what you do but the degree to which you do it. Tweaking knobs won't save your business. The corporate grave yards are littered with dead companies that cut payrolls 10 percent when a 40, 60 or 80 percent cut was needed. Survivors trim all fat!

Use zero-based budgeting. Historical expenses don't tell you what to spend this year. A zero-based budget helps answer three important questions: (1) Should we even be involved in this activity? (2) Are we spending too much to perform this activity? (3) How much should it cost?

Cash-Raiser Tip #14

SHRINK SHRINKAGE

Theft, scrap and obsolescence can cause you double-digit losses. Business owners see huge profit jumps through shrinkage controls. If you can't stop your thieves, call in security pros who can, with new computerized control systems that detect leaks more effectively.

You can't totally trust check expense records, invoices, purchase orders and other paper trails to tell you what's coming in and going out. You must pay closer attention. A supermarket chain plagued by losses in one of its stores discovered that its manager had added his own personal "extra" checkout, thus funneling about 10 percent of the store's huge sales directly into his own pockets. The chain discovered this only on their third inspection of the store. Are your profits going out the door?

Cash-Raiser Tip #15

BUY BETTER

You make money in your buying, not your selling. Well-run companies get the absolute lowest price and best deal from every supplier!

When did you last hit your suppliers for lower prices or better terms? When did you last get competitive bids? How do you know you are getting your best possible deal?

Sloppy buying costs you every single day. So check new suppliers for new prices. And once you have your best price, try to beat it by another 5 percent. Bargain on everything: Stationery, printing, freight, hotel rooms. These savings mount quickly, and you can haggle lower prices more times than you would believe, which translates into plenty of extra dollars.

Cash-Raiser Tip #16

RETHINK YOUR PRODUCTS

Are you a manufacturer? Can you reduce material costs by reducing scrap or using less material to make your product?

A kitchenware manufacturer found out almost too late that he could easily substitute cheaper aluminum for copper on his kitchenware products. Had he been using aluminum since he started in business, he would have had another $1.5 million in his bank account, or four times what he now owes creditors!

Rethink your product. Can you substitute less expensive components? Can you re-engineer production to cut scrap and waste? Use value-analysis to examine what your product and each component is designed to do, and to help you avoid scrap and substitute less costly materials.

But cheaper is not always smarter. Cheap can increase your production costs or decrease the perceived value of your product and the price you can get for it.

Don't think you know your manufacturing costs, or that you can't lower these costs. This thinking bankrupts companies!

Cash-Raiser Tip #17

SLASH PAYROLL

I've worked with many troubled companies and cannot recall one where labor costs could not be reduced by 10 percent.

Would a 10 percent payroll cut help your cash flow?

If you don't think you have flab in your payroll, you are defying Parkinson's Law: Work automatically expands to occupy those available to do it.

The quickest and most common way to reduce payroll is through forced layoffs. How much can you cut? Figure out how your labor costs increased as a percentage of sales. How do they compare to industry averages? What should they be with zero-based budgeting and strict job justification?

Don't hatchet good employees unless you first reduce costs by:

■ encouraging voluntary resignations, no-hirings and early retirements

■ eliminating or reducing overtime

■ rescheduling work and paid vacations

If these alternatives don't sufficiently cut your payroll, make full-time employees part-time, cut bonuses and benefits and reduce salaries.

Understand the implications of your payroll-cutting strategies. Tell your employees the reasons for your new policy, your cost-cutting goals (in dollars and cents) and the alternatives you considered.

Employees put up with great hardships if they see the hardships as necessary, and policies as fair and equitable. But they also want to see a light at the end of the tunnel – a time when they can again receive their just rewards.

Do you want more manpower for less money?

■ **Use temps** to even out peaks and valleys. You'll pay more per hour, but have lower overall costs compared to full-timers with too little work to keep them steadily and profitably busy.

■ **Hire apprentices and senior citizens;** they are the best labor buys in the market today. The young are anxious to learn. Senior citizens have a wealth of experience, a strong work ethic and will often work for less.

■ **Leasing employees** cuts expensive fringe benefits. Check with employee-leasing companies in your area, and you may save 10 to 15 percent by eliminating employee perks. You also avoid the risk of falling behind on your withholding taxes, a big consideration when cash is tight.

■ **Cut pension costs** with less costly alternatives: 401K plans and SEP or SARSEP programs. Also, age-weight your pension plan. Review these ideas with your pension advisor.

Cash-Raiser Tip #18

SLIM YOUR OWN PAYCHECK

Sacrifice must start at the top. Cut your employees' paychecks, but cut much more from your own.

If you run a multimillion-dollar business, you may not see the need to save your company a few more bucks by reducing your own salary. Those few dollars may not be monetarily critical, but when the boss won't sacrifice, he cannot expect others to.

My cases are sometimes only greedy owners who drain their businesses without considering or caring what their business can afford to pay them. They then wonder why they lose money. It's an easy trap to fall into. A first-time owner swaps a $250-a-week job for a business with a $5,000 weekly cash flow. If you've never before had your hands on $5,000, it's tempting!

Sal was one victim of champagne taste. Sal's music store grossed a healthy $600,000, but I had only to scan the expenses to see why it lost $68,000. There was Sal's $50,000 salary, and another $30,000 off the books. And Sal's wife drew a hefty $25,000 salary, and seldom worked.

Sal drained his music store of more than $100,000. But what did Sal give his business in return? Few turnarounds can afford a hefty owner's salary and survive.

Sal agreed to cut his salary from $50,000 to $38,000 and to keep his hands out of the till, but, of course, he continued stealing from his own business. Sal's business eventually failed, and he's now back at his old job as a department-store stereo clerk.

Your paycheck tells a lot about your determination to save your business.

Cash-Raiser Tip #19

CANCEL ALL PERKS

Chauffeur-driven limousines, wasteful "business" trips to strange and exotic lands where no business is ever conducted, bills from lavish restaurants and hotels, personal magazine subscriptions or roses to the wife or girlfriend on the company tab – are all business destroyers.

Playing expense account games is okay when making money, but a fool's game when you must hunker down and scramble for pennies.

Trade in your new, leased Caddy for a used Chevy, and people will take you more seriously. Until then, you're only the emperor who wore no clothes. You too will eventually be left without a kingdom.

Cash-Raiser Tip #20

TALK TO YOUR LANDLORD

Even sophisticated business owners don't negotiate for rent concessions when business is bad.

If your rent is 5 percent of sales, a one-third rent reduction will boost profitability nearly 2 percent. That's money!

Troubled companies can negotiate dynamite rent concessions, as some of my recent successes prove:

- A large Denver software firm reduced its rent $70,000 in a two-year workout.
- A struggling Boston floral wholesaler won a 25-percent rent reduction (a $60,000-a-year savings).
- A Boca Raton dance studio slashed $12,000 a year from its $30,000 lease.

Landlords aren't charities, but they will lower rents when they are without negotiating power and fear that you will move out or go bankrupt, leaving them with an empty space and no rent.

You have bargaining power when you pay high rent and your landlord has no prospective tenants anxious to pay what you pay. Perhaps you can take advantage of plummeting real-estate prices and the fact that once-desirable commercial spaces now beg for tenants.

Check your bargaining power. Does your landlord have chronically vacant space? Does he or she rent comparable space for less than you now pay?

If you can't cut rent, can you instead cut space? That worked for a business-forms publisher, who downsized from 40,000 square feet to 30,000 square feet simply by rearranging warehouse pallet racks. The business saved $80,000 a year! Would $80,000 a year help save your business?

Know the bargaining points: Will your landlord let you sublet idle space? Can you avoid "soft" costs, such as merchants' association advertising? Can you reduce property taxes or insurance?

Your landlord is only another supplier. Space is no more sacred than any other commodity, and a lease can be revised to what you can afford to pay.

Cash-Raiser Tip #21

STOP INSURANCE WASTE

When a clothing manufacturer told me he paid more than $40,000 a year for fire insurance, I asked, "How much do you owe your creditors?" "About $500,000," he replied. "And what would you collect from your insurance company if your business burned down?" I inquired. "About $300,000," he again answered. "So why spend $40,000 a year on insurance to protect only your creditors?" I asked.

Buy insurance to protect your equity in the business, not your creditors! When you are insolvent, you have little or no equity to protect, so you can cancel product liability and public-liability (premises) insurance and other liability policies. After all, if you are now insolvent, you are judgment-proof.

Review your insurance coverage with other agents. Your own insurance agent may find reasons to continue coverage and your hefty premiums. Buy only insurance you absolutely need, and you may halve your insurance costs.

More ways to save on insurance:

■ Many states let you save 20 to 40 percent on employee health and disability policies by following a few simple safety procedures. The increasingly popular wellness programs also can save you money.

■ Can you buy insurance cheaper through your trade or professional association? Chamber of Commerce? Probably.

■ Disability policies – one of the most expensive types of insurance – can be dramatically reduced by extending the benefit waiting period from 30 to 60 or even 90 days.

■ Have a risk-management firm survey your company for ways to reduce liability and insurance premiums. It can pay big dividends.

■ Shop employee-health plans. Premiums can vary by as much as 50 percent. HMOs usually offer the best rates.

■ Review your coverage. What does it cost? Do you need it? How can you save money on it? Look for unnecessary or overlapping coverages. Check what you'll save with higher deductibles. Check premiums from other insurance companies.

Cash-Raiser Tip #22

SLASH PROFESSIONAL FEES

Lawyers and accountants can pillage and plunder your bank account overnight – particularly when you are in trouble. But even healthy companies can go broke from insane legal fees. You need good lawyers and accountants in a workout, but handing most of your cash to these professionals is not the way to save your business.

Bid out your legal and accounting work. You can save without sacrificing quality. Handle what you can yourself. Use a law student for routine in-house work. Avoid litigation at all costs. Lawsuits are insanely expensive. If you must defend a lawsuit, pick a lawyer who will handle the case economically.

Demand detailed billing, and question suspicious costs. Some professionals make mistakes; others pad their bills. Review each charge. Was it necessary? Is it reasonable? Could it have been handled by someone less expensive within the firm?

Use arbitration, mediation and other litigation alternatives for faster, cheaper and less stressful results. Write arbitration clauses into your contracts.

Don't overuse your professionals. Call your professionals sparingly. Time is money – right out of your pocket!

Cash-Raiser Tip #23

SAVE BANKING AND FINANCE CHARGES

Banking has become very competitive, so shop banking services as you do other products and services. How can you shave banking costs?

■ Look for discounted or free banking services such as free or low-cost checking, free advice seminars, payroll services, cash "sweeps" to interest-bearing accounts and phone transfers.

■ Negotiate lower interest loans as your company's performance improves and yours loan becomes less shaky. Loan rates are often tied to debt-to-equity ratios. Your lender may not commit in writing to lowered interest, but you and your lender should reach that understanding.

■ Leasing can free up needed cash and lower your monthly costs. So compare financing versus leasing.

Cash-Raiser Tip #24

TACKLE TRAVEL AND ENTERTAINMENT COSTS

Travel and entertainment costs (T&E) torpedo budgets, and yet are the most controllable of all costs. You can cut T&E by 50 percent or more without losing sales.

■ Challenge every trip. Is it really necessary? Can you accomplish your goals through correspondence, telephone or teleconferencing? Most business trips are unnecessary, as few business deals require face-to-face meetings.

■ Can fewer people travel? Can one person handle matters rather than two or three? Can you arrange trips more economically? For instance, would multi-city trips avoid more costly individual trips?

■ Abolish expensive last-minute bookings. Arrange Saturday night stayovers. Know the tricks when you buy travel, or rely on a travel agent who will show you the money-saving ropes.

■ Travel lean and mean. A shoestring budget means traveling coach, budget motels and economy cars. You dine, but not at five-star restaurants.

■ Negotiate deals and hunt bargains. Travel deals abound! A good travel club can save you money. But don't hesitate to negotiate your own deal if you think you can do better. For instance, hotels routinely give as much as a 50 percent discount from their "rack" price if you book a large group or use them frequently – if you only ask.

Cash-Raiser Tip #25

ECONOMIZE ON ADVERTISING AND MARKETING

Is your advertising and marketing budget wasted? You can economize without weakening your marketing clout. Become a sharper marketer by examining what marketing works for you.

Create more powerful marketing with pennies:

■ Do you spend more than $1,000 a year on Yellow Page advertising? Read Barry Maber's book *Getting the Most from Your Yellow Page Advertising* (AMACOM). It's jam- packed with good suggestions on how to get bigger results from fewer dollars.

■ Can your suppliers help you with ad costs? Co-op ad deals between manufacturers and dealers are increasingly common.

■ Do you exhibit at trade shows? Carefully test their value. Most shows give a poor return on investment. If you do exhibit, choose your trade shows carefully. Exhibit in smaller booths with fewer frills, and spend more on pre-show publicity.

■ Monitor every ad for results. You must know where your business is coming from.

■ Set up an in-house ad agency to save at least 15 percent on your ad costs. All you need is an ad agency letterhead and one or two outside clients. It's a practical idea if you spend more than a few thousand dollars a year on advertising.

Cash-Raiser Tip #26

CALL IN THE EXPENSE REDUCTION PROS

How many ways are there to save money? I've only scratched the surface. My goal was to sensitize you for the need to cut costs by pinpointing the few, more obvious opportunities.

Expense reduction has become a science, as every expense has its own savings potential. While smaller expenses, such as telephone, delivery, postage and supplies, seem penny-ante, collectively they can waste enormous dollars.

You probably don't know every trick to lower your expenses (I know I don't), so you may be amazed to learn how much money you can save with some very simple strategies.

Nor do you have to become your own cost-reduction expert, because you can now hire such professionals. These expense-control experts scrutinize every expense, spot the waste and show you how to avoid it. Two excellent firms are *Expense Reduction Analysts* and *Cost Control Consultants Corp.* There are, however, others you can check out. Since these firms earn a percentage of what they actually save you, if there's no savings, there's no fee!

Call in these professionals today if you want to squeeze dollars when you don't even see dimes!

☑CHECKPOINT

1. Can you collect your outstanding receivables faster?

2. What excess or idle inventory, equipment or real estate can you turn into cash?

3. What additional borrowing power do you have?

4. What hidden or intangible assets can you exploit for fast cash?

5. Do you have spare space to lease or sublet?

6. Can you coax your customers to prepay so their money is in your pocket today?

7. Can you raise prices slightly?

8. Can you sell more to more customers?

9. What must you trim to turn your flabby company into a lean-and-mean organization?

10. Do you need help achieving your cost-cutting goals?

9

HOW TO JUMPSTART YOUR EMPLOYEES AND CUSTOMERS

Penning to paper corporate plans, budgets, policies, strategies and objectives won't make them happen.

It only happens when you can inspire your employees to achieve ambitious goals and deliver outstanding performances. It happens when you sway customers not to abandon you, but instead to throw their support behind you because your company is user-friendly. It happens when you convince creditors and lenders that your past problems will remain in the past. It happens when you make stockholders applaud your small gains, confident that this is not just another company destined for the trash can. It happens when you make positive things happen, or at least create the perception that positive things are happening!

Just as you must create financial stability, you also must create organizational stability. You may find this considerably more difficult than regaining financial stability, because to succeed you must develop a "people" philosophy. Many managers fail because they deal with people as "things." This erodes their relationships with employees and customers, the two groups they most need in good times and bad!

Destroy your relationships with your employees and customers, both of whom are essential for a successful workout, and you have nothing with which to rebuild. Each group has its own stake in your success, and each has good reason to support your company. But when you ignore their needs, you lose their support and usually your company.

So you must learn how to pull together your employees and customers. Win their support and make them essential players in your comeback.

John Mahoney, an old college friend and fellow-turnaround pro, tackled a classic case of organizational dry rot when he came aboard as president of a fast-failing, $20-million-a-year women's clothing retailer. Mahoney recounts:

"Employees were jumping ship or just didn't give a damn. Suppliers cut our credit, dwindling our inventory, causing lost sales and evaporating goodwill. Once customers see empty racks, they don't come back. Competitors? They hovered like vultures. One anxiously awaited our auction to pick up our inventory at a knock- down price. Two others busily solicited our best employees. Others besieged our landlords at our best locations so they could take our choice spots. It was crazy, and it was hell!"

Sound familiar? When you operate defensively, it either pulls you, your employees and your customers together, or it pushes you apart. Creating a climate for success under dismal circumstances is never easy, but always necessary. You must deal in hope!

MOTIVATE YOUR CREW

Bask your company in the right attitude, and your employees will know theirs is a company that will succeed.

All companies want and need motivated employees and improved productivity, but a turnaround company is particularly vulnerable because morale is usually rock-bottom. While you can eliminate extra people and cut salaries, real success comes when you also turn your people around so they don't just work for you but with you!

The crisis stage is when you first come to grips with your problems. This is when your employees are most demoralized. Employees in this fix care less about their work than about their own security. Why not? They work in a shaky environment and never know when they'll be out of a job. A middle manager for a large catering firm that just filed Chapter 11 asked me, "How can I be excited about my company when I may get a pink slip or a 20-percent pay cut next week?"

Motivation suffers when cutbacks must be made, so get your firings done quickly and all at once. Let your remaining employees know you have no further cutback plans. Rumors abound in a troubled organization, so let your employees hear the facts straight from you. The only way to overcome employees' uncertainty, anxiety and fear is through your personal integrity and your ability to communicate straight facts.

You may not need to terminate employees; your best employees may leave on their own. You must then make do with the less valuable and less employable, achieving a turnaround with fewer as well as less capable people. You can often keep your best people if you offer them more responsibilities in the turnaround and attractive incentives if the turnaround succeeds.

When I first come into a case, I try to identify those few key employees most vital to the business. Frequently, they are more important than the owner to the future of the business. Employees can know more about what's really going on.

I then develop an incentive program that ties these critical employees to the business throughout the workout. I may give them 20 percent of their pay as a deferred bonus – if the company attains certain performance goals. Whatever I offer, it is always significant, specific and tied to measurable performance. That's how you must harness your key troops. But I never offer ownership in the company. You don't want your employees as minority shareholders or partners who can cause you major headaches later.

Should you cut pay to preserve jobs, or sacrifice jobs to maintain salaries? Sometimes the answer is to do both. Pay cuts must be temporary. Layoffs are the answer to achieve long-term savings. A $30,000-a-year employee won't hang on forever for $25,000. She may for a month or two to avoid the upheaval of a new job, but eventually she'll move on. Employees will more quickly tolerate fringe benefit cuts than salary cuts, because lost benefits are less visible than a smaller paycheck.

Labor unions try to protect employees in a workout and more readily accept salary cutbacks than layoffs. But winning bargaining concessions from a labor union is always difficult because unions expect everyone else to sacrifice as much as possible before salaries or jobs are touched. A Chapter 11 bankruptcy's power to wipe out an oppressive collective bargaining agreement is a formidable weapon in negotiations and must sometimes be employed with an inflexible union.

Labor unions have more recently become pro-active in employer workouts and can enormously influence how employees react to the situation. Unionized employees take their cue from their union, not from management. So nurture the union representatives to effectively transmit their motivation to the rank and file. Chrysler, the first major corporation to appoint a union official to its corporate board, clearly understood the power of the unions.

How your employees react to layoffs and salary cutbacks is as much psychology as economics. A 10-percent salary rollback sells easier when employees see you and other executives taking a 40 percent cut and creditors losing 70 cents on the dollar. Your employees, more than anyone else, must be convinced there truly is an "equality of sacrifice." They must perceive it as equality. A $25,000 employee cut to $20,000 is hardly sympathetic to a CEO whose $250,000 salary is hacked to $200,000. The sacrifice must be functionally equal, not just mathematically proportionate.

So cost-cutting begins at the top. Eliminate the high-level positions first. (That's where most of the overhead flab is anyway.) Employees applaud when top managers take it hard on the chin. Even if it doesn't revitalize morale, it definitely helps neutralize antagonism.

But spilling executive blood doesn't always appease employees who must still shed their own. Employees rightfully believe they are in the worst position to sacrifice for the organization. It's relativity. A clerk-typist who counts $10 bills in a pay envelope can't relate to lenders and creditors who are losing millions.

Stabilizing morale is not enough. You also must shock your troops into positive thinking, people redirected from failure toward success. Their attitude largely mirrors your attitude.

To succeed, recondition employees to think about opportunity, profits and growth instead of only problems. It won't happen overnight, but it must happen if you want to go from a defensive to a forward-moving company.

Coaxing employees to think about profits and opportunities will be far tougher for you than for the manager of the healthy firm. Few employees relate their work to overall profits. Employees always want a more prosperous employer but seldom want to work harder to make their employer more prosperous.

Results come fastest when employees see a direct benefit to themselves through financial incentives tied to meaningful performance appraisals. And it's smart to substitute wage-and- benefit cuts with recognition rewards as a benchmark of recovery. Give bonuses as conditions improve, and restore salaries and benefits as soon as possible.

Effective incentives are meaningful when tied to individual performance, not corporate performance alone. Sales commissions and productivity incentives, for example, produce much better results than across-the-board incentives. Establish your incentives before you make your cutbacks so that your employees can see the upside as well as the downside to the situation.

Incentives are your carrot, but you also must carry a bigger stick. Employees must see that you're less tolerant of poor performance and that you'll quickly terminate employees who perform poorly.

With the carrot and stick approach, your employees realize they must either yank their oar harder or they're out. It's a powerful motivator for any turnaround. And to further kickstart your organization, replace weak people with strong, productive employees – a long overdue exercise for most companies.

Turnaround companies, like other companies, must be people-sensitive, but must be even more performance- and survival- sensitive. Terminating poorly performing but loyal and long- standing employees is one unhappy duty of corporate flab trimming.

Scrap affirmative action and other red-tape laws and policies that restrict your ability to keep the employees you need rather than the ones Washington wants you to employ. You need the best. You can't be a welfare program when you're a step away from your own welfare check.

Incentives alone won't achieve a climate for success. Monetary rewards are vital, but they never create the crucible of enthusiasm you need. Barry Sullivan, another turnaround pro, superbly exemplifies a corporate leader who knows how to create a climate for success.

Sullivan took control of First Chicago Corporation when First Chicago, then the nation's eleventh-largest bank holding company, was under heavy attack by such financial service giants as Merrill Lynch, American Express and Sears. Besides implementing innovative marketing changes, Sullivan jump-started First Chicago by encouraging an open atmosphere and a teamwork approach through a collegial management style, new compensation policies and personal example.

Sullivan delved into every corporate nook and cranny. He scrutinized everything from budgets to selecting the art to decorate the bank's walls. Sullivan created this new corporate climate by changing just about everything from the physical environment to internal communication to employee participation in managerial decision-making. In exchange, Sullivan was blessed with people who showed up for work each morning with a refreshingly positive attitude.

Leaders like Sullivan understand how well employees can respond to even the small wins in the turnaround process. You must constantly spotlight the gains, even when the gains are modest.

One of my own clients, Jon Humphreys, makes it a point to take the crew of his cabinet shop to lunch whenever something positive happens, such as a sizable new order or a sales increase.

Another company on the rebound from slumping sales raffles away to a lucky employee a free vacation trip whenever sales hit a certain mark. These are nothing more than symbolic gestures, but symbolism lifts spirits.

Shortly after the devastation of Pearl Harbor, General Jimmy Doolittle launched a stunning bomb raid on Tokyo. The raid inflicted negligible damage, but for the first time since the war began, Americans had cause to smile. Victory can come with small, symbolic punches!

Honest, open and frequent communication is the cornerstone of this new corporate climate. This communication is not through fancy corporate bulletins or memos filtered through five layers of management. It happens when you meet face-to-face with all of your employees. If you want results, roll up your sleeves and talk with your people. Don't talk to your people.

Don't forget that your employees have a great stake in your company's survival, so don't callously leave your employees in the dark about corporate events. Believe me, nothing will alienate your employees more than when you are distant and unresponsive to their concerns.

The constant theme I hear from employees, regardless of size or type of business is, "We gave this place many years of our lives, and we depend on it to feed our kids and keep a roof over our heads. We damn well have a right to know what's going on!" And they're right.

Tell your employees what is going on: This is what good communication and courageous managers are all about. And they tell them even when the news is bad. It's their involvement that creates jumpstart organizations.

You may think you communicate effectively but give employees only lip service. Employees are naturally cynical to whatever you tell them, and this is particularly true when your company is in deep trouble and the truth may only encourage employee defection.

After all, even rats have the good sense to abandon a sinking ship. Still, good managers accept the right of employees to share the bad news with the good, even if tempered with a dose of optimism.

Meet frequently with your employees. Keep them abreast of developments; try to learn from them. In troubled times, your natural instinct will be to insulate yourself from your front-line troops. This is more tolerable in the good times, but fatal in the bad when you critically need constant feedback from all employees.

Listen to them! It's the only way to know what's really going on. If your crisis brings you and your employees together for the first time, you'll be surprised how valuable their observations and recommendations can be!

Don't tell your employees merely what is happening. Explain why. You may understand why things are the way they are, but do your employees? Some years ago, I was trying to straighten out a small Pittsburgh wrought-iron accessories manufacturer. The manufacturer couldn't obtain credit from the manufacturer of a brass-assembly screw, so he switched to an alloy screw available from a supplier who would extend credit.

The alloy screw didn't quite work as well as the brass screw, and the employees couldn't figure out why the company suddenly dropped the easier-to-work-with brass screw in favor of the alloy screw. The plant buzzed with rumors that the boss had lost his mind, until they were finally told why the decision to switch screws was made. Suddenly, the boss was an innovator and survivor, not an imbecile. Unless your employees understand what you're thinking, you, too, will look like a dunce.

Motivation builds when your employees more actively participate in the turnaround. Why not divide your employees into task forces, and assign each a specific project? Why not have key employees rotate on a special workout committee?

One large magazine publisher, now in his second year of a workout, encourages teamwork through a ten-member employee counsel that meets monthly for shirt-sleeve sessions. Granting employees a greater role in corporate governance is hardly a novel idea, but what better time to implement it than during a turnaround, when your employees sense the need to more strongly control their own destiny.

END BAD POLITICS

Your best intentions and best efforts are meaningless when your organization is riddled with bad politics. Enthusiasm, cooperation and unity of purpose can't happen in an environment of internal feuding, backstabbing and politicking. A polarized company is a company divided, and one that's nearly impossible to save.

How healthy are the politics in your company? In tough times, they can become bizarre and totally disruptive. An example of crazy politics involved a sinking $20-million-a-year shipping firm. In one office sat its young president, who had inherited half the business from his father. In the next office sat his disgruntled sister, who had inherited the other half. Neither brother nor sister spoke to each other for more than three years, and each functioned through completely autonomous staffs who spent much of their time creating a divided camp. In this case, the roadblocks to a successful turnaround were quite obvious.

Power plays within the troubled organization, regardless of form, are always disruptive. From top managers to warehouse clerks, everyone must work together closely. If you don't have that basic harmony, you must make changes to develop a cohesive team.

Do you have a larger business? Your problem may be a board of directors that's either too passive or too domineering. It either fails to adequately control events, or it takes away the flexibility you need to do the job. Politics, regardless of form, must be straightened out when it impedes your ability to make the changes necessary for survival.

Conflict often results from poor organizational structure. Your company may be too top heavy, or offer employees too little support. The structure of your organization must be reshaped so that necessary changes can be swiftly implemented, and the results of change accurately and quickly measured and communicated back to the top.

Changing the organizational structure is never enough. You also need the right people in the key spots. These key people must take their direction from the top, and force it to the lowest rung of your organization. But you are fooling yourself if you think the answer to your people problem is simply to play with neat little boxes on a piece of paper. As one observer remarked when handed the fourth draft of a newly proposed reorganization: "Different tree, same monkeys."

Put it all together, and you have a five-point strategy for getting the most from your people.

1. Demonstrate strong, optimistic leadership.

2. Establish clear goals and strong incentives.

3. Communicate constantly and honestly.

4. Encourage employee participation in the turnaround.

5. Eliminate organizational politics and roadblocks.

CREATE A USER-FRIENDLY COMPANY

Survivors treat their customers as number one, and give them more than they ever had before. Of course, customer-driven firms seldom fail in the first place because they sincerely believe their customer is their lifeblood and run their business accordingly. You must especially put your customer on the pedestal in troubled times so you will have the sales to rebuild your business.

Penn Central, Baldwin-United Corporation, Rolls Royce and W.T. Grant are four corporate relics. Each turned its back on its customers. Seven out of ten firms play ostrich and hide from their customers when they are in trouble. These firms function with a bureaucracy-driven philosophy, a mindset to serve their needs before their customers' needs.

Cosmetic changes won't save these firms. They badly need a new corporate philosophy, one in which the customer truly comes first. If your customer is not number one, you too must quickly learn to march to the beat of a different drummer.

Distressed companies are especially vulnerable to more aggressive competitors who are better able to satisfy the always- fickle customer. The way to lose the battle is to let your customers and sales disappear because you succumbed to pressures to "de-market" rather than market. Cash poor companies almost always cut back first on advertising, promotion and other marketing efforts considered less vital to their survival. That's a mistake. To raise cash, they slash customer service and cut product quality, which are only bigger mistakes!

Turnarounds need strong sales, but sales seem secondary when you're fighting so many other problems. Yet your customers will dump you in droves if they no longer get the products or services they want, when they want them and at the prices they want them at. Customers shop winners, not losers. Strong competitors trading on your vulnerability will move in for the kill.

You must counteract your vulnerability with even more powerful marketing and better customer service. Each powerfully expresses that your company is alive and well. You cannot let customers believe you can no longer properly serve them, or they will leave you. Strong marketing and top-notch customer service dispels that thought.

A large, long-established Boston drug wholesaler slogging through Chapter 11 illustrates: Five competitors hit the road to steal their retail accounts. They dangled lenient credit, extra discounts and even free vacations. The firm's sales manager recounts a common tale: "In the first two months alone, we lost 60 of our 465 accounts. To strike back, we designed our own re-energized marketing program, and added three new salespeople to stay very close to our customers. Despite our cash problems, we invested $60,000 for a promotional campaign to win new customers. Our competitors, convinced we were down for the count, couldn't believe we could bounce back and grab their customers! At first, we had too many financial and operational problems to worry much about sales, marketing or customer retention. We simply became sloppy and took our customers for granted. But, when you're in business, you can't become sloppy no matter what your other problems are."

Look like a survivor. Customers, like employees, will jump ship out of insecurity if they sense that you're weak. How can you send that message when you're not at all sure it's true? Sometimes it's with mirrors. Years ago, a client's printing firm was failing fast, and his competitors, like vultures, hovered for the kill. "XYZ Printers won't be around long, so why not send us your printing?" was their war cry. So, for $600, we had a billboard prominently placed beside XYZ's plant announcing: "Under Construction _ New and Expanded Facilities for XYZ Printers."

Of course it wasn't true: XYZ could barely scrounge up the $600 for the sign. But it worked. We sent pictures of the "construction site" to every XYZ customer. XYZ's competitors were dumbstruck, and, of course, XYZ's customers believed the message. After all, seeing is believing. Look successful to stay successful, even if you are not successful.

You also need super-smart marketing when you don't have big bucks for a marketing campaign.

With cash tight, make your advertising and promotion more effective and economical than before. Your marketing plan also must match your turnaround plan. Well-targeted marketing must replace "smother 'em" marketing. Pareto's law says 20 percent of your customers will generate 80 percent of your sales. This means you target that 20 percent! Cater to these all-important customers even if you must neglect your smaller and less profitable accounts in the process. You can no longer be all things to all people. Once you identify those customers vital to your future, then marshal your shrinking resources to forge even stronger relationships with them. Downsizing will lose you some marginal accounts, but that can be healthy if it helps you hold those few big customers you need to rebuild.

Make your advertising budget work extra hard for you. Avoid public relations, community image-building, institutional and other "soft" advertising. Every advertising dollar you spend must produce direct, measurable and very profitable results.

SELLING IN TROUBLED TIMES

Use precise cost to sales evaluations. Make sales compensation match performance. I usually switch salespeople from salary to commission, if only to eliminate the non-producers who never earned their salaries in the first place.

Salespeople do sell more aggressively when their paychecks are on the line. One university study of troubled companies showed sales staff cutbacks had surprisingly little impact on overall sales.

Apparently Pareto's law was hard at work again. Surviving corporations remain market-oriented, and they direct their managerial energies to satisfying the customers that count. Misguided organizations harness large sales forces to replace the once-valuable customers they lose. Spend more time and effort to keep the customers you have, not the customer you may get. It pays bigger dividends.

Do you sell through sales reps? Then you will probably have to re-energize your rep groups. How well are they now performing? Sluggish sales may be the fault of a weak sales organization. You may have the wrong reps, or they may have lost interest and enthusiasm for your line.

This frequently happens when a company gets into trouble. Good reps want winners and don't like being associated with losers within their trade. Only new products, promotions and services can keep your rep organization on its toes in troubled times.

Good communication is no less important with your rep groups than with employees. Your reps must know your plans and how you will correct problems they must deal with (late or spotty shipments, poor quality, weak sales support). Your reps also are concerned, of course, whether they will be paid. Forward their commissions more frequently, so you have one less obstacle between you.

Your sales reps are your goodwill ambassadors to your customers. They must field the complaints, handle the embarrassing rumors and convince your customers that yours is a company to do business with. Your job is to tell them why all that is so. Not only must you convince them that it is true but, most importantly, you must make sure your reps spread the right words.

HOLD YOUR PRICES

Too many companies get into trouble because they underprice. This error is about five times as common as overpricing. The pressure to boost sales and keep customers happy is what leads you to lower your prices on the fallacy that low-profit sales are profitable when added to your present sales. Low-profit sales seldom cover the creeping costs necessary to support them.

A faulty pricing strategy sabotaged A&P supermarket's turnaround.

After years of struggling against young startup chains, A&P went "deep discount" and ignited the one of the most costliest, most disastrous price war in food retailing. A&P lost more than $40 million in only six months.

It discovered too late that reduced prices force competitors to retaliate with even lower prices. When you slug it out on the basis of price alone, the victory inevitably goes to the company with the greatest staying power. That's not going to be the barely alive turnaround company.

Turnarounds that cut prices should cut their costs instead. In fact, for most turnarounds it's smarter to increase prices. Modest, well-timed price hikes rarely hurt sales, but can add considerably to your bottom line. Couple it with improved customer service, and you have a winning combination.

MARKETING 101

Energizing customer relationships comes only with a new commitment to product quality and customer service. You can't cut back on product quality or service and think you can get away with it. Customers will react badly to shoddy products and service.

If surviving companies teach us anything, it is that the turnaround is one last opportunity to look at your products and services the way your customers do. It also may be your last opportunity to regain the competitive edge by building that better mousetrap.

Energizing your company also means energizing your products and services. Again, remember Pareto's law and focus on your key products or services. Product proliferation may have grown and killed your company. If you never learned to exploit your many products or services, you then do poorly with all.

Downsizing to your core products is your surest route to survival. Few companies have the resources needed to shotgun a wide variety of goods or services. When they try, the customer invariably ends up with too little – and that means an unhappy customer!

Stress your important customers, product lines, services and distribution policies. Don't waste your precious resources on the unimportant. Simmons Mattress shrunk from 8,000 dealers to fewer than 5,000 important dealers they could profitably pay attention to. Simmons concentrated its resources on building stronger dealer relations, and stepped up both its own and its dealers' promotional programs to boost sales. Simmons also improved quality and increased prices. Simmons' comeback followed a basic survival strategy: "Thick on the best, to hell with the rest!"

To redirect your marketing program, answer these six questions:

1. Which customers should you concentrate on?

2. Which products or services should you concentrate on?

3. What marketing strategies (advertising, promotion) most effectively and efficiently reach your customers?

4. What new services, products or programs can strengthen key customer relationships?

5. What can you do right now to look like a survivor?

6. What resources can you commit to your marketing program?

If the purpose of business, as Management Guru Peter Drucker suggests, "is to create a customer," or, as Stanford's Harold Levitt puts it, "to buy a customer," then the responsibility for energizing these philosophies throughout your organization is on your shoulders as the turnaround leader. You have the primary responsibility to your customers. You must show every employee how to acquire new customers, keep existing ones and rebuild on a foundation that recognizes the customer as the source of everyone's paycheck. You must energize your employees and your customers, as well as create a link between them through which flows improved products, services, systems and policies.

Employees who truly care about the customer are important for any company. They are doubly important for troubled companies, where employees and customers must both be adaptive and flexible as they deal with your limited resources. You develop this cohesion.

Troubled companies become user friendly because their customers are not only their most valuable asset, but their one remaining asset. Business survivors keep their customers happy by staying close to them, very close. Winners listen to their customers, service the socks off them and make sure they always feel important. Their reward is the continued chiming of their cash register.

If you believe, as you should, that the business of business is customer service and satisfaction, then you must energize your business in that direction. This managerial philosophy is embraced by the movers and shakers within successful turnaround companies. You do this when you:

■ Develop a sense of purpose and a shared view of what your company is about.

■ Instill a sense of pride that your company is the best at what it does.

■ Create a success climate by navigating your people away from problems and toward opportunities.

■ Build the motivation machine that inspires ordinary employees to perform extraordinarily.

■ Energize your organization with a user-friendly, customer-first, service-driven philosophy.

■ Fashion new products, services and programs to regain the competitive edge and to show that your company has a real future.

Where, when and how do you begin this mission? "When" is easy. Start right now! "Where" also is not difficult. Don't send a letter or another catalog. Don't even phone. Get in your car or hop a plane, but see every important customer. And when you're in trouble, there's hardly a customer who's not important.

Maybe you only need to walk the floor of your own retail business, or stop at a few tables if you're a restaurateur for eyeball-to-eyeball contact. You get the idea. There's no substitute for frequent and meaningful contact. Let your customers know you appreciate their business. Find out what problems they may have with you and what you can do to better satisfy them.

But satisfying your customer is hardly enough. Deliver more! Give your customers more than they expect, more than they paid for and more than your competitors could possibly give.

Stay in close touch with your complaints department. That is where you'll hear the seeds of discontent, and it's there that you must begin plugging the leaks in the dam to implement change.

Whether you keep your customers won't depend as much on the nature of their problems with you but on how you handle them. Customers can be very understanding (if they are in business themselves, they have had their own share of troubles) if you explain the reason for the problem, how you will remedy it, and sincerely express your concern for how it affects that customer. Most unsatisfied customers will give you another try. Normalizing relations with an unhappy customer must be highest on your priority list.

Here's an example of what I mean: A mid-sized manufacturer of household items in Duluth, Minnesota, found itself surrounded by several cut-throat competitors. This manufacturer had the smallest sliver of the market and, being small, it had its rough spots. Deliveries were late, product quality was uneven, billing errors were common, and customer complaints were becoming rampant. A new sales manager found the sales staff either avoided or ignored complaints. Rather than face the problems, they turned to the less-productive task of hunting down new customers to replace those lost.

A no-nonsense policy finally emerged: Every customer who complained to the company had to be called by his or her sales rep the very same day. All sales reps were required to phone in daily to get their messages. Most importantly, every effort was made to resolve all complaints within three days. And to salve the wound, complaining customers were given a small concession (an extra discount or some free goods) on their next order.

Before long, sales began to rebound. Not surprisingly, much of the sales increase came from those customers who previously complained! In fact, the complaint department soon became the place the sales reps congregated, confident they could turn the complaints into new orders! Within two years, the company had captured 35 percent of its market. Yes, it still got complaints, but also many more orders.

Your customer-first system won't come together overnight. But you may improve service by 2 percent a month. Bind yourself to your customer slowly and deliberately. In the meantime, listen to your customers. Customer satisfaction is not measured by you. It's measured by them.

This chapter has a simple – but enormously important – message. The format for success positions employees and customers as the two most important resources. If you want your customers to support your business, your employees must support your customers. You must support them both. And when you do, you have the foundation for a successful business. A very successful business!

☑CHECKPOINT

1. Do your personnel policies promote good morale?

2. Do your employees perceive you and other top managers as sacrificing to save the business?

3. What incentives can you offer your employees to increase productivity?

4. How well do you communicate with your employees?

5. What bad politics pollute your business? What can you do to end them?

6. Are you paying the most attention to the customers critical to your survival?

7. Have you primed your sales organization to sell even more for you in troubled times?

8. Is your marketing cost-effective? Targeted to the key accounts?

9. Have you created a user-friendly, service-driven philosophy?

10

HOW TO TURN
YOUR BUSINESS INTO A
CREDITOR-PROOF FORTRESS

Vulnerable businesses stand the best chance to fail. Well-fortified, creditor-proof enterprises usually survive. That's how I see it!

If you reviewed my 1,000 cases, you too would find it amazing how resilient the well-protected business is compared to those that are exposed and unprotected. That is why this chapter preaches this important rule: you, not your creditors, must have the upper hand and strongest bargaining position. And that happens only when you turn your business into a creditor-proof fortress.

You may not see the need to protect your business even when creditors breathe down your neck. You may think your business needs no protection. You may think there's nothing you can do to protect it. You may think it's too late to protect it. You may think incorrectly on all counts!

Believe me, solid defensive positioning will give you the upper hand when it comes time to combat your creditors. You have complete control over your businesses future, no matter what your creditors do.

Without defensive positioning you are exposed and vulnerable. Your creditors control the show. You must dance to their tune. Is that the way you want it? Not if you are a survivor!

Survivors do everything possible to creditor-proof their businesses. Survivors protect themselves before they go into business. Survivors continuously fortify themselves once in business.

BUILDING YOUR FORTRESS

Timing is critical. Building a strong financial fortress takes time, and you build the strongest fortress when you defensively position your business before serious problems arise and you have angry creditors chasing you. Still, it's never too late to try.

Fortifying a client's business is always one of my very first objectives. I know that I'll eventually go eyeball-to-eyeball with creditors. When I do, I want them boxed in so they must accept our deal. You can achieve this only by convincing creditors they will get far less – perhaps nothing – if they refuse your deal. And to be truly convincing you must show your creditors that you can stay in business regardless of what they do. You, not your creditors, must have the options.

How can you turn your business into an impregnable, creditor- proof fortress? With these six vital building blocks:

Building Block #1: Use a corporate shield

Building your fortress begins with the right business organization. There are over 15 million businesses in America. Four million are unincorporated. Their owners sit on a literal time bomb. When they fail, as most will, their owners may lose not only their businesses, but everything they own personally.

Using a corporation to operate your business is essential today because only a corporation protects your personal assets from your business creditors. Only the foolish, naive or unknowing jeopardize their personal assets. Don't be among them. Limit your creditors' recourse to your business only. Don't let them follow you home. It will cost you dearly. Even if you have no personal assets to lose, why subject yourself to a personal bankruptcy when it is so easily avoided?

It costs only several hundred dollars to incorporate and a few extra dollars for accounting and maintaining corporate books and records. There are commercial firms that will incorporate you for under $50. Investing those few dollars is a tremendous bargain when you consider how effectively a corporation protects your personal wealth from business failure. A corporation is the best insurance you can buy today! Don't discover that too late.

Early in my legal career I represented a young pharmacist who had just gone bust with his two unincorporated drugstores. When the smoke cleared, Joe and his family had lost their $300,000 home, two cars and a host of other personal assets to their business creditors. "You don't need the hassle of a corporation," his naive lawyer had counseled when he set Joe up in business. Dumb, dumb advice. Don't you fall for it!

What can you do if your business is unincorporated and heavily in debt? Act fast. It may not be too late to protect yourself.

Quickly incorporate and transfer both your business assets and liabilities to your new corporation. Then gradually pay down the debts that belong to your unincorporated business. You will have the cash flow, as your new corporation will simultaneously build its own liabilities. Once you've fully paid the debts of your unincorporated business, you are left only with corporate creditors, and your personal wealth is no longer endangered. This takes careful planning and good legal advice to make certain you do not violate any laws.

I can tell you about one chap who incorporated his Reno, Nevada, surgical supply store only several weeks before liquidating it under an Assignment for the Benefit of Creditors. Nearly all of the debts predated his incorporating, so the creditors had the legal right to collect from the owner personally. But the creditors never checked to see if the business was incorporated when the debt was incurred. They simply assumed it was incorporated from the start and never pursued it further.

If you're not incorporated, do it immediately. Confining your creditors to the fewest possible assets means they can look only to the business for payment – not to you!

For purposes of liability protection, it does not matter whether you use a regular "C" corporation or an "S" corporation. They differ only in their taxation. Your accountant can guide you on this. You also may consider forming a limited liability company, now recognized in about 25 states. But never operate as a proprietorship or partnership.

A corporation limits your liability only when you avoid personal guarantees on the corporate debts. This can't always be avoided, because banks and other lenders rarely lend to small businesses without an owner guarantee. But you can escape most guarantees on other corporate obligations if you follow the strategies in Chapter 19.

Building Block #2: Isolate winners from losers

If one corporation is sensible, then two, three or ten corporations may make even more sense.

If you own several businesses, incorporate each separately. One failed business won't endanger the other healthy business. It's the smart way to creditor-proof a growing conglomerate. Only fools put all their eggs in one basket.

The corporate graveyards are littered with once-thriving companies that vanished because they foolishly operated all of their businesses under one corporation.

Beware the law of probability: Even the clever businessperson eventually saddles himself with a loser. And that one loser can easily destroy everything.

Here's another lesson learned too late. Joan and Harry, a young Texas couple, once owned three thriving Mexican restaurants in the Dallas suburbs. Their fourth restaurant? A disaster. Enormous losses from this poorly located fourth restaurant soon tumbled the three profitmakers because all of the restaurants were in the same corporation. A common mistake? Sure, but don't you make it!

Your goal is to isolate your potential losers from your present winners. If you incorporate each business separately, you can safely shed your losers while building on the strength of your winners. This gives you maximum protection when you're small and most vulnerable. Larger companies can't as easily shed their losers. Tax, financing, creditor and operational factors may require a one-corporation structure. But you may never become big unless you do isolate your sick ventures from your healthy enterprises while you are growing!

You may find it equally smart to split your existing corporation into separate corporations! Confine your liability- prone activities to one corporation and have your more valuable assets owned by the less vulnerable corporation.

Think! What is the heart of your business? Where and how are you most likely to incur liability? How can you separate one from the other? Think very carefully. This survival-thinking saves businesses!

Plenty of Main-street ventures are organized precisely this way. A Tampa superette chain operates each of its 16 stores through a separate corporation. Each fully stands on its own with no financial or legal entanglements with the other ventures. This is smart, defensive positioning.

I encouraged a $12-million-a-year Denver electrical-component manufacturer to become two separate corporations. One would serve the industrial market, the other the consumer market. This too is smart defensive positioning!

If your business is in the first stages of a downturn, see how you can legally spin essential assets into a new, debt-free corporation. Confine creditors only to the least important, most expendable part of your business.

Smart operators function through multicorporations, even when they operate small, simple businesses. Saving an ailing business then requires only minor surgery to remove the few sick parts.

Building Block #3: Shelter key assets

The building-block strategy, by using corporations, limits your creditors to the assets of your business. Multiple corporations isolate your sick businesses from the healthy business.

Here is your third creditor-proofing strategy: Keep your operating company asset poor so creditors stand to gain nothing when they go after you.

Real estate is an important asset that should never be owned by an operating company. Why needlessly expose a valuable building to business creditors? Own real estate personally or title it in a separate real estate trust, corporation, limited partnership or another entity that keeps it beyond the reach of your business creditors.

Good advice? You bet!

Unfortunately, Lucy didn't think so. A once-prosperous owner of a thriving restaurant on the beautiful intracoastal waterway in Fort Lauderdale, Lucy wisely snapped at the chance to buy the building from her landlord. Contrary to my advice, she titled the property in her restaurant corporation. When Lucy's restaurant fell from grace as Fort Lauderdale's fashionable dining spot, her restaurant failed. But her trade creditors, owed about $600,000, had few worries. They grabbed the big equity in her real estate.

Lucy will never again give her creditors that opportunity. Now $600,000 smarter, Lucy owns her real estate outside the operating corporation and safe from creditors. A still smarter Lucy similarly titled her chairs, tables, furniture, equipment and even her valuable liquor license to another outside entity. Any future creditors could chase only empty space. Too bad Lucy hadn't taken my advice before she lost $600,000.

Nobody wants to hurt creditors, but it's nevertheless more comforting when you can lose nothing, and your creditors can gain nothing should push come to shove. That's the real world!

Does your corporation hold assets that would be safer titled outside the corporation and beyond creditor reach? Real estate? Expensive equipment? Patents? Trademarks? Copyrights? Distributorship or franchise rights? If you want protected assets, title them outside your business and lease or license their use to the operating business. That's savvy strategy!

Building Block #4: Debt shield your business

I love big, friendly mortgages. They are high on my creditor- proofing list and a great tool to help save your business. A business, heavily encumbered to a friendly lender can become a debt-free business overnight. Magic? No. Only some basic law turned to your own advantage.

Assume your business's assets are worth $100,000, and your brother has a $100,000 mortgage secured by those same assets. Suppose you also owe general creditors $200,000. Because your brother's mortgage has priority over all other creditors, including your general creditors, there would be absolutely nothing left for your general creditors if they seized your assets or pushed you into bankruptcy. Your unsecured creditors then lose their bargaining power, and you have precisely the business-saving leverage you need to survive.

A "friendly" mortgage or debt shield offers you enormous survival power. This one strategy has helped me save hundreds of once-troubled businesses. But to work, your friendly mortgage must cover the liquidation value of your business assets. Too small a mortgage leaves your creditors equity to chase, and you do not have adequate protection.

A "friendly" mortgage has a "friendly" mortgage holder willing to protect you and cooperate with you so the mortgage becomes a defense shield. It may be a relative, a friend, a loyal supplier, a friendly bank or an affiliated company. How do you create your friendly mortgage?

- If you loaned tons of money to your business, why not secure your loan with a mortgage on your business? (See your lawyer to structure this correctly.)

- Do you owe a friend or relative for loans, wages or fees for services? Why not secure these obligations?

- Do you have a favorite supplier you want to protect and who in turn will, protect you?

- Do you owe your banker on an unsecured line of credit, or have you secured your loan by a mortgage on your home or other personal assets? Is it a banker you can work with? Why not also give him a hefty mortgage on your business?

Understand a little law, and you'll see how effectively you can shelter your business with a friendly mortgage. You can never lose control because your friendly mortgage holder can legally foreclose and resell your business assets, perhaps to a new corporation you organize. It's one way to solve nagging, unsecured creditor problems, when less extreme measures fail. Later chapter 5 explore this strategy in greater detail.

Building Block #5: Control your lease

If your location is vital to your business, your lease may be your most important and valuable asset.

One good way to protect your lease: Have a separate corporation be the tenant in your lease. This corporation can then sublet the space to your operating company as a tenant at will.

You are vulnerable when your troubled business holds the lease because the bankruptcy court can sell your lease; even without landlord approval and even if your lease prevents an assignment or a transfer to a new tenant. So in bankruptcy it's easy to lose control of your valuable location, and with it your business.

I learned that costly lesson as a green legal pup trying to bail out a client's fashionable gift shop perched in a very popular Boston mall .

My business-saving strategy started by protecting the business with a hefty friendly mortgage. I figured I could then negotiate a great deal from the creditors, who were owed more than $300,000, as they then had no equity in the business to chase.

Boy, was I wrong!

What I blindly overlooked was the fact that my client was paying a bargain $20,000-a-year rent on retail space worth more than $60,000. And the lease had twelve more years left.

Before I could catch my second wind, the creditors threw the gift shop into bankruptcy, and sold the lease to a competitor for a whopping $200,000. The creditors were nearly fully paid, and my client was out of business!

I never again made that mistake!

Now when I come across a business with a valuable lease, I rush to protect it. I write the lease to one corporation set up for that purpose and sublet to their operating company as a tenant at will. They can then evict their failing business and sublet the space to a new startup corporation. Or they can sell the lease and pocket the profit if they don't want to go back into business. Or they can negotiate with their creditors, assured the creditors can't put a big value on their lease.

When your lease is not an asset of your troubled business, your creditors can neither claim the lease nor sell it. Your creditors only option is to liquidate your other assets at public auction. They cannot sell your business as a going concern for those bigger dollars. When creditors must settle for those few auction dollars, you gain bargaining power, an important building block for your creditor-proof fortress.

Building Block #6: Shelter the goodwill

The guts of any business is not its machinery, inventory or receivables. It's the relationship of a company with its customers.

When you are the heart and soul of your business, the one person your customers and suppliers want to do business with, you can never really be put out of business. That's why you must always control your key business relationships. If your business fails, you can transfer those relationships to another business, whether it's your own startup or someone else's business. And someone else may be willing to pay you a hefty sum for those goodwill relationships and the profits they represent.

So a key rule is to avoid long-term customer contracts when you're in trouble. As with a real-estate lease, customer contracts can be sold by a bankruptcy court to a buyer willing to assume them. Without a long-term contract, there's nothing to sell; your customers can discontinue business with your defunct company and transfer their business to any place you designate.

Developing strong relationships with key customers and suppliers is always good business, but it is essential to survival when you're in trouble. Goodwill is the cement that holds your fortress together!

Who are your key accounts? Your vital suppliers? When they want to do business with you, and only you, you are indeed the heart of your creditor-proof business!

Now let's put our various fortress-building strategies into perspective. Imagine for a moment approaching your creditors and challenging them to take everything you have.

Sounds silly, doesn't it?

But with a creditor-proof fortress, you literally can offer creditors everything, because there's nothing to take. Why?

- Because your business is incorporated, your creditors can claim only your business assets, not your personal assets.

- Because your businesses are separately incorporated, your creditors can claim only assets owned by your ailing enterprise, and they must leave untouched your flourishing businesses.

- Because your most valuable assets are safely titled outside your failing corporation, your creditors have few assets to claim.

- Because those few assets are encumbered by a friendly mortgage, creditors can claim no equity in those assets.

- Because your lease is securely held by another corporation, your creditors cannot make claim to it or sell your business as a going concern.

- Because you are your businesses most valuable asset, your key customers and suppliers will take their business wherever you go, not wherever your creditors say to go.

The six fortress builders give you, and not your creditors, total control. And you must be in control when you want to turn your debt-saddled business into a debt-free money machine on your terms!

BLOCKADING CREDITORS AND BILL COLLECTORS

Entrenched within your creditor-proof fortress, you can deal with your creditors from a strong position. Begin your defense by freezing payments to creditors on past-due bills to plug your cash drain. You must stonewall creditors so you don't bleed to death. You know how it is. Creditor A, owed $4,000, pushes for $500 a week. Creditor B, owed $7,000, hassles you for $350 a week. Creditor C squeezes $1,000 a month on your long overdue bill. To recoup his $6,000, Creditor D withholds your trade discounts. You are soon repaying creditors two dollars for every dollar you earn. You can't stay in business when you try simultaneously to pay loans, replenish inventory and pay operating expenses, and settle back bills.

Dribbling payments to creditors on past-due bills accomplishes nothing. It's a fool's game. You'll repay your creditors thousands of dollars and still be in debt. And since you can as easily restructure $500,000 in debts as $400,000, what do you gain by squandering $100,000 to pacify creditors before you seriously tackle your problems? You won't win popularity contests by dribbling those payments. Creditors will still call you an S.O.B and deny you credit.

You must be equally tough with lenders who will try to drain you of what they can before your bankruptcy. Of course, lenders who hold your assets as collateral can more easily coerce payment than unsecured creditors, who can only sue to collect. Still, secured lenders, who accelerate payment on shaky loans, also drain your business and must be resisted.

Prioritize your debts and expenses: Suppliers, utilities, professional fees, back rent, insurance, loans, taxes. What do you owe each? How overdue is each? What debts are personally guaranteed? What debts are secured?

Your objective is to pay no more than what you absolutely must to keep your doors open. Pay expenses in the following order:

1. Payroll and payroll taxes

2. Rent and utilities

3. Secured loans and leases on essential assets

4. Purchases of essential supplies and inventory

Use common sense. For instance, pay a few dollars to a small, nuisance supplier if it helps you concentrate better on your larger creditors. Or pay personally guaranteed debts if it frees you of personal liability.

PUT ON A BULLET-PROOF VEST

You may fight creditors for months before you finally pull the trigger to escape your debts. This is your final window of opportunity to fortify your business before your big battle. The trick is not to let creditor pressures get the best of you, so you can focus on the main objectives of the turnaround.

Preserve your sanity by hiring a hardy soul with a deaf ear, a bullet-proof vest and a fast tongue to handle the creditors. Don't you "dance" with the creditors. Nothing is more time- consuming and depressing than to listen to clamoring, hostile creditors.

You can't think positively or work creatively when preoccupied with protecting your butt from the searing heat of creditors. But a thick-skinned employee, whose life savings are not wrapped up in the business, can leave behind emotion. Find someone with the stomach and the cunning to play the game! The title of controller or vice president/accounts payable allows your employee to interface authoritatively with creditors. Find someone who can pacify creditors so they won't harass you, and yet has the good judgment to warn you about particularly onerous threats. Where do you find this character? It may be one of your employees, or you may need to look outside your business for the right individual. I have a ready roster of battle-hardened veterans ready to don bullet-proof vests for my clients. They are worth their weight in gold.

One memorable case of mine involved a defunct travel agency that stranded hundreds of tour travelers when it didn't pay the hotel bill. Bombarded with scores of threatening phone calls, my clients, Jan and Pat, barely escaped nervous breakdowns when one of my veteran "accounts-payable specialists" answered their telephones and took control of the situation.

Protecting clients from creditor hassles is one of my firms most important functions in a turnaround. I insist creditors call me, not the client. Creditors will talk to me because they know I will give them straight answers. My accounts-payable staff logs hundreds of creditor calls each day. These are distracting phone calls our clients avoid in order to give their businesses the attention and positive focus they badly need. Guide your business with a clear mind and a positive attitude. Find a sterner soul to handle the guns so you can steer the ship.

SEVEN RULES TO TAME CREDITORS

Follow some basic rules, and you can effectively handle hundreds of hounding calls from angry creditors seeking one simple answer to one simple question, "Where's my money?" Violate these rules, and you make costly mistakes, lose creditor confidence, pay what you shouldn't, or grant costly concessions. Post these seven rules by your telephone and inside your checkbook:

Rule #1. Forget phony excuses.

No, your check is not in the mail. No, your accountant does not have your checkbook. No, your dog didn't eat the bill. You can't pay because you don't have the money and you need time to put together a workout plan that's fair to all creditors. Now, that wasn't too difficult, was it? Your creditors will respect your straight talk and won't badger you every day. You will be spared making lame excuses and losing credibility.

Perhaps you don't want to save your business, but need time to pay back taxes or guaranteed debts, recoup your investment or only need to grab a few more paychecks until you can find a job or start a new business. Your promise of a workout plan is still not a misrepresentation, because your workout can be, and often is, a plan to liquidate your business.

To defuse creditor pressure, I routinely ask creditors for a 60-day collection moratorium while I analyze my client's situation and formulate a workout plan. Most creditors agree because our request is reasonable. When 60 days pass, I inform creditors that a plan is nearly completed and will be on their desk within 30 days. This wins me 90 hassle-free days. Creditors may eventually receive an unacceptable plan, but it's a plan, and that's all I promised. If they reject the plan, I request 60 days more to modify the plan hoping it will be more acceptable. You can stall for several months without ever using the tired, "I-lost-your-invoice" cliche that nauseates creditors.

Rule #2. Don't let creditors intimidate you.

Most creditors are reasonably patient, but more than a few will try to intimidate you into a fast payment.

They may threaten to push you into bankruptcy (they almost never do). They may threaten lawsuits (you can tie them up in courts for years). They may threaten to report you to the credit bureau (haven't you lost your credit already?).

Ignore creditor threats! Let pushy creditors know they will be paid after more patient creditors are paid. This counterthreat works! Collection agencies and attorneys play roughest because their client has already been tossed around. And these professional collectors are unconcerned about your goodwill and future business.

No matter who chases you for money, fight back and refuse payment. You need to protect yourself and your more cooperative and patient creditors who are waiting in line for their fair due.

Rule #3. Refuse override payments.

Creditors have their own tricks. They may try to deduct earned discounts, promotional allowances or other purchasing incentives from your overdue bill. As a C.O.D. customer, always demand the same price and allowances as cash customers receive. Credit returned goods against future purchases, not your past bill.

Trivial? Hardly. Override dollars can mount up mighty fast. Pay no override or extra payments toward your past-due bills. A troubled stationery retailer let his wholesaler apply more than $1,000 a month in trade discounts to his past-due $90,000 bill. In three years, the wholesaler recovered $36,000 more than other creditors. This was neither fair nor smart. Insist your suppliers give you every dollar in trade concessions, and pay nothing on arrears unless it's part of an overall settlement.

Rule #4. Don't give your creditors security.

Never secure creditor obligations with a mortgage or a guarantee. Creditors who hold a mortgage on your business or your personal assets are in too powerful a position and can only hurt you.

Creditors may wave a big stick and threaten a lawsuit, or dangle the carrot of leniency in exchange for security. Refuse! The only time to give a creditor a mortgage is when it's a friendly mortgage that defensively shields your business.

An "unfriendly" mortgage only protects your creditor, ties your hands and limits your options to rescue your business.

Rule #5. Ignore business termination threats.

I laugh when suppliers say they won't sell on C.O.D. terms without payment on account. Few suppliers enjoy a monopoly. And even when they do, it's poor economics to pay more on your back bills than the new goods can produce in profits. Nor should you favor important creditors over less vital suppliers.

No supplier wants to lose your business. Reduce your fears about losing an important supplier by shopping for replacement suppliers in advance. Shop carefully, and you may find even better deals!

I often hear how vital certain suppliers are, and why they "must" be paid during the workout. The product or service is vital, not the supplier. There are always other suppliers. When suppliers threaten to discontinue business, I need only call their many competitors who are anxious for business.

Rule #6. Listen. Don't talk.

Loose lips sink ships and businesses! Watch what you tell your creditors. You may unwittingly say things that will later hurt you. For instance, admit that you are insolvent and your creditors can throw you into bankruptcy. Nor should you reveal who your other creditors or suppliers are to a disgruntled creditor, who may solicit their aid to throw you into bankruptcy. Tell your creditors only four points:

1. You are now experiencing problems and cannot presently pay.

2. You will pay C.O.D on future orders.

3. No unsecured creditor will receive preferential payments; all general creditors will be treated equally.

4. You will offer your creditors a fair and equitable plan to resolve your debts within a month or two.

Rule #7. Follow these rules.

Conspicuously post these rules. Read them daily. My clients do. I closely monitor their checkbooks to make sure they play by these rules. Those who don't lose their checkbooks. It's that simple. It's a necessary discipline, because every wasted check to creditors hurts your chance for recovery. Yes, it's you on the firing line, and you must face the hostile creditors day after day, so it will be tempting to write a check to get rid of a pushy creditor. But survivors say no.

TREAT CREDITORS FAIRLY

While you must keep your creditors unpaid, you must be sensitive to their position and respect their rights.

Your creditors are only businesspeople like yourself; they too are trying to make good in their own business. They extended you credit in good faith, and you must treat them fairly if they are to cooperate with you. Even unpaid, angry creditors can be turned into friends if you:

Show loyalty.

Nothing angers a creditor more than ignoring their bill while you buy from someone else for cash. Let your suppliers know immediately that you will continue to buy from them – but only if they remain competitive on price and terms and cooperative with you on the workout. Creditors won't take your loyalty for granted.

Avoid preferences.

Creditors stay patient only when other creditors stay patient and when they are not losing the upper hand through their patience. Creditors rightfully get angry when they discover that other creditors are being paid while they are not. Assure your creditors that if they are going without payment, so are your other creditors. Remind creditors who demand payment that you will treat all creditors equally. That's only fair.

Your secured lenders may not let you pay your unsecured creditors during the workout, so your cash goes to them rather than to your unsecured creditors. If payment in violation of this order only causes your lender to foreclose, you have a credible reason for not paying general creditors. Why not make your secured lender the bad guy who won't let you pay your bills? It's a strategy that has worked for me many times.

Stay 100-percent honest.

Creditor cooperation is earned only when your creditors trust you and believe in your honesty. Thirty years in this business has given me an opportunity to rub shoulders against plenty of cheats and crooks who lost their companies only because their creditors distrusted them.

Bad checks are dishonest. Don't juggle an overdrawn checkbook. Bounced checks always spell trouble. So do false credit applications. The truth may lose you credit, but lies only invite fraud charges. Obtain credit honestly, or go without it.

And don't buy heavily on credit when you know you can't pay. Hustling credit from new and unsuspecting suppliers, or loading-up before you go belly-up, is bad business. Not only will it destroy your business, it will destroy your reputation and can get you into serious legal trouble.

Assume your creditors are closely watching your every move. Forget shady tricks or questionable practices. Don't move inventory or equipment suspiciously. Even innocent transactions can be misinterpreted, and the smallest transgression magnified.

HOW TO OUTWIT COLLECTION AGENTS AND LAWYERS

Stalling your creditors won't work forever. Eventually you will deal with collection agencies and lawyers representing creditors who believe that fast action is the best action, and that the squeaky wheel gets the oil.

Large, impersonal, automated corporate creditors move quickly to collect. Their computers have no ears. You must instead find a real person you can talk to when you're not paying because:

- The goods were defective, late or were never received, or the service was unsatisfactory.

- Your payments were not properly credited.

- You have merchandise for return.

These claims can stall your account for 60 to 90 days while your claim is investigated.

Turning your account over to a collection agency or attorney joins the battle. Collection agencies are far less threatening than attorneys, and also are more easily handled. Collection agencies may be national firms such as Dun and Bradstreet, or local agencies. They may serve all industries or just one industry, such as the jewelry or the garment trades. Whether big or small, collection agencies skillfully extract money from recalcitrant and unknowing debtors who are easily harassed and intimidated.

Collection agencies succeed mostly through their ability to intimidate by creating an illusion of enormous power. In reality, collection agencies are as powerless as their clients. Nasty letters and harassing or angry phone calls are their only weapons.

I'm relieved when a creditor hires a collection agency. I know the account will be tied up for several months before I must contend with a still nastier lawyer.

Consumers are well-protected from abusive collection practices by federal law. Commercial accounts are less protected. Collectors, for instance, may badger you at home, evenings and weekends. Slamming the phone in the caller's ear is one practical remedy. Report illegal notices that look like lawsuits to the Federal Trade Commission. Others may threaten to forcibly repossess unpaid merchandise. Goods once sold to you remain yours whether paid for or not. The bill collector may show up at your business and can stay there until you ask him to leave, which you should do quickly. Don't let a bill collector intimidate you into writing a check.

A lawyer, whether hired by the creditor or a collection agency, will soon appear. A good collection lawyer can be a pesky thorn in your side, but lawyers vary greatly in style and effectiveness. Passive lawyers write collection letters. Aggressive lawyers sue with little or no warning and push their claims aggressively.

You will then need a lawyer to stall the lawsuits inexpensively! Find a young, lawyer smart enough to tie up cases without costly legal maneuvers. A $5,000 legal bill to defend a $10,000 claim destined to go absolutely nowhere is nonsense.

My law firm defended countless troubled business clients against garden-variety creditor suits. My computers constantly pumped out inexpensive, but efficient boiler-plate defenses. My clients would eventually straighten out their financial problems or go bust while the case stagnated, so why needlessly run up legal fees? Use common sense with your lawsuits, or your legal fees will kill you faster than your creditors!

How swiftly can events unravel for you? If your creditors are now sending you dunning notices, you can probably delay matters for many months. Pesky collection agencies and lawyers can consume a few more months. How much more time do you need to turn your headache business into a debt-free money machine?

☑CHECKPOINT

1. *Is your business well-fortified from its creditors, or is it exposed and vulnerable?*

2. *Are you squandering money by paying bills you will never fully pay?*

3. *Is someone handling your creditors so you can spend your time rebuilding your business?*

4. *Do you observe the seven key rules in handling your creditors?*

5. *Do you fully respect your creditors' rights and treat them fairly and honestly?*

6. *Do you know how to defend yourself against creditors?*

11

WORKOUTS AND CRAMDOWNS: TACKLING YOUR PROBLEM LOANS

Once your company is stabilized, you can begin to tackle the liability side of your balance sheet and completely restructure your debts.

Your two key objectives in a financial restructuring are to keep your creditors at bay and reduce your debt to tolerable levels, preferably through a "voluntary" debt-restructuring that avoids either a Chapter 11 reorganization or a bankruptcy liquidation. But digging yourself out from debts accumulated from years of unprofitable operation is tricky. Whatever the situation, your successful workout must convince creditors they are being treated fairly and equitably in relation to other creditor groups. Your creditors also must see themselves treated fairly in relation to others expected to sacrifice when a business goes bad, such as stockholders and employees.

Before you start your financial restructuring, you must understand your options and the alternatives available to you. You also must know what concessions to bargain for and how to negotiate so you get the relief you need from your debts.

The workout can be long, tedious and often complex, and can exhaust you because while you fight your creditors, you also must hold your business together with too few assets. Big corporations organize in-house management teams to oversee their debt restructuring. Smaller companies rely more on their professional advisors, who better understand the workouts and can design a more objective and workable financial arrangement.

Debt workouts are the product of good negotiating skills. Similar situations can produce markedly different results only because of the parties involved and their abilities to maneuver in a classically adversarial situation.

But the best deals happen when each party negotiates in good faith and understands the other parties' interests and options.

A debt workout differs from most other business and legal negotiations. The workout usually involves many parties with conflicting interests and rights. Creditor groups, as hostile to each other as well as to the debtor company, can become vultures that fight for their share of the spoils. This polarization within creditor groups often jeopardizes a successful reorganization and forces many companies to resolve their problems within the more stable environment of a Chapter 11.

Less experienced debtors also may fear or avoid open discussion of their situation, or not disclose information critical to a well-planned workout. There are few secrets in a workout, and secretive actions bring a predictable and unpleasant reaction. Surprise or unexplained moves also provide little advantage. A debt workout, like a chess game, doesn't require a move to predict what your opponent will do. Poor communication may spur your opponent to act counterproductively. And these reactions cannot always be undone.

A debt restructuring usually involves three major groups of creditors:

- Secured creditors

- Unsecured or general creditors

- Tax obligations

Obviously, you must handle each creditor class very differently, because each has very different rights, alternatives, concerns and options. This chapter tackles your secured loans. The following will give you some tips on how to handle your general creditors and taxes.

RESHAPING YOUR DEBTS

Your primary goal should be to restructure your overall debt so that your total debt fits your assets. It also must match what you can pay and when. Of course, even when you reach those goals, you must stay profitable to be completely out of the woods.

Your balance sheet cleanup begins with your secured obligations, those debts for which the creditor holds a mortgage or a pledge of your company's assets as collateral security.

Bank loans, government or SBA loans, acquisition loans from sellers of a business or loans from other asset-based lenders are all common examples. Equipment leases technically differ from secured obligations, but as a practical matter, they are treated similarly.

Tackling secured creditors is the most critical first step in the overall debt workout, because secured creditors can foreclose on their collateral and easily close your business. While your unsecured creditors can only sue to recover their debts, your secured lenders must be handled very carefully because of their enormous self-help power.

Secured lenders do enjoy a strong bargaining position, but that doesn't mean they won't cooperate with a business-saving solution if you can't pay your loan. Your lenders don't want your business, they want their money. Lenders hate the foreclosure hassle, and too many foreclosures reflects poorly on a loan officer. No lender, however, can sit idle while your loan falls further and further behind.

Adopt the right attitude. Be cooperative and realistic without humbling yourself before your secured lenders. Some lenders are unreasonable and act illegally, so to survive, you must know when to cooperate, when to fight and how to excel at each.

The biggest mistake is to avoid your lenders when you have financial problems. Lenders can forgive a defaulted loan, but not an illusive, irresponsible borrower. Lenders cooperate only when you come clean and offer fast, fair solutions.

TAKE A "NO-NONSENSE" LOOK AT YOUR "NONSENSE LOAN"

Are you victimized by a nonsense loan or a loan that you can never pay? A nonsense loan may never have made sense from the start, and was doomed for default even before the ink dried on the loan papers. A nonsense loan also may have been a once-sensible loan that became unworkable as your fortunes changed. Most troubled loans were unsound to begin with. There are hundreds of examples: A seller unloads her $100,000 business to a dimwit buyer for $300,000, financing $250,000. The seller later wonders why the buyer defaulted. A hungry supplier overloads a new account, only to find his mortgage doesn't magically guarantee payment. A venture capitalist finances a hi-tech startup built on a overly optimistic business plan. Each of these self-victimized lenders predictably finds themself in a workout, hoping to recoup a tiny fraction of what he is owed.

The SBA wrote the book on nonsense loans. My files are loaded with SBA blunders. It's understandable. The SBA only makes loans smart banks turn down. The SBA's too-lenient lending policies put as many people out of business as into business.

No genius is needed to foresee a problem loan. I'm now trying to bail out a $400,000 bank loan that financed the purchase of a Texas convalescent facility. The nursing home needed a $1.2 million annual income just to pay the loan. But fully occupied, the nursing home could never gross more than $800,000. How could a smart businessman and astute banker ignore such basic math? A $5 pocket calculator would have saved the bank the $200,000 loss that I, unfortunately, will soon hand them.

Nonsense loans have no winners or losers. Borrower and lender both lose. The business owner loses his or her business and maybe some personal assets. The lender loses part or all of the loan. How it happened is a learning experience. What can be done? You and your lender must think clearly so that you both come out as well as possible under the circumstances. Winning for you is saving your business. Your lender wins if he ends up with more than if you had failed. Within those parameters, you and your lender must carve your new deal.

You can carve a new deal. Why not? Loans aren't chiselled in stone, they're only ink on paper. Don't hesitate to tear up your loan and start fresh with an entirely new deal if that's what it takes for you and your lender to come out winners.

This lesson was not lost on Stu, a street-smart young Boston entrepreneur whose telephone-equipment leasing company started with a $1 million loan from a Boston bank. Before long, the leased telephone industry was loaded with cut-throat competitors that destroyed Stu's profits. When Stu fell four months behind on his $140,000-a-year interest payments, the bank threatened foreclosure. That's when Stu and I began a crazy game of bluff with the lender. Stu had no hope of paying the loan. The bank had no hope of getting paid. And we all knew the score. One month after our first meeting, the bank cut it's loan from $1 million to $100,000. With one stroke of the pen, $900,000 in pressing debts vanished. Magic? Nope. Charity? Hardly. Stu and the bank objectively concluded that they were both victimized by the same bad loan.

There was, of course, more to the story. Stu benefitted from a three-step master strategy that can reshape any nonsense loan.

Step 1: Convince your lender that he will get more in a restructured loan than in foreclosure.

Step 2: Cut your loan to about the liquidation value of your pledged assets.

Step 3: Repay according to what your business can afford to pay and keep growing.

This simple formula certainly saved Stu's telephone company. Stu's assets were worth only $80,000 at auction. And Stu couldn't afford to pay more than $2,000 a month. Stu's new $100,000 loan is proportionate to his assets, and the $2,100 monthly installments fit nicely into Stu's budget. A larger debt or a bigger payment would still be a nonsense loan.

Sure, we had several heated skirmishes before the bank signed. Stu's bank even started foreclosure until the appraiser confirmed that Stu's assets would fetch no more than $80,000 at auction. Our offer of $100,000 suddenly became an attractive alternative. Your secured lenders have no more power to extract blood from a turnip than did Stu's. Remember that when you negotiate with your lenders!

HOW TO DEFANG YOUR LENDER

Lenders with problem loans are instinctively defensive. Their immediate objective is to secure all past-due payments, protect their collateral, shore up their loan with even more collateral, and then liquidate the loan at the first possible opportunity. This is their master strategy to recover as much as possible. Grab the initiative. Forewarn the lender about your upcoming problems, and offer to reshape your loan to your lender's advantage. When you take the initiative, you can bargain for and win concessions denied seriously delinquent and uncooperative borrowers.

But cooperative or not, your lender must decide:

- Should he foreclose now, or cooperate, and hope for a larger recovery later?

- What temporary and permanent loan concessions should be granted?

Your first objective is to buy time so you can start your turnaround with your lenders' cooperation. You want a grace period of reduced or canceled payments until your cash flow improves and your company stabilizes. This gives you the time to negotiate an entirely new loan for your overall workout plan.

You will probably negotiate your loan workout with your lender's workout team. Your loan officer may be there, as will the lender's legal counsel. Lenders worry about lender liability suits, and legal counsel keeps the lender from these rocky shoals. Counsel also neutralizes your own attorney. Lenders want an equal fight. Workouts also are highly technical, and thus require legal guidance. Most importantly, the lender's attorney adds a somber tone to the situation, a reminder that your lender takes your loan problems very seriously. In short, the lender's attorney is master intimidator and resistance-crusher.

With their guidance, your lender decides whether to work with you or foreclose. If your lender's collateral consists chiefly of inventory or accounts receivable, he will worry that you will deplete these assets during your workout, and he will be in a worse position if he must foreclose later.

A recently liquidated Pennsylvania discount-clothing chain supports this concern. Their lender, a Philadelphia bank, recovered only $1.4 million on its $12 million loan. When the company filed Chapter 11 two years earlier, its assets' liquidation value was $3 million. Delay in foreclosure cost the bank $1.6 million. For lenders, the "cooperate-or-foreclose" decision is a "damned-if-you-do, damned-if-you-don't" situation. Convince your lender that forbearance and cooperation present less risk and more potential gain than foreclosure.

Lenders foreclose for different reasons. Your lender may be uncooperative because regulatory agencies are pressuring him. Or huge losses this year may encourage him to absorb your loss so he starts clean next year. A new loan officer may want to charge your bad loan to his predecessor rather than carry it in his files. Lending institution politics creates irrational decisions in a game played by irrational thinkers following irrational rules.

Your role as a guarantor is another important consideration. For example, a bank suddenly foreclosed on a furniture manufacturer's $300,000 loan, barely one month overdue. Why? The owner was getting divorced, and the bank wanted to attach his home before he lost it to his wife.

Convincing your lender that you will remain financially strong as a guarantor is as important as demonstrating your company's continued financial strength. If your lender has recourse to other strong guarantees (such as the SBA), your lender will prefer to collect under these guarantees. Why cooperate with you when a simple demand letter to the guarantor gets them fully paid?

Preferential payments to other creditors may encourage foreclosure. Lenders won't tolerate other creditors paid at their expense. And an IRS lien gives the IRS a first lien on accounts receivables generated after 45 days of the lien. The bank must foreclose to protect its rights to the pledged receivables unless you file Chapter 11. Fraud, embezzlement or other dishonesty also invite foreclosure. Lenders do not cooperate with thieves.

Despite strong reasons to foreclose, you can turn your lender into an ally. Prior relationships are important. Trade on it, and your lender's may be more lenient and reasonable. But lenders are people and therefore unpredictable. Attitudes and policies vary within the same bank. Pinstripe suits only look alike.

Start out with a positive attitude, and anticipate cooperation. Consider the many factors in your favor. First, lenders dislike the adverse publicity from closing a business. Nor can your lender be certain that in time you won't repay more than what the lender would fetch by immediately foreclosing. Remember, your key is to convince your lender that cooperation offers more long-term benefit than risks. So your lender must believe that your company can be quickly stabilized without draining pledged assets. Back up this proposition. Make your case.

Provide your lender with cash-flow statements to demonstrate how your company will finance itself, and stay afloat without depleting the lender's collateral. Show the outside financing that will cover your deficits. Furnish the lender frequent asset appraisals to more easily monitor its collateral. Set benchmarks by which you and your lender can determine whether your company is recovering to your mutual satisfaction. Show your lender why there is absolutely nothing to lose and everything to gain by cooperating. Show why time and patience are as much in his interest as your own. That's the formula to turn your lender into an ally!

Deal collectively with your secured lenders. Don't shield your lenders from one another or conceal other loan defaults. Successful workouts are built on coordination and cooperation between all secured lenders, especially when they all share the same collateral. Secured creditors don't want other lenders paid when they are not. Collectively, they can design a more unified and equitable solution to your problem.

PREPARING FOR BATTLE

Be smart. Battle your lender only when your personal assets are protected. Otherwise your lender may attach your assets without warning, or insist they be pledged in exchange for cooperation and forbearance on foreclosure.

Money deposited with your lender is particularly vulnerable. Your bank can automatically grab all funds in your checking and savings accounts, as well as funds from any loan guarantors deposited with the bank. Keep account low when you have a nervous lender.

Your lenders will try to shore up their shaky loans, and push for more collateral: More business assets, more personal assets, or newer, stronger guarantors. When your lender thinks your present collateral may not cover the loan, it probably won't. So why jeopardize more of your assets when it only improves your lender's position and weakens your own?

Refusing to pledge more collateral won't bring a faster foreclosure despite threats to the contrary. Well-secured lenders foreclose most quickly because they know foreclosure will get them fully paid. Under-collateralized lenders need more patience. Your lender will dangle attractive concessions for more collateral. Temporarily suspended payments, lower interest or fresh advances are common concessions. But these inducements are not worth risking more of your personal wealth on the gamble that your business will succeed. Strengthen your lender's hand, and you have a well-secured lender ready to foreclose at the drop of a hat. Why not, when he now has the security needed to be paid in full?

How do you politely say "no" to a pushy lender? Title your property with your spouse. You may pledge more assets, but what if you and your spouse are having marital problems? Your spouse will naturally be uncooperative, and probably refuse to encumber marital property. You see the strategy: You be the nice guy. Make somebody else the "heavy." Whatever your story, arrange your financial affairs so you no longer control assets that the lender may want pledged. When your assets are safely protected from lender seizure you are in a safe position to battle your lender.

LOAN-SHRINKING STRATEGIES

Lenders howl loudest when asked to cut their loans. But you must shrink your loan when your business is over-financed or when your loans exceed what your business is worth. When you're in over your head, you must dump debt. Some examples:

- *A small meat-processing business, with assets worth about $100,000, owed its banks $240,000 and its general creditors $150,000. I re-negotiated the bank loan from $240,000 to $135,000. The general creditors, in a poorer bargaining position, accepted $15,000, or about 10 cents on the dollar. The company finally had a sensible balance sheet.*

- *A Tennessee homebuilder's assets were worth only about $75,000. Their secured lenders were owed $300,000, and the trade creditors another $100,000. They settled for $60,000 and $10,000, respectively, because it beat what they would get in bankruptcy.*

- *A Boston men's clothing shop owed the SBA more than $300,000, but only $20,000 to trade creditors. The business could have been sold for about $100,000. Hard bargaining drove the SBA to settle for $100,000, with full payment for the few general creditors. Another company suddenly made financial sense!*

Downsizing your debts to match what your business is worth is common sense, but even veteran business people often struggle with loans they can't fully repay. Their struggles continue for as long as their creditors let them continue. They build neither equity nor net worth in their own businesses. Their future, in reality, is only a paltry paycheck, not a debt-free business that has a value.

What is your business worth? What would you pay for it as a buyer? Forget your businesses book value or liquidation value. The workout is your opportunity to buy your business back from your creditors at a price another buyer would pay, with 100-percent financing.

The value of your business on the open market is the maximum debt you can allow. Your goal, however, should be to cut your debts to no more than the liquidation value of your assets.

Overly indebted business owners don't always see this point. You may not either. But if your home was worth $100,000 and was mortgaged for $200,000, you probably would see the need to reduce your mortgage by $100,000 before you realizing any equity. You also would see that it would be smarter to abandon your house to the bank and buy another house where your mortgage payments would start to build equity. You don't always see this as quickly with a business.

Some owners intentionally choose to struggle with debts far beyond the value of their businesses. Henry, a South Florida car-wash operator, is a hardworking chap who mortgaged his car-wash business to a bank for more than $350,000. Because the neighborhood badly deteriorated, Henry's business is now worth $150,000 tops! My proposition to Henry: Force the bank to cut their mortgage to $150,000 so Henry could begin to build some net worth, and be free of strangling interest payments. Not Henry, who dutifully sends the bank its full payment every month. Henry's loan balance will drop to $150,000 in about the year 2073. Will poor Henry be around to celebrate?

Henry believes his business will rapidly increase in value, but I doubt it.

Sam, an Atlanta supermarket owner, offers another perspective when he tells you he's not overly bothered by the $460,000 his supermarket owes the bank. This is despite the dismal fact that his rickety business isn't worth $200,000. Says Sam, "I know my business will never be debt-free. Heck, I can barely afford the interest payments. But who cares, as long as I can take home a salary. To me, my business isn't net worth, it's a week's pay." Unless you are a Sam, start building a net worth in your business. Cut your loans to the bone.

Where do you start? Estimate your assets' liquidation value from the point of view of liquidators.

Lenders and debtors do disagree on liquidation values. Asset appraisal involves guesswork, and there always is a margin for error. The nature and condition of your assets as well as location and seasonal demand are a few of the many factors that can influence what your lender will recover. Raw material, unfinished goods or questionable receivables are particularly difficult to value. You never know what your assets can be peddled for until they are auctioned.

Your strategy should be to depress the lender's potential recovery. Negotiate when your assets have the lowest value. Accounts receivable, for instance, are worth considerably more to your lender than finished goods, which are worth more than raw materials. When I re-negotiated a lamp manufacturer's $2.2-million bank loan, I rigged their production schedule so that nearly $3 million worth of lamps remained unassembled. A pile of lamp parts had considerably less value to the bank than completed, ready-to- ship lamps. My strategy stopped foreclosure as the bank patiently waited for the lamps to be completed and shipped. They could then foreclose on the receivables, and maximize their recovery. I never gave the bank that opportunity. Assembling lamps only as needed, our inventory remained mostly just piles of lamp parts. This is the defensive positioning you need when you must beat down your lenders.

Your leases, copyrights, patents, franchise rights, customer lists and other intangible assets may be worth more than your tangible assets. Few lenders can capitalize on these assets because the value is destroyed in a forced closing.

Liquidation costs, including auction and attorneys' fees and other foreclosure expenses, also significantly reduce a lender's recovery on liquidation. Factor these costs into your negotiations.

Smart lenders don't try to auction troubled companies. They know they will get much more for them as going businesses than as distressed assets. Prolonged negotiations with your lender gives him more time to scout buyers, who will pay more for your business if they can take it as a going concern. If your lender controls your lease or corporate stock, he can force the sale of your business. So a lender's cooperation may last only until a buyer appears who will pay those bigger bucks for your business.

TURN CHOKING PAYMENTS INTO BITE-SIZE INSTALLMENTS

Reducing your debts is only one objective. You must simultaneously restructure your loan payments to what you can afford.

Over-financed businesses usually cannot meet their payment schedule. They must reduce their debt and realign their monthly payments. But even modest loans can choke you.

Stranglehold loans are especially common in an era of high-interest, short-term loans. But no matter how it happens, your loan payments must still leave you adequate working capital and enough cash to rebuild your business.

Starve your lenders, when you have a cash-hungry, insolvent company. It will put more money on the table. It did for Classic Clothes, finally poised to make money after three years of windfall losses. The business had a secured $120,000 bank loan ($4,600 monthly payments) and a swarm of general creditors owed another $140,000. Since Classic was easily worth $160,000 under the hammer, I temporarily left the $120,000 bank loan intact. In an out-of-court workout, I compromised the general creditors' debts down to $20,000. Classic's financial statement improved, but not its cash flow. Classic was left with only $1,500 a month after expenses; it couldn't possibly cover the $4,600 bank loan without going broke.

I negotiated a deal whereby the bank would defer all principal payments and accept interest only for three years. Classic quickly began to accumulate cash. It wasn't very much, but enough to rebuild Classic's inventory so it could become a moneymaker.

What can you afford to pay on your loans? What will a conservative cash-flow projection show? You may be poorer than you think!

Classic Clothes certainly was. If the company had continued to feed its bank $4,600 a month, it would dig a deep hole and within one year, it would have been dead. Cash flow is king! It must be to you and your lender. Classic Clothes will refinance its loan when its cash flow improves, but for now, the company is making money and over the hump.

Can you reduce your strangling payments? Try these four propositions on your lender:

1. Extend your loan.

The easiest proposition is to extend short-term loans to long-term obligations. This common strategy saved Ajax Cleaners from a cash-consuming, three-year, $200,000 bank note. Ajax turned its $7,000-a-month payments into more easily handled $4,000 installments by extending its loan to seven years. Extending business loans to seven or even ten years is quite common in a workout. The loan may be "ballooned," or fully due in three to five years, but you gain breathing room when you go to a more manageable 10-year payment schedule!

2. Defer principal.

Promise your lender he will faithfully receive interest, and he may freeze principal payments until your business is back on its feet. How much of each monthly payment is principal? It may be significant, as it was for Broadway Drugs, a small New York chain saddled with a $500,000, three-year-loan. The loan badly hurt Broadway, which never had the spare cash to build its inventory and sales to a profitable level. When Broadway's suppliers wouldn't extend more credit, we turned to the bank and renegotiated an interest-only deal for two years. The savings on loan payments turned into inventory that increased Broadway's sales by 40 percent. Like Classic Clothes, Broadway's losses soon became comfortable profits.

3. Suspend all loan payments.

A temporary moratorium on all payments is a very tough sell, but lenders will go along if it is the only way to save their loan.

Well-collateralized lenders will resist because they can fully recoup by foreclosing. Shaky loan lenders may play the waiting game if they see brighter prospects ahead and too small a recovery from pressing collection today. Yet, well-collateralized lenders also can be patient because they do have a comfortable cushion to cover the accruing interest. That's why a young and savvy loan officer for a textile importer's bank suspended for two years all payments on a $300,000 loan. Why not? The bank collateral was worth more than $800,000 and covered the accrued interest by a very safe margin.

4. Refinance short-term business debt with long-term real-estate loans.

If you own real estate, this may be a shrewd move. Wareham Restaurant, for example, sidestepped back-breaking monthly payments on a $400,000, five-year equipment loan by refinancing its real estate. Wareham spread its payments over 25 years and, as a bonus, saved 3 percent on interest. Wareham's monthly payments dropped 70 percent, releasing enough cash for Wareham to soon open two more successful seafood restaurants at the Cape Cod's gateway.

Again, go through the drill. What can you afford to pay on your loans each month? How can you renegotiate your loans to match what you can pay? How can you negotiate even lower payments so you can pocket the difference? There are ways!

MORE WORKOUT TIPS

Coaxing a lender to restructure your loan successfully takes a mix of arithmetic, psychology, bluff, luck and know-how. Lenders, of course, have their own tricks.

Caught in a cross-fire between losing part of their loan and a foreclosure that will get them even less, some lenders push the patience pill. "Stick with it," they chant. "Someday, someway, your business will succeed." Catch the hidden message?

Carl needed no bright lights! Carl's faltering Minneapolis steak house owed the bank $1.2 million or about $800,000 too much for Carl, who figured his business was worth about $1 million if sold as a going business to a generous buyer. Carl also knew that his business wouldn't bring more than $400,000 at auction. Armed with these appraisals, Carl set out to restructure his loan to about $600,000.

Borrowers suffer from payment paralysis, but lenders hear only what they want to hear. Carl's banker suffered from this affliction. Carl explained how his unmanageable loan soured his incentive to continue with the business. "Cut the loan to $600,000, and extend the payments for three more years," he asked, knowing his alternative was to foreclose and end up with a far bigger loss.

The bank pretended not to hear a word, feeding him the classic pep talk. "Keep working at it. Eventually you'll make it."

But why should Carl stay with the business? How could he? His business had no equity. Nor could it make any money for him with those hefty loan payments. One more payment, and Carl wouldn't have the money to buy even one more carrot. Optimism is easy to preach. But it can be fatal. Two days later, he warned the bank by certified letter, "Rewrite the loan, or I'm filing for bankruptcy." Suddenly, the bank's hearing improved. He got his new loan!

Lenders will do anything to save their loan balances. They will extend your payments as long as necessary if it will get them fully paid. Extending loans endlessly, of course, is reasonable to the lender. Virtually any loan can someday be repaid if you choose to spend the rest of your life in serfdom, working only for your lender.

Your lender also may see a bright future for your business, a day when it can fully repay the loan. Such hopes certainly danced in the mind of Carl's banker. Perhaps next year, or in five years, Carl's restaurant would be a big success and worth the loan balance. The bank would then be back in the driver's seat and in a position to hold out for full repayment.

Strike when you have poverty on your side. Be decisive. Act decisive. You're offering your lender a win-win deal: The lender will get substantially more than at foreclosure. That's winning! You will get a loan you can live with. That too is winning!

Never give your lender additional collateral in return for loan concessions. Lenders love more collateral, and always press for more when they sense you don't want to lose your business. A lender will extend or defer loan payments on a shaky loan for a second mortgage or your wealthy father-in-law's guarantee. Lenders always want more collateral when they doubt whether their present collateral will cover their faulty loan. Keep the upper hand. If your lender had plenty of strong collateral and was certain of repayment, you wouldn't dare bargain.

Each case must, of course, be decided on its own merits, but I never allow my client to give his or her lenders additional collateral, particularly if its personal assets.

Jimmy, a young owner of a Boston landscaping firm, was stubborn and refused my advice. Jimmy owed his bank $120,000 on a loan only secured by four sputtering trucks and a heap of nearly worthless landscape equipment. At auction, the bank might recover $25,000.

I asked Jimmy what his business was worth to him. "About $50,000," he replied, estimating the trucks and equipment to be worth about $25,000 to $30,000, and the goodwill another $20,000. My pitch to the bank? Cut the loan to $50,000 or take the equipment. I knew Jimmy could easily buy or lease new trucks and start again in a new corporation, and for far less then $50,000.

Grass grew fast under Jimmy's feet. He let the bank turn his vulnerability to its advantage. The bank ignored my demands to reduce the loan and counter offered with $100,000 and extended payments for another year if Jimmy's mother gave the bank a second mortgage on her home as additional collateral. Jimmy jumped at the deal.

New England grass dries up in September; Jimmy's payments to the bank also dried up in September. Within two months, the bank had foreclosed on Jimmy's business and his mother's house.

The way to bargain your way out of a bad loan is to bargain with cash.

Lenders saddled with bad loans are motivated to go to the bargaining table when you wave money. The shakier the loan, the less cash you must wave. I've negotiated plenty of loan buyouts for as little as 10 cents on the dollar. I was successful even when the lender may have realized 70 or 80 cents on the dollar through foreclosure. Perhaps the lender wanted to avoid the foreclosure hassles, or saw less recovery from the collateral.

I always suggest a cash offer should be about 30 percent below what you think the collateral is worth at liquidation. Let your lender negotiate for more if he believes he is in a stronger bargaining position.

Arrange your financing before you approach your lender, so you can make a firm cash offer. But watch the risk factor. Avoid pledging more personal assets or incurring greater personal exposure for the replacement financing. Don't just cut your debt. Limit your downside.

There are other tradeoffs for negotiating a reduced loan. Larger companies may swap debt for equity. The lender receives shares in the company and cancels some or all of the loan. "Puts" and "calls" allow either the lender or the company to later sell or buy back the shares for a pre-determined price.

When your lender becomes a shareholder, he benefits from any future upturn in your company's fortunes. You, in return, have a manageable loan. Your lender avoids an immediate loss. You avoid foreclosure and a lost business. Converting lenders to partners works especially well when your company is over-leveraged and needs more equity financing.

A highly leveraged New York bioengineering firm cured its defaulted $1.5 million bank loan when the bank converted 70 percent of the loan into a 35-percent ownership in the promising company. It was a smart deal. Why should the lender foreclose and recover only 20 or 30 cents on the dollar? And why kill a business with such strong growth potential? Today, the bank's interest is worth $25 million. It was a very smart deal for both parties.

But don't act too hastily when your back is against the wall, you can give away too much of your business to a pressing lender. You usually can do better if you can find third-party financing to buy out the lender for a discount. Had the bioengineering firm shopped for new financing, it may have found someone to advance the $1.5 million to buy out the bank for as little as 10 percent of the company. And the bank may have accepted $1 million in cash, requiring even less of the company to be sold.

Negotiate with your lender as if it were a third party, rather than someone with the power to padlock your door. You won't get the best deal when you're frightened.

If your business has a strong future, trading shares for less debt can ease your financial problems and get you even more financing.

Last year, I helped a fast-growing California software company convince its lender to accept 40 percent ownership in the company, cancel $1.2 million on its $2-million loan and advance another $1 million. These deals happen every day!

Do you think you can interest your lender in owning a piece of your company? Then give it a try. Your deal will depend on the strength or weakness of your loan, your growth potential, your lender and your ability to negotiate the best deal.

There is a symbolic message when a lender turns stockholder. Other creditors, employees and stockholders see it as a sign of confidence, a signal that someone truly believes you have a future!

WAVE THE BIG STICK

Waving wads of money or stock certificates to appease a pushy lender isn't always the solution. When you deal with an unreasonable lender, you must wave a big stick.

There are, in fact, two big sticks that can bludgeon a stubborn lender. The bigger stick is a Chapter 11, which allows you to lower your loan to the collateral's liquidation value. But don't rush too quickly into bankruptcy court, for the many reasons I point out in Chapter 13.

The Chapter 11 stick worked for Decorator Wallcoverings, a Midwest wallpaper manufacturer saddled with a $2-million bank loan against assets worth about $500,000 at auction. After several months of dickering, the bank refused to reduce the loan below $1.5 million, so Decorator filed for Chapter 11. The bankruptcy court judge, convinced that the bank had no more than $500,000 in collateral, reduced the loan to that amount. The $1.5 million balance was then treated as unsecured debt. The bank eventually received another $225,000, or 15 percent of that amount, as an unsecured creditor's dividend. The lender would have done appreciably better had it worked outside the bankruptcy court.

Lenders are painfully aware that a bankruptcy court can force a reasonable settlement when they are unreasonable. Of course, your lender can still collect on your personal guarantees, or foreclose on collateral not owned by the Chapter 11 company. So whether your lender will get hurt in Chapter 11 really depends on whether it has good secondary recourse outside the corporation.

The lender-liability lawsuit can be another powerful weapon in your arsenal. Lenders who mistreat their borrowers lose bundles every year. You can sue your lender for considerable damages and have your loan canceled if your lender:

- Committed fraud or misrepresentation.

- Changed your loan terms without your consent.

- Exercised unreasonable control over your business.

- Failed to make promised loan advances.

- Made adverse comments about you as a borrower.

- Defaulted your loan without good cause.

- Negligently disposed of your collateral.

The mere threat of a lender liability suit can often persuade a lender to see things your way. That's why I have a good lender-liability lawyer review my cases when I suspect lender liability and I need leverage to negotiate with the lender.

In one case, I walked into a major Manhattan bank with a well-documented lender liability case. The bank completely misled my client, breached its written commitment to make further advances and controlled every aspect of my client's construction business. The bank knew exactly what lay ahead in court once it read our lawsuit seeking $10 million in damages. To settle, the bank canceled its $800,000 loan and paid our $125,000 in legal fees.

You may have other good defenses. For instance, never assume your lender has a valid mortgage. Common legal defects frequently render a lender's mortgage, but not necessarily the obligation, entirely worthless. Defects can, at the very least, delay foreclosure and require your cooperation to correct. Always have your lawyer carefully review your loan documents. A serious defect means bargaining power!

Tough tactics have their place, but I still prefer the carrot. Lender cooperation can be used to your advantage in a workout. Since your secured lender controls your assets, he can perform a variety of tricks to help you extricate your business from those nagging tax and trade claims. Lender cooperation has its value.

Parlaying lender cooperation saved a large New Hampshire textile manufacturer. The business owed its lender about $4 million and its trade creditors $8 million. With the liquidation value of the business less than $3 million, I was confident I could negotiate the lender's loan from $4 million to $3 million. But rather than attack the lender, I instead waited for the lender to foreclose on the business and resell its assets to my client's new corporation. This completely eliminated the $8 million due to unsecured creditors. My client, through his new corporation, then assumed and repaid the entire $4-million loan. It was another win-win situation. The manufacturer regained solvency, and the cooperative lender was amply rewarded with full payment. A lender on your side can pay big dividends!

WINNING WAYS TO GET EVEN MORE MONEY

Let me share another secret: Lenders will loan you even more money when you are at the threshold of bankruptcy.

Advancing you a few additional dollars now may keep your business alive so you can repay those bigger dollars later. A timely infusion of additional capital to get your distressed business through its financial crisis can be a shrewd move for you and your lender when:

- The additional capital is absolutely vital to you survival.

- Your lender can be satisfied that the new loan will be repaid.

- Your lender will lose money if your business fails.

- The additional loan is small compared to what the lender can lose if you fail.

Your lender may not advance you more funds because he has no more funds to advance. Or your lender cannot advance more against a defaulted loan for regulatory reasons. But even here, the lender may agree to subordinate its security interest on your collateral to accommodate new secured financing. Subordinations should always be in your grab bag of concessions when you meet with your lender.

Trade creditors, particularly your larger creditors who have more to lose if your lender calls your loans, are your best loan candidates. And if your general creditors won't give you a loan, they may make your loan payments to keep you operating because this increases their own chances of getting paid.

A wholesale-grocery store recently advanced more than $80,000 to keep a struggling Florida restaurant afloat until its peak- selling season. It worked. The restaurant not only survived but it repaid the wholesaler the $80,000 and more than $150,000 in past- due bills. Had the business failed, the wholesaler would have lost almost everything. A pool of creditors similarly loaned a boat- repair shop $50,000 to cover its note payment in the slow winter months. Another smart move. In the next two summers, the boat yard repaid the $50,000 as well as the other outstanding bills due its supporting creditors.

Your creditors have a big stake in your business, maybe more than you do. They may decide their stake is worth protecting with a few extra dollars.

KNOW WHAT'S INSIDE THAT PINSTRIPED SUIT

A successful loan bailout involves more than numbers, or even legal and financial one-upsmanship. Those things provide the framework within which to tackle the problem loan, but loan workouts are still very much a people game. Personalities and psychology are important ingredients.

Every successful loan workout represents a logical solution to a bad situation between the borrower and the lender. It takes a borrower and lender, working together in good faith, to find that logical solution.

Failures? They're usually disagreements about what is logical. Invariably, it is the lender who sees the proposal as illogical.

Lenders may all wear pinstriped suits, but you must know what's inside that suit. Lenders never react identically to a problem loan. Some lenders are exceptionally reasonable. Others take a consistently hard stand: Pay or foreclose is their only policy.

You must know what's inside that pinstriped suit before you do battle. As a batter checks out a pitcher, you too must anticipate whether beanballs or spitballs are likely to come your way!

A few phone calls can get you the answer. Lenders have reputations. Others, once in your position, have sat at the lender's mahogany desk pouring out their troubles. Did Mr. Pinstripe throw them highballs or sinkers? Find out.

But your biggest danger is not your lender but that you won't see your loan as a problem.

At a recent loan-workout seminar, one banker confessed, "I have seen too many businesses struggle to make impossible note payments and then throw in the towel because they had nothing left but the loan. Their shelves stood empty, working capital was gone, valuable accounts had abandoned ship, and they had nothing, including desire, to rebuild with. It's unfortunate. Had these owners intelligently tackled their bad loans in time, they would be in business today." How true!

☑ CHECKPOINT

1. *Do you have too big a loan in relation to your assets? A loan you cannot repay?*

2. *How must you restructure your overall debts to shape a healthy balance sheet?*

3. *Are you fully protected from your lender?*

4. *What loan concessions do you need?*

5. *What defenses or counterclaims can you use as leverage against your lender?*

6. *How can your lender help you in your debt restructuring? What is that cooperation worth?*

7. *What do you really know about how your lender will react to your problem loan?*

12

HOW TO SETTLE WITH CREDITORS FOR PENNIES ON THE DOLLAR

Only when you are confident you can restructure your secured loans should you tackle your excessive unsecured debts, trade payables and tax obligations. But cleaning up these creditors may be considerably more complicated and tiring than wrestling with your problem loans, because many unsecured creditors is a less manageable situation than one or two secured lenders. Preserving good relationships here also is critical, as you need cooperation and support from key suppliers.

To your advantage, unsecured creditors are relatively powerless compared to secured lenders because unsecured creditors stand in line for payment after secured creditors and taxes. Few workouts make much money available to unsecured creditors, granting debtors more strength and negotiating power when confronting them. Creditors lose interest once they see that a recovery is unlikely, and they stand to recoup very little from the liquidation. So creditors owed billions of dollars do accept pennies on the dollar to settle, because pennies are better than nothing.

What you owe is a statistic when you are in trouble. What you can afford to pay or what creditors can squeeze out of you is reality. Your creditors must settle not on the basis of "what ought to be," but "what is."

Understand these realities and you can turn your poverty into the power to slash overwhelming debts into pennies-on-the-dollar settlements — giving yourself a fresh start. And you can win these settlements, whether in Chapter 11 or through a non-bankruptcy workout.

My Garrett Group specializes in debt-restructuring and has handled hundreds of pennies-on-the-dollar deals, but I can prove the point with just a few quick examples:

- *A Bronx nursing home owner settled with his general creditors for 15 cents on the dollar, payable over three years. More than $700,000 in debt shriveled to $100,000.*

■ *Creditors of a 20-store San Diego discount clothing chain accepted 10 cents on the dollar plus 20 percent of the company's stock to forgive nearly $7 million in long-overdue trade debt.*

■ *A Syracuse hardware store owner negotiated $200,000 in trade debts down to a more manageable $24,000. And this small sum was payable over two years.*

■ *The owner of a New England chain of pet shops convinced its creditors to accept $90,000 and cancel more than $220,000 in trade obligations. The creditors obliged because they realized that cocker spaniels, canaries and guppies fetch remarkably little at public auction.*

These aren't spectacular examples, but they are typical of the humdrum settlements beleaguered business people and their creditors negotiate hundreds of times a day.

These examples should encourage you, but I warn you: Negotiated settlements with unsecured creditors can be a challenge because these creditors are so numerous, they represent a variety of relationships with you and your business, and they seldom share the same stake in whether your business survives.

Begin your debt-restructuring by evaluating the politics of your situation. Understand key relationships between you and your creditors, and understand the politics between creditors:

■ How many creditors must you deal with?

■ How much do you owe each?

■ Which creditors are critical to your business?

■ Who are the largest creditors, and will they control the outcome?

■ How friendly or hostile are relations between you and your creditors?

■ Which creditors will benefit most from your survival?

■ How cooperative or adversarial are the creditors with each other?

■ What credit associations or law firms are involved in the workout, and what is their usual approach in a workout?

Only when you are armed with this information can you forecast whether settlement negotiations will be cordial or hostile, whether one or two creditors will dominate events, or whether there will be a leader for other creditors to follow. Develop a feel for the dynamics of your situation, and you'll gain a sense of how best to approach your creditors.

START WITH AN OUT-OF-COURT DEAL

Surprisingly few businesses attempt to restructure their debts outside bankruptcy court. That's a big mistake! An out-of-court workout gives you the same opportunity to cancel part of your debt, extend payments, or both. As with Chapter 11, your creditors must agree to your workout proposal. This may involve one creditor, several major creditors or every general creditor.

I typically attempt an out-of-court workout before filing Chapter 11 bankruptcy. Only when the out-of-court workout fails do I try another debt-reduction strategy. But I fight to make an out-of-court settlement work because these non-bankruptcy arrangements are nearly always more advantageous than a Chapter 11 reorganization.

One big advantage of the workout compared to the Chapter 11: It keeps your financial woes relatively private, and you avoid the public announcements that accompany a Chapter 11. This is a vital consideration when your customers will shun a supplier with financial problems or you have employees who will abandon an unstable job. Customers and employees are less aware of out-of-court workouts. Chapter 11, on the other hand, causes a public-relations nightmare.

Out-of-court workouts also have other advantages. You are unconstrained by the many rules and restrictions of a Chapter 11. A workout provides greater flexibility in carving out deals with your creditors. A Chapter 11 requires a more rigid reorganization plan that treats all general creditors equally. The workout can be much more creative and adaptive to what will bring you and your creditors together.

The third and biggest advantage of a non-bankruptcy workout: You will save a fortune in legal fees and costs. A Chapter 11 bankruptcy spawns enormous legal and professional fees. You can reach the same result out of court for a small fraction of the cost.

Privacy, creativity and **economy**: Three compelling reasons to work a deal with your creditors outside of bankruptcy court.

Still, an out-of-court workout may not be your solution. Because a workout is a voluntary arrangement between you and your creditors, it won't stop legal action by your holdout creditors. Nor will it stop all creditors. Only Chapter 11 can stop a bank foreclosure or tax seizure. Chapter 11 also is necessary when too many unsecured creditors reject your workout proposal. A Chapter 11 then forces your plan on these holdouts.

The number of unsecured creditors and the amount you owe each creditor will greatly influence whether an out-of-court workout will succeed. Fewer creditors greatly improves your odds, because you can generally manage these few creditors without a Chapter 11. Twenty or thirty creditors is controllable. One-hundred creditors may need Chapter 11 for a more orderly process and to bring the holdouts into line.

The amount you owe each creditor also influences the outcome of your workout. You may have one-hundred creditors but owe your five largest creditors 80 percent of your total debt. Because your out-of-court workout may involve only these five large creditors, you again have prospects for an orderly out-of-court workout.

But even when the odds for success are poor, do try an out-of-court workout first, particularly if you don't have tax or secured creditor problems. I've successfully negotiated out-of-court deals with as many as 600 creditors! Because we are well-experienced in debt-restructuring, the Garrett Group has negotiated some terrific creditor arrangements for clients of every size and from virtually every industry.

For instance, a Georgia hi-tech firm had 180 trade creditors who agreed to 50 cents on the dollar, payable over two years. Three weeks of hard-ball negotiation cut the struggling firm's debts 50 percent, from $1.2 million to about $600,000. Yes, we have a handful of holdouts who are owed about $50,000. Some may sue for full payment, but they can be tied up in court for years. Eventually they too will settle cheaply. They always do.

THE PENNIES-ON-THE-DOLLAR FORMULA

To succeed, your workout plan must convince your creditors that it is 1) **Feasible**: You can pay as promised; 2) **Fair**: Your plan treats all creditors equally and proportionately; and 3) **Equitable** Your plan beats the alternative – what creditors would receive through forced liquidation of your business. Always build your plan on these three essential elements, or it is doomed.

Learn terminology before you design your pennies-on-the-dollar plan. Out-of-court workouts also are called **compositions**. A **composition** may include a **consolidation**, an **extension**, or both. Under a consolidation, creditors receive less than full payment on their obligations. An extension stretches payments out over time. A composition may, for example, offer creditors 20 percent of what is due as full settlement. This may be payable over 24 months. So the two key negotiating points are:

■ **How much** will you pay?

■ **When** will you pay it?

What will you pay? Secured lenders consider the liquidation value of their collateral as the bargaining threshold. Unsecured creditors also must consider what they would receive under a forced liquidation of your business. Because your unsecured creditors can force your business into involuntary bankruptcy and liquidation, it is an alternative they will consider.

How much would your general creditors receive if your business were liquidated? It's easy to calculate: Estimate the liquidation value of your business assets, then deduct your secured debts, unpaid taxes, accrued wages, attorneys' fees, liquidation costs and all other priority claims that must be fully paid before your unsecured creditors get a dime. From what is left, you can approximate what your unsecured creditors would share pro-rata.

For example, if your business would liquidate for about $300,000 and you owe $200,000 to your secured creditors and other priority claims (including liquidation costs), then your general creditors would share about $100,000. If you owe these creditors $1 million, then each would receive about 10 percent of what they are due. A successful plan out-of-court workout must obviously offer these creditors something more.

This calculation gives you the minimum amount to offer. But how much higher should your offer go?

The formula I've successfully used for hundreds of workout plans starts negotiations by offering creditors about 5 percent more than they would receive under a forced liquidation. In the above example, creditors would share $100,000 (10 percent of the $1 million owed), a sensible first offer would be $150,000, or a 15 percent dividend. Always offer creditors more than what they would get under liquidation, or they will liquidate your business, even for revenge. Make your first move generous, but not too generous!

How high can you go to settle? Ask yourself, how long you are willing to work solely for your creditors? Your most generous plan pledges to your creditors every dime in profits for those years. You cannot realistically commit more than three or four years' profits to discharge your past debts. Who can logically mortgage their future for longer? Still, your creditors may insist that you do, and you must then consider it smarter to start again. Nor can you pledge more than your projected profits. No company can afford more. Between the minimum and maximum settlement offers lies reality. Where you end depends on your negotiating talents.

Creditors may see your approach as reasonable, but disagree on other points.

First, general creditors, like secured creditors, may disagree with the estimate of your business's liquidation value. Obtain liquidation appraisals from recognized-commercial auctioneers. Your accountant can value your receivables; other appraisers can value your intangible assets, such as trade names, leases, copyrights, and patents. Creditors also may probe the accuracy of your liabilities. Your attorney or accountant should schedule your priority debts for general creditor review.

What do you do if your general creditors would receive absolutely nothing under a forced liquidation? This often happens when secured debts and/or taxes are high, and the assets have a modest value. Offer your unsecured creditors 15 percent on their claims as your opening bid. I've negotiated a few 5 and 10 percent plans, but these are rare. If your creditors can't get at least a 15 percent dividend under liquidation, then the dump-buyback discussed in chapter 14 may be the right medicine for you. Or bite the bullet and give your creditors that 15 percent to win them.

Creditors in larger cases also challenge future profit projections and what share of those profits should be earmarked for creditors. Creditors also may push you to invest more of your own money to boost the dividends available to your general creditors. My advice is to refuse, even if your business seems to be recovering and the risk of loss is negligible. Always confine creditors to the business assets. Don't expose your own.

When creditors question profit projections, they also usually question expenses. Big owner salaries, fancy-fringe benefits and other costly perks catch a creditor's eye. Conversely, your creditors may paint too rosy a profit picture for your company, and thus commit you to an overly generous dividend. You may paint yourself into this same dangerous corner when you become too optimistic about your future. Be conservative. Don't delude yourself or your creditors with an unrealistic settlement offer. Remember _ poverty is power! So look perennially poor. Creditors get greedy when they smell money!

Optimism kills businesses. Glowing financial projections usually dim and become obsolete even before the workout plan is approved. More than once I have renegotiated a revised plan within a month or two of creditors approving the original plan.

A case in point: A 30-store California ladies apparel chain that originally settled with its creditors for 50 percent. The promised dividends, like an airborne parachute, descended to 30 percent, then 20 percent, and finally to 10 percent. The retailing empire continued its downward slide, and the unsecured creditors never saw a dime. The case reminds me that projections are only predictions, and predictions seldom come true. It also should remind you.

Who can accurately project what any company will earn or can comfortably pay two or three years in the future? It's appreciably more difficult for the more volatile workout firm, whose future must be considerably brighter than its past. Overly eager creditors can project future earnings two or three times greater than what you may project, leaving you too far apart for settlement.

Offering general creditors a stock dividend can resolve this problem. As stockholders, your creditors become beneficiaries of your future fortunes. Your creditors may accept some ownership interest to cancel their debts if your company has that bright future and a stock potentially marketable at a big profit.

You also can design a formula plan. For instance, you can guarantee your creditors a minimum dividend plus a bonus dividend based on a specified sales or profit performance. Formula plans appear equitable, but they can produce serious problems later. Your formula may not reflect the actual cash available for dividends. You may intentionally avoid reaching your performance level to avoid creditor dividends. You also may encounter difficulties in drafting, interpreting or enforcing your formula.

To raise more cash for dividends, creditors may force the sale of valuable assets, or even entire "cash producer" divisions or subsidiaries. You must fight when these assets are the foundation of your future.

Creditors see no sacred cows. Chrysler was nearly forced to sell its highly profitable tank division before its creditors relented. It was the tank division that rejuvenated Chrysler. Airlines often forfeit their best air routes to raise cash for creditors. Most then wither and die. My client's 30-store discount clothing chain was forced to sell three valuable locations to generate an additional $250,000 for secured lenders. It hurt the chain's bottom line considerably. Smaller luxuries, such as fancy company cars, idle computer systems and other symbols of corporate flab, are ever-obvious targets for alert creditors anxious to wring another dime from the ashes.

Many less significant points can be negotiated when settling with creditors. For instance, if you extend payments over time, will your creditors want interest? Interest at the prime lending rate is reasonable, but remind creditors that if your business goes bankrupt, they will wait two or three years for a check from the bankruptcy court that bears no interest.

Smart creditors know a promise is not a payment and may demand a mortgage on or security interest in your business. A mortgage gives your present creditors a priority over future creditors should you fail later. The mortgage also lets them more easily enforce the payment plan. Concede this point, but refuse personal guarantees to ensure payment.

Most general creditor workouts combine extensions and consolidations. The debtor company negotiates to pay a percentage of the total indebtedness over time. Treating creditors equally is essential, but you can offer creditors alternative plans. For example, you may offer each creditor the choice of a 10 percent immediate cash dividend or a 20 percent dividend payable in three semiannual installments.

Allowing your creditors to choose among options dramatically boosts your chances for acceptance. Creditors no longer see it as "take it or leave it," but instead see it as "which offer should I accept?" Psychology is all-important when you want your creditors to sign on the dotted line.

Creditors who are owed less than $500 are usually fully paid, as their involvement makes the settlement process too cumbersome. Small creditors with little at stake are less inclined to accept a settlement and instead play spoiler to a successful workout. Larger creditors then routinely buy the claims of smaller creditors to avoid their obstructing an orderly workout.

Compositions or informal out-of-court workouts are generally conditional on acceptance by creditors who are owed at least 90 to 95 percent of the outstanding debts. Fewer acceptances leaves too many unresolved claims. Holdouts may have their claims defended against or acquired by other creditors to protect the company and the plan. If you can reach agreement with a significant percentage of your creditors, but too many holdouts still remain, then a Chapter 11 can force your plan on your few dissenting creditors.

If your overall debt is not excessive and you only need time to pay your creditors, your settlement should propose an 100 percent payment. This will be either on a stand-by or extension basis.

Stand-by means your creditors agree to suspend collection for a specified time. The stand-by is the right strategy when time alone is your problem, such as when you will sell property to pay your debts. Under a temporary stand-by, creditors agree to a moratorium in which they will not press their claims until the settlement plan is accepted or rejected.

What will your deal to creditors look like?

HEAD TO HEAD

You and your creditors must open lines of communication early in the workout to organize manageable procedures for negotiating the settlement plan.

But negotiations need not be complicated. If your company is small, you may simply send your creditors a letter outlining your financial problem and include a proposed settlement agreement (the plan) to accept and return. This informal approach works best when you have few creditors, and you owe relatively small amounts. Your creditors won't pursue more formal proceedings because there's not enough at stake.

With higher stakes, you need direct creditor negotiations. When you have many creditors, they should, for negotiation purposes, be represented by a committee of three to twelve of the largest creditors. The size and complexity of the workout will determine the size and composition of the committee. The creditors' committee that serves all creditors has several roles:

■ Determine your company's financial condition.

■ Audit your company for fraud, embezzlement or other dishonesty.

- Review your cash flow and profit projections to negotiate settlement.

- Consider alternatives to a workout, such as bankruptcy or forced sale of your company.

- Identify special problems or cash-raising opportunities.

- Negotiate the final settlement plan.

- Recommend the negotiated settlement to other creditors.

- Monitor your company's progress.

- Enforce compliance with the plan.

To function effectively, you must work exclusively through the steering committee, which in turn must communicate continuously with all creditors. Since you negotiate through the committee, you are spared the pressures of general creditor contact. Creditors will patiently await the final outcome of your negotiations if they are kept abreast of events by the creditors' committee, so you should encourage this communication.

No matter how your creditors become organized, settlement negotiations involving heavy debts are usually long, tedious and frustrating. And while numbers are convincing, creditors do bring to the bargaining table more than a calculator. Anger, suspicion, irrationality, doubt, desire for vengeance and other nasty emotions always surface when people lose money.

Twenty creditors see your situation 20 different ways. On the right side of the table sits the "Cynic," who is convinced you pillaged, plundered and raped your business. Creditors may think the worst until you prove differently. So explain how your business got into trouble. Point out the problems that caused your losses. To diffuse creditor suspicions, invite them to inspect your books. Creditors usually decline, but resist inspection, and creditors will push harder to find out what you are hiding.

Across from the cynic, the "Moralist" chants, "You owe me $1,000, I want $1,000. Anything less is immoral and unconscionable." His tune is "what ought to be" never "what is." Be patient with this character. You can only present the facts until they finally sink in. After all, even saints can be broke!

The "Avenger" snarls at the other end of the table. Sure, he's upset about the $50,000 you owe him, but he's demanding vengeance for the $500 bounced check on your last order. Getting down to business for the avenger means adjusting small, irritating items first.

Squirming next to the avenger is the credit manager of a big supplier who only worries how to explain to his boss losing the $80,000 you owe. Is he gloating? A competitor at the table probably lost even more.

The lawyers in the crowd think secret thoughts of how they would come out far richer under a bankruptcy that guarantees to produce even bigger legal fees.

You find these and other stereotypical characters on every creditors' committee. So when you do negotiate with your creditors, be guided by a famous line of Don Corleone in *The Godfather*: "Never get angry. Never make a threat. Reason with people."

Reason with people. Good advice! But it's not enough when you go head to head. Try five more essential strategies when you negotiate with your creditors:

1. Play for time. Creditors, like fish, must tire before you can easily reel them in. Anger and emotion run highest at first. In time, your creditors will move on to new problems and even fresher losses. When you become yesterday's news, creditors will quickly settle on more favorable terms. That's why I wait several months before pushing my initial settlement offer. But for the deal I want, I may have to wear the creditors down for a few more months. Persevere. Creditors need time to recover from the maddening thought that they are about to lose money. That's when you strike!

2. Recruit friendlier and more influential creditors as a nucleus of support to inject a positive tone into the proceedings, to neutralize opposition and to win converts to your cause.

3. Meet with your holdouts individually and find out why they oppose your proposed settlement. "Eyeball-to-eyeball" may produce results unobtainable through a steering committee. A directly confronted creditor can't hide in the crowd, but must tell you why he won't accept your settlement. When objections are on the table, you can deal with them.

4. Bypass obstacles. Why let a credit manager or some other middle manager nix your proposed deal? They answer to someone else. Jump heads when someone who represents a creditor on your workout becomes unreasonable. Reach the ear of someone higher within the creditor's organization. Don't stand on formalities and protocol while fighting to save your business. The tenacious S.O.B. survives!

5. Use your professionals when you don't see eye to eye with a creditor. Your lawyer may have better luck with the creditor's attorney. When negotiations strike out at your level, switch negotiations to the professional level. Also, try reversing events. I've had many cases where I couldn't strike a deal with the creditors' lawyers, while my client won quick agreement from his creditors.

SELL FUTURE DOLLARS

You may convince creditors your plan is fair, feasible and equitable, and they may still turn you down. You may show that your company can pay what you promise, and they may still turn you down. To get your deal, you need even more powerful motivators. One hot button is the future profits your creditors will reap by doing business with you in the years ahead.

This magic ointment to salve the creditors' wounds worked miracles for Nathan, a street-smart operator of a large San Francisco seafood restaurant that was choking on more than $400,000 in trade debts and was on the verge of bankruptcy. On the other hand, Nathan's recently renovated restaurant enjoyed strong sales and was threatened only by its big bills.

I figured Nathan's creditors would never see even $20,000 in a bankruptcy, so I suggested that Nathan offer his creditors $20,000 as an initial offer and let the creditors negotiate from there. But Nathan only laughed. He instinctively knew how to handle creditors. And I learned a valuable lesson from him in an austere Boston law office adorned with parchment prints of old whaling ships and 15 angry creditors, all anxiously awaiting deadbeat Nathan.

Arriving an hour late, Nathan calmly sat down at the huge conference table as his creditors fired their threats, innuendos and insults. Each salvo hung Nathan's head a bit lower, like a scolded puppy that had stained the new oriental carpet.

Finally, Nathan's creditors ran out of steam. Nathan, in turn, slowly stood up and countered, "I politely listened to you for the last hour. Now please hear me out."

Turning first to Sam, the meat supplier owed more than $80,000, he began, "Sam, how much business have you done with me since I started my restaurant?" Sam didn't know, but Nathan did. "$1.6 million in the past 12 years," snapped Nathan. "So why argue with me now about a lousy $80,000? If I stay in business — you know it's finally booming – how much more business do you think you will get from me in the next 10 years?" Again Sam shrugged. "Probably another $2 million before I retire," Nathan estimated. "Before we're through doing business together, you will have pocketed $3.5 million of my hard-earned money. I wish I had your $80,000, Sam, but I don't. Why not simply call it a small extra discount on my past purchases or a bonus for my future business?"

Now Sam played the dejected puppy as Nathan painted Sam the ungrateful tightwad. Sam's $80,000 bill literally vanished before our eyes.

Nathan next tackled Harry, his disgruntled produce supplier, who 20 minutes earlier screamed murder for his $40,000. The curtain rose on Act Two. "Yes, Harry, I do owe you $40,000, but in the past eight years, I gave you $957,000. In the next 10 years, I'll give you maybe another $1.5 million.

$2.5 million! Not bad, Harry. The $40,000 I owe you is not even 2 percent of the business we'll do together. Since when is 2 percent a big discount, Harry?"

Nathan's other creditors wriggled in their chairs as Nathan confidently pitched each creditor in turn. The message was clear. What Nathan owed his creditors was but a tiny fraction of the business Nathan did with his creditors. Nathan was no longer the bad guy. Creditors instead saw him as a valuable account.

I'll never forget the finale. Nathan's largest creditor blurted, "OK, Nathan, old buddy, what do you propose as a settlement?"

Nathan mulled the question. "I would never insult you by offering a few measly bucks to share. Just send me a canceled bill, and I will charter a cruise for all of us. We can then properly launch our next 10 years of profitable business together and resume our long-standing friendships." Toasting Nathan, the meeting adjourned and with it, $400,000 in unpaid bills.

Nathan later lamented, "That damned cruise will cost me $25,000. "But under the circumstances," he chuckled, "I can afford it." I never sent Nathan a bill. Nathan should bill me for this important lesson in the art of persuading creditors.

Can Nathan's strategy work for you? How much business do you do with your creditors? What future business can they anticipate from you? Make your creditors see your business as an important future asset to them!

PLAY POKER

Poker and creditor negotiations are both games of bluff.

What happens to your creditors if they do not accept your deal and throw you into bankruptcy? They may derive satisfaction worth the few dollars they would lose. But creditors weighing a 20 or 30-cents-on-the-dollar deal will remind you that unless you cough up more, you will end up without a business.

Your creditors do have something to lose if you fail, but so do you. Bluff! Take a lesson from Joe, the struggling owner of a computer repair company who played poker very skillfully when confronting his major creditors. After preliminaries, Joe threw his proposal on the table. "Settle for 25 cents on the dollar, and I can have your checks next week."

Because Joe's business had turned the corner and was finally making money, the creditors assumed Joe would pay substantially more to save it. Their feelers tested Joe to find out just how badly he wanted it. Then they would know how far to push Joe.

Harriet, another master negotiator and credit manager for one of the larger creditors, patiently listened to Joe and quietly countered, "Joe, you don't want to lose your business. And you know we won't accept 25 percent. But we might take 30 percent now and another 10 percent a year for the next seven years."

This was a creditor looking at a few pennies on the dollar if she didn't strike a deal cajoling Joe to pay every dime he owed.

Joe thoughtfully put down his cigar, extracted a prescription vial from his vest pocket, and popped a few saccharin tablets, which the creditors assumed were life-sustaining nitroglycerin for a bad heart. Joe slowly drawled, "The truth is, I would rather quit the game and retire to Florida. I'm not getting any younger. With a bad heart and all... The only reason I'm here is out of concern for all of you. I'd hate to see everyone get screwed if I walked away from my business."

Convincing? You bet. Joe's master bluff forced his creditors to think about their own downside.

Within a few moments, Joe had his deal. Riding down the elevator, I asked Joe how much he would have paid the creditors to keep his company alive. "Probably 50 or 60 cents on the dollar. But did they have to know that?" he smiled.

Tom, on the other extreme, played a poor poker game. Tom's furniture store owed his suppliers $300,000. In this case, I represented a supplier that was owed $25,000. Ten of Tom's major creditors met at my office to negotiate a settlement with Tom and his wife. Tom began by sketching his heart-wrenching tale of how his business ended up in trouble. He then offered the creditors 15 percent immediately and 10 percent for each of the next two years, or a total settlement of 35 percent.

We checked Tom's finances and knew that because his business was overfinanced to the SBA, we would get absolutely nothing if it failed.

So why did Tom make so generous an offer? Tom desperately wanted to stay in business. Foolishly, he showed us that desire. Tom admitted he would do virtually anything to keep his business. (his wife crying whenever we threatened to close him down hardly helped their cause.) Tom soon agreed to 25 percent down, financed by a second mortgage on his home, plus another 15 percent for each of the next five years. Tom didn't solve his problems. He only spread his debt but will still pay his creditors 100 percent. As we would receive nothing in bankruptcy, it was a ridiculous deal.

Tom should have handed us the keys and said, "The keys are yours. I have a great new job in California, but since I want to help you out, I'll listen to any reasonable proposal."

My own client, a major North Carolina manufacturer, would have jumped at the chance to settle for 10 percent and so would have Tom's other creditors. But Tom showed no poker face and that cost him hundreds of thousands of dollars.

Emotions on both ends play a part. Creditors reject even the most generous settlements if they distrust the owner. Conversely, creditors generally cooperate with honest, hard-working troubled-business owners. Creditor distrust and resentment often forces the liquidation of many viable businesses that offer their creditors generous dividends.

Did you antagonize or alienate your creditors? Did you issue bad checks? Furnish misleading financial statements? Con extra credit long after it was obvious you could not pay? Will creditors believe you milked your business or were too casual in your concern for your creditors?

Ample opportunity exists for the breakdown of good relationships between you and your creditors during the workout. One trouble spot is switching to a new and competitive supplier. Or your creditors may not see you sacrificing as you continue to draw your high salary and big perks. Small things rankle creditors, like a manufacturer who showed up at his Chapter 11 creditors' meeting driving a new Jaguar. The fact that the car was leased to him personally did little to appease his creditors, who were about to lose hundreds of thousands of dollars to the man behind this symbol of wealth.

Your situation is even more serious when creditors won't settle because they lack confidence in your management. A poor or non-existent turnaround plan, unmet projections or continued operating losses don't inspire creditor confidence. Creditors then believe they may gain more by immediately liquidating your business.

Larger companies can recruit a new chief executive or financial officer to bring a fresh perspective, credibility and vigor to the restructuring effort. Someone who can say, "I did not create this mess, but I can clean it up," develops a very different relationship with creditors than those who created the mess.

TACKLING YOUR ONE LARGE CREDITOR

Perhaps you do not have many creditors, but only one or a few troublesome creditors.

A deal with only one creditor can be more imaginative than when you settle with all creditors because you no longer need an "equal" deal. You will negotiate the same points with one creditor as you did under a general composition, but your personal relationship with that one big creditor, rather than the terms, usually decides whether you will succeed.

One-creditor settlements can be both creative and complex. For example, I recently worked out a settlement with a major creditor for a large New York fabric store that owed $125,000 to a Danish textile manufacturer.

The manufacturer knew that with the retailer in bankruptcy he would receive about $25,000 or a 20 percent dividend. Through hard bargaining, we finally settled for $50,000 with $10,000 to be paid immediately, $35,000 payable over two years and $5,000 in inventory to be returned for credit. The debt cancellation also was conditional: The retailer had to buy at least $250,000 a year from the manufacturer over three years. Of course, these purchases would be C.O.D.

These deals cannot be structured with an all-creditor group. A one-creditor plan may introduce many more terms that can satisfy both you and your creditor.

Still, one-creditor deals depend more on the attitude and management style of the creditor than on the financial considerations.

Time and time again, I have seen creditors cancel most of their debt on the strength of only one sincere phone call. Others may stubbornly or angrily ignore the best arguments for settling and push for full payment. Why one creditor may be such an easy sell and another remains unyielding is puzzling. The answer may be that smart debtors first involve their creditor in their business problems and then strike for the deal.

An example was the Kendricks, a father and son team whose failing fuel oil business still grossed several million a year. For years, the Kendricks purchased their oil from one wholesale distributor, now owed about $400,000. The Kendricks were shrewd; they involved the wholesaler by soliciting his advice and guidance on how to straighten out their faltering business. The creditor was soon deeply involved in the business as a confidant, and no longer considered himself an adversary.

When the Kendricks sat down to talk about their debt, the wholesaler must have subconsciously felt some responsibility. Wasn't he part of their team? Had the wholesaler been kept at arms- length, he would not have been as cooperative.

Creditors react to more than numbers. Put yourself in your creditor's shoes. Would you accept your proposition? Say "yes" and you have a deal to sell.

9-POINT DEBT-SETTLEMENT CHECKLIST

Keep this handy checklist at your fingertips when you sit down with your creditors. Here are the nine key negotiating points and counterpoints:

1. How much will you pay?

Initially, offer about 5 percent more than what your creditors would get in a bankruptcy. Gradually raise your offer by 2 percent increments. Demand even greater creditor concessions.

2. How much now and how much later?

Pay immediately only what your business can afford to pay without investing more of your money. Limit future payments to what you can comfortably pay, considering cash flow and profitability.

3. What length of payments?

Don't commit to more than two to three years. Convince your creditors that it's not worth it to you. Total payments to creditors should never exceed your cash on hand and two or three years' surplus cash flow.

4. What about return goods?

Merchandise returned to suppliers for credit is as valuable as cash and should be bartered the same as a cash payment.

5. What about a mortgage to secure future payments?

A mortgage on your business assets is a reasonable creditor demand. Use it as a bargaining tool for other concessions. Also, insist that your creditors subordinate their mortgage to any future financing you may require.

6. What about interest?

Payouts beyond two or three years may require a reasonable interest.

7. Will you personally guarantee the payments?

Refuse!

8. What about future purchases?

Creditors may condition their settlement on your future business, but make certain that you buy at the same price as cash customers and that you can buy what you agree to buy. Give yourself a comfortable margin for error.

9. What about giving creditors' shares in your company?

Never give creditors more than 25 to 30 percent of the shares in your company. And do negotiate for a buyback option that allows you to reclaim 100 percent ownership.

When you walk out of the creditors' meeting, add up the score. Ask yourself these tough questions: Is your business really positioned for that fresh start? Can your business now survive and prosper? If not, your creditors may only need a stronger dose of "business-saving medicine."

RESOLVING TAX PROBLEMS

Do you owe taxes to the IRS or state taxing authorities? You're not alone. Many distressed businesses do. It's an easy trap to fall into.

Caught in a cash squeeze, you may have used withholding or sales taxes to cover your operating expenses. Financially troubled companies can owe hundreds of thousands of dollars in back taxes before the tax collector starts breathing down their necks. These businesses only accept their "temporary problems" as a crisis when the IRS padlocks their doors or levies their bank accounts.

Handling the IRS is tricky. The right strategy will depend on several factors: How much you owe, the severity of your financial condition, your personal exposure and wealth, your workout plan and, finally, how closely the IRS is on your trail.

If you owe the IRS a substantial amount and want to stall collection, pay the oldest quarters first. This delays IRS detection and gives you more time to implement your overall workout plan and the final resolution of your IRS problems. However, you will then pay current quarters late and incur further penalties. If you only need a few months to fully pay your back taxes, then it's wiser to pay only the current quarters to avoid more penalties.

Next consider how much you owe. If, for example, you owe the IRS several hundred-thousand dollars and have little personal wealth, you probably will never fully pay the IRS. Why belabor strategy or throw a few dollars at the IRS? Whether you owe the IRS $2 million or $1.9 million is academic when you have no personal assets or income to pay the taxes. Your strategy here may be to sink your company, pick up its few assets for pennies on the dollar and begin again with a new corporation.

If you want to walk away from your business without personal tax exposure, as you should, and you cannot pay the full tax, then pay at least the employees' withholding or "trust fund" taxes. As an officer or owner of your business, you are personally liable for unpaid trust taxes, but not the employer's contributions. To ensure that your payments are applied to the trust portion, you should clearly mark this on your checks. Trust taxes are about two-thirds of the total taxes, so paying only the trust taxes will save you money. For instance, if your total taxes are $6,000 a week, you would save about $2,000 a week by not paying the employer's contribution. You would save about $25,000 if you plan to close your business in three months.

The IRS quickly catches its scofflaws. You may avoid payment or filing your returns for several quarters, but eventually the IRS computer will catch you. An IRS agent may knock on your door after you miss even one payment. The IRS can be disturbingly efficient.

What the IRS will do about your delinquent taxes will depend on your total tax liability, the delinquency period, the prospects of having the taxes paid quickly, and, most importantly, your attitude and cooperation.

Your IRS agent will insist on timely payment of all future taxes and that you make weekly deposits into a bank tax depository account. Miss one payment, and the IRS will quickly close your business.

What repayment agreement can you negotiate with the IRS? The IRS doesn't consider itself a bank that makes long-term loans. It will pressure you to pay quickly, even if it destroys your business. Unless your back taxes are fully paid within several months, you should anticipate seizure of your business. The IRS won't wait longer, particularly if you have an easily liquidated business that can fully pay your taxes if seized.

You can forestall action. Convince your IRS agent that you are attempting to borrow or to sell your business. Also, pay a small amount on the past liability each month to show good faith and to buy more time. Nevertheless, your agent will want to close your file as rapidly as possible, whether your bill is paid or not. Unless you have a payment plan for the delinquent taxes, the IRS will seize your business or force you to file Chapter 11 which transfers your case to the IRS Special Procedure Division. Your agent, of course, has one less case to worry about.

Chapter 11 gives you six years to pay the back taxes. Why would the IRS push you into Chapter 11 and a six-year payment plan when it will refuse a two-year installment agreement? Because IRS collection agents are not equipped to handle long-term payout arrangements except under a bankruptcy proceeding.

Here are two more valuable tips to slow down the IRS: 1) Do you have a good excuse for your tax delinquency? Sickness? Business interruption? Other casualty? Business reversals beyond your control? Make your case. IRS agents are human. 2) Is your business heavily encumbered? Convince the IRS that it will get little or nothing under seizure. IRS guidelines discourage seizure of overencumbered businesses, but agents may still seize or threaten seizure if the they believe they can frighten you into payment.

The IRS also will not seize your business if you can post a bond or pledge other assets equal to the equity in your business. This is a smart strategy when you need time to pay the IRS. But never pledge collateral worth more than the equity in the business, nor should you pledge personal assets unless you are absolutely certain you can eventually pay the taxes. Gambling your personal wealth on a sick business is always a bad gamble. Even when you are certain you can pay the taxes, limit your pledged personal assets to those taxes you are personally responsible for and not the non- trust taxes.

If you can't reach an installment agreement with the IRS, file for Chapter 11 before the IRS seizes. Filing for Chapter 11 later is usually a hollow victory because by then, your business may have been too seriously disrupted.

If you do owe excessive taxes, you'll find an out-of-court deal with your secured lenders and general creditors futile unless you can simultaneously solve your tax problems.

Your business is never safe when the tax collector is after you. The IRS will levy your bank accounts. To protect your funds, you must continuously relocate your accounts to new banks the IRS does not know about. If the IRS has your accounts receivable list, their agents will levy every receivable. This will devastate your cash flow and your customer relations.

State-taxing authorities can be equally tough. For instance, sales taxes can mount rapidly, and you may owe your state even more than you owe the IRS. Most states follow IRS procedures when enforcing their tax claims, and will need a similar counterstrategy.

If you or your business has tax troubles, read my *How to Settle with the IRS for Pennies on the Dollar.* This eye-opening book reveals every possible strategy, tactic and trick for defending yourself against the tax collector. My best advice: Don't play games with taxes. Pay your taxes on time because the tax collector plays by the roughest rules.

☑CHECKPOINT

1. Can an out-of-court settlement with your general creditors be your best debt-reduction strategy?

2. What would be a fair settlement with your creditors?

3. What problems may hamper a settlement? Why may creditors object to your proposition?

4. What arguments can you make that would most persuade or convince creditors to accept your offer?

5. What is your strategy on back taxes?

13

BEWITCHED, BOTHERED AND BEWILDERED ABOUT BANKRUPTCY?

Troubled companies and a Chapter 11 bankruptcy go together like bread and butter. Mutt and Jeff. Horse and carriage.

That's the trouble. Too many failing businesses automatically think they'll find their solutions in the hallowed halls of bankruptcy.

They usually are wrong.

Maybe you, too, are ready to file Chapter 11 to gain protection from your creditors and a new financial start.

Don't run into bankruptcy too fast. First understand the pitfalls you face. Know when you should file Chapter 11 and when to avoid it. And to improve your odds of surviving a Chapter 11, know what really goes on in the dark halls of bankruptcy.

Before we start, here's a quick primer to the two major types of bankruptcy: Under Chapter 7 of the Bankruptcy Code, you liquidate your distressed business. A Chapter 11, on the other hand, lets you rehabilitate your business by reorganizing your burdensome debts in an agreement with creditors. Chapter 11 also allows you to reject contracts, and can help you raise fresh credit and capital.

If a Chapter 11 can do all that for the failing company, why do only 15 percent of Chapter 11 companies successfully reorganize? Why do 85 percent fail and liquidate in Chapter 7? Interesting questions?

More astoundingly, the few companies that do survive Chapter 11 are usually larger companies. Statistics show that fewer than 10 percent of the survivors are small firms. But most survivors disappear within three years. These companies probably never really resolved their problems in a Chapter 11.

It's because of these dismal results that I say a Chapter 11 is usually the wrong medicine for most small, sick businesses. Still, most small-business owners hastily jump into a Chapter 11, convinced it's their only solution, or their best solution, when it's nearly always their most fatal move!

So why the mad rush into a Chapter 11?

The answer is that less savvy business owners are too easily prodded into a Chapter 11 by a bankruptcy attorney unfamiliar with less drastic and far more effective cures for a sick business. For these lawyers, a Chapter 11 is the medicine that spells the big fees. It also is the medicine that can ultimately kill your business.

WHEN A CHAPTER 11 CAN BE YOUR BEST FRIEND

A Chapter 11 has plenty of downsides, but before we focus on the negatives, here are five situations in which a Chapter 11 can be the right business-saving remedy:

1. You need a Chapter 11 to stop creditors from seizing, repossessing or foreclosing on your assets.

When persuasion fails, a Chapter 11 is the only way to stop secured lenders from foreclosure.

Just as unsecured creditors cannot sue a company in a Chapter 11, secured creditors are similarly enjoined from foreclosing on a Chapter 11 company without court approval. And the bankruptcy court will protect you from foreclosure if the court believes the lender is adequately protected. But the burden is on you to show that your lender will not be hurt by any delay in foreclosure.

I file about a third of my Chapter 11 cases to stop lender foreclosure. We may have little or no difficulty controlling unsecured creditors, but when loan obligations go unmet, lenders can become pushy. Still, a Chapter 11 doesn't always resolve problem loans or permanently stop foreclosure. If your lender can convince the court that its collateral is shrinking in value, or that you are falling further behind, then delay will hurt your lender, and the court will allow foreclosure.

Even when your lender can convince the court to allow foreclosure, a Chapter 11 may cool your lender and create the calming atmosphere within which to negotiate a new and more lenient loan arrangement.

And if you press the right strategies in a Chapter 11, you can give your lender plenty to worry about. For example, a Chapter 11 can bludgeon your secured lenders to cooperate with you under threats of "cramdown," which reduces your lender's loan to the liquidation value of its collateral. The cramdown makes a Chapter 11 a worthy tool for restructuring the overfinanced company plagued with uncooperative lenders.

But it's still far preferable to negotiate a new and more workable loan without Chapter 11. Why suffer the expense and hassle when you and your lender can as easily and more cheaply sit down and amicably reach the same outcome a bankruptcy judge would force upon you?

I can usually cut a deal with a recalcitrant lender and avoid a Chapter 11, but only when the lender is convinced we otherwise will file a Chapter 11, and appreciates what can lie ahead for him in bankruptcy court.

2. You need a Chapter 11 to stop the IRS.

It will stop the IRS dead cold! In fact, it's the only weapon that can completely tame the IRS.

Consider that once you file a Chapter 11 the IRS (and other taxing agencies) must:

- Stop all further collection efforts.

- Cancel any seizures or levies against your property.

- Return any seized property still in its possession.

In Chapter 11, you automatically have up to six years to repay your back taxes, a big benefit. Chapter 11 makes absolute sense if you can't repay your taxes as quickly as the IRS demands. But if you owe the IRS far more than you can possibly fully repay within the six years, then a Chapter 11 may not be your answer.

While it is technically possible in a Chapter 11 to settle with the IRS for less than the full amount owed, these cases have a high failure rate. There are probably better ways of dealing with the IRS. Turn to Chapter 14 for a few ideas.

If you owe a relatively small tax bill that you can't immediately pay, try to resolve it without a Chapter 11, particularly if you have no other significant creditor problems. Why spend $10,000 or $15,000 in legal fees to file a Chapter 11 that blockades the tax collector's $25,000 bill? It's bad economics and needless aggravation. It's better to borrow, even at a high interest, and pay the IRS.

But use common sense. Never borrow against personal assets to pay the IRS (or any other creditor) if you question the survivability of your business. It's wiser to file Chapter 11 rather than risk your own wealth.

On the other hand, for your Chapter 11 to succeed, you also must have the financial ability to pay your delinquent taxes in six years. If you continue to lose money, you lack that ability. If you fall further behind on your taxes after you file Chapter 11, the bankruptcy court will close you down quickly.

The IRS may not be your only tax problem. You also may owe on state-meals tax, sales tax, gas tax or many other types of taxes. Fortunately, a Chapter 11 cures these tax ailments the same way it does unpaid federal taxes.

Filing Chapter 11 to stop the tax collector is an everyday event. Probably half of all small-business Chapter 11s are due to serious tax problems, so you will have plenty of company in the halls of bankruptcy if taxes are your problem.

3. You need a Chapter 11 to resolve general creditor problems.

You may try, but you can't always successfully restructure trade debts through an out-of-court workout. Your creditors may be too hostile, too unmanageable or too numerous.

If you have only a few creditors and enjoy a reasonably good relationship with them, then an out-of-court debt restructuring should work for you. You can then avoid the long, complex and costly hassle of a Chapter 11. On the other hand, if you have many hostile creditors or are burdened with complex financing arrangements involving different classes of creditors, then a Chapter 11 may be necessary to control their competing claims and interests and create order from chaos.

You may reach an out-of-court settlement with most of your creditors but still have too many holdouts that threaten you. A Chapter 11 then becomes a useful weapon, as a reorganization plan approved by a majority of your creditors, binds those stubborn holdouts to the same plan.

A Chapter 11 forces your creditors to face the unhappy reality that they will never get fully paid. Time diffuses emotion, brings order from chaos and provides a forum where you and your creditors can and must talk!

Out-of-court workouts frequently are hammered out against the threat of Chapter 11. Because creditors aware of your financial problems will move quickly and aggressively to collect, your workout must be rapid and controlled, or you may be forced to file a Chapter 11. But the mere threat of Chapter 11 may coax even your most hostile creditors to the bargaining table. If you do bluff Chapter 11, be prepared to follow through.

For your Chapter 11 to succeed, you will need approval of your plan from a simple majority of your general creditors who are owed at least two-thirds of the total unsecured debt. For instance, if 100 voting creditors are owed $100,000, then 51 creditors who are collectively owed at least $67,000 must accept your plan. You may need to offer your creditors several increasingly generous plans before you gain the necessary votes. You also need similar approvals from the other classes of creditors affected by your plan, such as secured creditors, taxes, and priority claimants. However, it is usually easier to gain their approval. The bankruptcy court also can approve your plan even if you fail to win the assent of one or more classes of creditors if the court believes your plan is fair, equitable and feasible overall.

In contrast to a Chapter 11, out-of-court workouts need virtually all creditors to accept. A deal with creditors collectively owed $500,000 is meaningless when you have other creditors owed another $500,000 still chasing you. You can forget a Chapter 11 and fight the dissidents only if you cut a deal with creditors owed about 90 percent or more of your total debt.

Here's an instance where you should combine a Chapter 11 and an out-of-court workout into a pre-packaged Chapter 11. In a pre-packaged Chapter 11, you first attempt an out-of-court workout. In the earlier example, if 51 creditors assented to your plan that collectively were owed $67,000, the pre-packaged Chapter 11 would bind 49 non-assenting creditors owed $33,000 who could otherwise sue for full payment.

A pre-packaged Chapter 11 starts with an out-of-court workout agreement in which assenting creditors confirm they will assent to the same plan in Chapter 11, should one be filed. If you then gain enough assents to confirm your plan in Chapter 11, but too few for a successful non-bankruptcy workout, file Chapter 11. Your plan of reorganization should offer all creditors the same plan that the majority of creditors originally agreed to in the out-of-court workout. Because you have the necessary assents in hand, you can quickly emerge from a Chapter 11 with your original out-of-court plan forced upon all creditors.

The pre-packaged Chapter 11 allows you to first attempt a non-bankruptcy workout, a big advantage. You have nothing to lose. Should you later need a Chapter 11, you can conclude it quickly, assured of a favorable outcome. I call this a "dip" a Chapter 11 because you are in and out of court so quickly. This one debt- busting tactic can save you the considerable aggravation and legal fees of a typical prolonged, costly Chapter 11 in which you must hammer out your deal with creditors after you file.

4. You need a Chapter 11 to cancel burdensome contracts.

One feature of a Chapter 11 is its power to terminate burdensome contracts and leases. You may, for example, use a Chapter 11 to extricate yourself from an unprofitable supply contract, a lease on outdated equipment, or a real-estate lease. You can even cancel oppressive collective bargaining agreements if a labor union is the root of your trouble.

But be slow to file a Chapter 11 here as well. Creditors in burdensome or defaulted leases or contracts know you can bail out in Chapter 11. Like all creditors, most prefer to settle out of court rather than wait years for less in a Chapter 11 or a Chapter 7 liquidation.

A Chapter 11 allows you to reject or cancel any lease or contract that the court finds burdensome or detrimental to your financial rehabilitation. This remedy is one of the most important in Chapter 11. Without the ability to shed bad contracts and leases, many companies could never regain the profitability so essential to their successful reorganization.

Zayres, a large discount store chain with hundreds of shopping center locations throughout the country, was an all-too- common story. Like most fast-growth chains, many of its stores were unprofitable because they were in dying shopping centers. Zayres could have walked away from these long-term leases, but the landlord claims would have been staggering. Chapter 11 allowed them to instead abandon its loser locations and move ahead with its winners.

Fast-growth chains that eventually go into a Chapter 11 start with two or three profitable stores and rapidly expand. Predictably, many of their locations are mistakes, corrected through a Chapter 11.

Yours may not be a high-flying chain, but you may have other leases or contracts you must terminate to become healthy. Regal Men's Store, a profit-maker for 30 years in a downtown Cleveland store block, followed the crowd and relocated to a suburban shopping center. What a blunder! Business was bad, and losses were heavy. Stuck with a long-term lease at a bad location, Regal had only three options when the landlord wouldn't negotiate a settlement: **1)** Stay at the bad location, and face inevitable bankruptcy, **2)** Move and be stuck paying rent for the abandoned shopping center location (which would result in bankruptcy), or **3)** File Chapter 11 and reject the lease.

Regal chose to file Chapter 11. In their reorganization plan, they paid the shopping-center developer a small dividend. The contractor was then a general creditor, and his claim for breach of lease (a landlord's claim is for two years' rent) was a pittance compared to what Regal would have lost had it been forced to honor its lease obligations.

A Chapter 11 can work equally well for landlords. I once filed Chapter 11 for a landlord with only one asset – an old railroad depot leased to a now-thriving restaurant. My client leased the property for 10 years at a rent so low it didn't even cover the mortgage payments on the property. Soon the mortgage fell several months behind, so I filed a Chapter 11 to terminate the bargain lease. Rather than face eviction, the tenant negotiated a new lease. While the new lease didn't turn the depot into a first-rate money maker, it did give my client the cash flow needed to cover his expenses.

I have plenty of cases where a Chapter 11 allowed me to cancel leases and bad contracts that saved many businesses:

■ A Connecticut clothing wholesaler canceled an order for 20,000 winter coats when he decided more profitable leisure wear should be the cornerstone of its turnaround.

■ An Iowa electronics firm terminated twelve costly executive employment contracts and saved more than $1.3 million in annual salaries. These savings were critical for reorganization.

■ A Massachusetts Oriental-rug importer, re-focusing on mail order promotions rather than retail distribution, used Chapter 11 to escape contracts with its 10 retail sales reps.

■ A Florida ambulance service in a Chapter 11 became profitable only after it canceled unprofitable emergency service contracts with three cities. It also canceled leases on six ambulances. It now has fewer, but more profitable contracts.

Because Chapter 11 usually comes on the heels of big losses, it's not surprising that most firms must undergo radical change in Chapter 11. The ability to wiggle out of bad contracts allows that change.

5. You need a Chapter 11 to get credit.

More credit? Absolutely! It will surprise you, but many troubled firms get more credit after they file Chapter 11 than they had ever obtained before.

Why? Suppliers know when you are in financial trouble. Rumors spread quickly that a bankruptcy can be in your future. So your suppliers correctly reason that what they sell you on credit today may become 5 or 10 cents on the dollar several years from now. And creditors know they stand at the end of the line to get paid if your business fails or you file for Chapter 11, because in Chapter 11 they won't ordinarily fully recover the pre-filing debt. Inevitably, they wind up with only pennies on the dollar.

But extending you credit after you file Chapter 11 is another story. Your supplier now sits in a considerably more secure position because bills must then be paid when due. Even if your business fails, your post-filing creditors will get paid before general creditors who are owed pre-filing debts.

A Chapter 11's powers to protect post-filing creditors certainly helped Midland Foods, a large Ohio superette grossing about $2 million a year. After several years of huge losses, Midland was deeply in debt and without a dime in credit.

Soon after I filed Midland's Chapter 11, I asked Midland's creditors for about two weeks' credit. The creditors couldn't lose. They would be paid every two weeks, and their debt would be first for repayment if Midland failed. Because I could easily show there would be sufficient proceeds on liquidation to cover Midland's priority claims, the creditors had a no-lose proposition. Midland again had merchandise on their shelves and a chiming cash register.

A Chapter 11 also lets you refinance more creatively. For instance, with a Chapter 11 and court approval, you can safely lend to your own company and even grant yourself a mortgage on your business assets. Affiliated companies can similarly pledge their assets to secure new financing. Many other money-raising options, not usually possible or safe without a Chapter 11, become available because the bankruptcy court can grant new lenders and creditors priority over existing lenders. These creative and unconventional financing arrangements may be vital when your business needs fresh cash.

THREE CHAPTER 11 PITFALLS

A Chapter 11's promise of a brighter future dims considerably when you consider its three big pitfalls:

1. A Chapter 11 may scare away your customers and suppliers.

Do you have long-term customer relationships or customers with warranties or extended contracts? What will they think about your Chapter 11? Who wants an orphaned product or a deal with a potentially dead company?

That was my problem with a machine shop that manufactured one critical part for a Detroit automaker. Would a Chapter 11 be their solution? How could it be a solution when the automaker would surely switch suppliers at the first hint of bankruptcy? How could the automaker rely upon a supplier who might disappear? Our obvious answer was a quiet, out-of-court workout to shield the automaker from the machinist's problems.

Despite the potential loss of an important customer, a Chapter 11 may be an unavoidable alternative. If so, you need a fast and effective public-relations campaign to blunt customer concerns and rebuild their confidence in your future.

Don't think that word of your Chapter 11 won't get around. It will. A Chapter 11 spawns a rumor mill, no matter what your business or how small you may be. At the least, you can always count on your competitors to quickly publicize your problems to your customers, suppliers and employees. Damaging rumors and malicious misinformation can sink your company faster than your bad balance sheet.

2. You can lose control of your business in Chapter 11.

You always lose some control in Chapter 11. But creditors can ask the court to appoint a trustee to completely run your business if they can prove gross mismanagement or fraud. The creditors' committee, or the court, also can set your salary or control daily decisions you now routinely make. Bankruptcy constrains how you run your business because you need court approval to do anything outside the ordinary course of business. You also will find many business opportunities stalled or missed because you're in bankruptcy. And to closely supervise you, the court will require that you file biweekly financial reports and other mountains of red tape. This all takes time away from rebuilding your business, time you can't afford.

Bankruptcy is a hostile environment where many different players, each in their own way, can make your life miserable. There's the judge, the creditors' committee, secured creditors, the United States trustee (who oversees the administration of your case) and maybe a court-appointed examiner or trustee. Sharing management of your business with creditors and court officials is a bitter pill to small entrepreneurial business owners. It probably will be to you too. A Chapter 11 means handcuffs. Freedom from Chapter 11 is not unlike leaving jail.

3. A Chapter 11 is costly and time-consuming.

This is the worst part. A Chapter 11 is a hotbed of legal maneuvers, ploys and counterploys, all of which cost time and money. Chapter 11 is considerably more involved, expensive and cumbersome than are less legalistic, out-of-court creditor arrangements. A Chapter 11 can take several years (one to two years is average). Good employees who become frustrated by the process may move on to more free- wheeling companies. Sadly, these complexities and bureaucratic inefficiencies encourage the high legal fees that boost a Chapter 11 beyond the financial reach of all but the larger companies, which are blessed with big money and the organizational stamina to withstand the endless red-tape nonsense.

Any competent lawyer will want at least a $10,000 to $20,000 retainer to handle a Chapter 11. And this is for a small case. Do you own a $1-million-a-year business? Expect a $50,000 to $75,000 retainer. A $5 million company? Perhaps $100,000. You will pay not only your own lawyer, but also the lawyer to the creditors' committee and a small army of accountants, appraisers and other professionals. Out-of-court workouts also involve professional fees, but these pale against the whopping Chapter 11 fees.

A Chapter 11 is beyond the means of the smaller company because it takes nearly as much professional time and effort to reorganize a small business as a large corporation. This is one big reason why so many troubled smaller companies either attempt out- of-court workouts or simply close up shop rather than file a Chapter 11.

A Chapter 11 will seriously distract if you are you a small- business owner. Large corporations have layers of personnel and platoons of outside professionals to oversee a Chapter 11. A Mom- and-Pop business has just one layer - Mom and Pop.

Could you shoulder the entire burden of filing reports, negotiating with the creditors' committee, huddling with lawyers, accountants and consultants, spending long days in court and still stay on top of your business?

The advantages and disadvantages of a Chapter 11 are greatly magnified between large and small companies. Small companies can sometimes trade on their smallness and more personal relationships with suppliers and lenders. Still, larger corporations fare better in a Chapter 11. Small companies lack the big corporation's clout and leverage with creditors. And unlike the large corporation whose failure can sink many small suppliers and unemploy thousands, your small business has comparatively little impact on those it does business with. Unlike a Fortune 500 company kept alive by a benevolent Uncle Sam or dependent suppliers and creditors who cannot afford to let it sink, your small business is expendable!

HOW TO SURVIVE A CHAPTER 11

A Chapter 11 is strong medicine for any sick business. For most, the medicine is too strong.

One big reason is that few companies can finance themselves through a Chapter 11. While a Chapter 11 can ease credit and cash flow, cash shortages nevertheless usually stay a serious and chronic problem. Running on empty causes most reorganization efforts to stall. You must know how you will stay afloat in a Chapter 11, particularly when your secured lenders resist new financing attempts or won't give you access to your cash flow.

Relying upon Chapter 11 to stop a foreclosure will be a short- lived adventure if your lender can convince the court your collateral doesn't sufficiently protect him. If yours is a heavily encumbered company, you need lender cooperation to boost your odds for surviving a Chapter 11. This cooperation is best won before you run into court.

All in all, a Chapter 11 chiefly fails for the same reasons out-of-court workouts fail. Creditors stay hostile and uncooperative because they distrust you. These creditors then sabotage you whether you are in or out of a Chapter 11. Creditors will turn down even the most generous settlement offer when they dislike the debtor.

Chapter 11 companies also fail because they get chopped up in the Chapter 11 meat grinder. A Chapter 11 is a bureaucratic mine field. Your insurance lapses, your reports are filed late, or you make a cranky judge crankier. Suddenly, you're thrown into Chapter 7. A Chapter 11 is thin ice, and it's so very easy to fall through. Bankruptcy judges are unpredictable. Most bend over backward to keep companies alive, but others too hastily and arbitrarily close businesses, particularly the small business that clutters a busy docket.

A failed Chapter 11 usually is still the failure to become profitable. It offers only a temporary, safe harbor to redirect and rebuild your company. Most companies can't or don't take this opportunity. They see Chapter 11 only as an opportunity to get rid of creditors. Once relieved of your creditors, you may think your problems are over, but you are wrong. Your problems aren't over until you make enough money to pay for your past and finance your future!

The court and your creditors won't seriously question whether your company can make money. Your promises to pay dividends to creditors can be full of false optimism. Surprisingly few companies that emerge from Chapter 11 are profitable. The rest are only handed a second opportunity to snag a new round of creditors before they finally fail.

You may make money but not enough money. You then fail because you didn't lower your debts to what you could afford. Minor surgery on your debts solves nothing when radical surgery is required. I have seen too many Chapter 11 companies negotiate nonsensical deals with their creditors. Slashing your debts from $6 million to $3 million, for example, accomplishes nothing when your company can only support $1 million in debts. But when you are overly optimistic and anxious to get the ordeal over with, you and your creditors can reach hasty deals and ignore the hard, dismal facts. Smart creditors bargain for less, confident they will receive at least that much. More objective business owners would still own their business.

Closely examine companies that succeed in a Chapter 11, and thereafter, and you will see that they share six common characteristics. They all:

1. go into a Chapter 11 with sufficient cash and a nucleus of assets.

2. have a solid business concept on how to become profitable and rebuild.

3. enjoy creditor cooperation and support.

4. maintain a positive cash flow during the Chapter 11 and thereafter.

5. cure their underlying problems.

6. get out of a Chapter 11 as quickly as possible.

7. scrupulously behave while in a Chapter 11.

Without these key elements for reorganizational success, a Chapter 11 is overly risky. But even then, this doesn't necessarily mean a Chapter 11 should not be attempted. Some of these ingredients for a successful outcome may be found only after you file for reorganization. A Chapter 11 then becomes that safe harbor, a place to get your second wind and calmly see what you have to save, and how best to save it.

Time and time again, reorganizational success is phrased as "going back to basics." This means that the company is again emphasizing the keys to its earlier victories. The reorganized company redefines its purpose and its values and becomes the business it should have been in the first place.

HOW ONE COMPANY FOUND SUCCESS IN BANKRUPTCY COURT

How does a Chapter 11 really work? What mysterious processes transform a corporate cripple into a debt-free money machine?

It was no mystery to Al Jaspen, the beleaguered owner of West Palm Beach's Jaspen Photofinishing. It all started when Al's bank notified him that it was foreclosing on the mortgage on his business. Earlier that week, an IRS agent threatened to padlock Al's shop. And just that day the sheriff handed Al his sixth creditor lawsuit of the week. Al, after three years of struggling to build a successful business, saw only a bleak and penniless future. But Al was a survivor.

That same afternoon, the bank was told to forget its foreclosure and the IRS was told to forget the padlock. The lawsuits? Their new home was a trash bag.

Al waved no magic wand to make his creditors disappear. Nor did Al inherit a million dollars from his rich aunt in Toledo. Al had stronger medicine: A Chapter 11!

Al figured a Chapter 11 could work magic for him just as it had for such corporate giants as Braniff Airlines, Daylin, Wickes, Food Fair, Penn Central, and even Chase Revel, Inc., the one-time publisher of *Entrepreneur Magazine* and America's rags-to-riches guru.

Al's problems began months earlier when several of his large accounts went bust, sticking him with $140,000 in bad debts. Then Al's largest competitor slashed his prices, forcing Al to match him dollar for dollar until his profits completely vanished. The strain of a hefty bank mortgage, high overhead costs and plummeting sales skyrocketed Al's trade liabilities and unpaid taxes. When Al filed for a Chapter 11, his assets were barely one-third his debts. But it wasn't the end of the road for Al. A Chapter 11 proved to be Al's new beginning, as his future unfolded in six sweeping steps. Here is a brief synopsis of these steps:

1. First, a reorganization petition was filed under Chapter 11 with the local bankruptcy court. With the petition filed, Al's business came under immediate court protection, and his creditors were automatically restrained from further action against the business. The bank holding the mortgage on Al's business could not foreclose. The IRS couldn't seize his business. Creditor lawsuits were moot. Creditor debts would be resolved through the bankruptcy court. Other general creditors also could no longer demand payment as their prior debts were similarly frozen.

2. Next, I worked with Al to find new credit. With Al's past bills frozen, new suppliers gave Al limited credit because they had priority of payment if his business failed. Enough credit soon flowed again to ease Al's strained cash flow.

3. I then went to work on Al's old creditors. Shortly after Al filed for his Chapter 11, the court formed a creditors' committee of several of Al's largest unsecured creditors. They represented all general creditors for purposes of negotiating a plan of reorganization. After several meetings, Al's general creditors accepted $100,000 to be paid over three years in full settlement of the $300,000 they were owed. The creditors' committee recommendation to accept this plan won the support of enough general creditors to confirm Al's plan, and eliminate about $200,000 in debts.

4. Al's bank was a secured creditor with a mortgage on Al's business so it needed to be handled differently. Al agreed to pay the bank the entire $70,000 it was owed, but even here, Chapter 11 helped Al enormously. Since Al had missed several payments, his bank declared his note in default. In Chapter 11, Al was able to cure the default by paying these arrears, so Al's bank was forced to accept his "catchup" payment and reinstate Al's loan.

5. Since the IRS was a priority creditor entitled to payment before general creditors, it would have its $45,000 tax bill fully paid, but over six years – giving Al plenty of time.

6. Resolving creditor problems was only part of Al's Chapter 11 game plan. With his company in Chapter 11, Al whipped his operation into a money maker. Al slashed his payroll, expanded his lines, aggressively sold new accounts and sublet idle space to a professional photographer who stimulated even more business for Al. Al's losses gradually turned into respectable profits. Finally, the court approved Al's arrangement with his creditors, and Al was off to a new start. Chapter 11 let him:

- Resolve his financial problems while holding his creditors at bay.

- Reinstate the bank's defaulted loan rather than let the bank foreclose.

- Pay the IRS over six years.

- Obtain the credit needed to rebuild.

- Cut debts from $300,000 to a manageable $100,000.

- Take a long, hard look at his dying business and figure out how to make it profitable.

Al's problems may look familiar to you. Most troubled businesses face similar difficulties. You too may need a Chapter 11 to stave off foreclosure. Or you may need to whittle down staggering debts due general creditors. Or you might want to plug the profit drain caused by unfavorable leases or contracts. Any financial problem has a remedy in a Chapter 11. And any company, large or small – whether incorporated, a proprietorship or a partnership – can use Chapter 11's broad protection to help turn their debt-ridden business into a money machine.

But, there may be even easier, more pleasant ways to make all that happen.

HOW TO BURY YOUR DEAD BUSINESS WITHOUT BANKRUPTCY

Maybe you don't want to reorganize your business in bankruptcy, but prefer to quietly and discreetly bury it. Don't do it by filing bankruptcy. Chapter 7 gets you nothing but mountains of red tape, avoidable legal fees and a bankruptcy trustee who will look for reasons to sue you.

So what is the right way to bury a dead business?

Make an Assignment for the Benefit of Creditors (ABC). Under an ABC you transfer your assets to an assignee, who liquidates your business and then pays creditors their share of the liquidation proceeds.

While the process is similar to bankruptcy, an ABC offers you several important advantages compared to bankruptcy:

- **ABCs are simpler:** With an ABC you avoid complex and formal court proceedings. An ABC is as simple as signing a piece of paper and handing your assignee the keys and a creditor list.

- **You usually incur no fees with an ABC.** The assignee takes his or her fee from the liquidation proceeds of your business. On the other hand, a business bankruptcy can cost you several thousand dollars in legal fees.

■ **ABCs are less troublesome:** In an ABC, you do not have to be concerned with preference claims against yourself because preference claims apply only to bankruptcy. Assignees also are less likely to pursue fraudulent transfers than are bankruptcy trustees, because assignees lack a bankruptcy trustee's strong recovery powers. Moreover, you appoint the assignee. While the assignee must fairly represent the creditors' interests, you would not logically appoint one likely to hassle you.

You cannot force your creditors to go along with an ABC. Dissatisfied creditors can still petition your business into bankruptcy. But they seldom do unless they have suspicions of wrongdoing, fraudulent conduct or significant preferential payments to other creditors.

In fact, I have found that most creditors prefer an ABC to bankruptcy because it gets them their money faster, and usually more money, because an ABC is less costly than bankruptcy.

A business already liquidated (such as in a bank foreclosure) should still make an ABC so its creditors can be properly notified that it's out of business and someone is protecting their interests. This stops creditors from forever chasing you for payment.

Now you see why I always use an ABC when I want to quietly bury a dead business.

Every state allows Assignments for the Benefit of Creditors. The procedures and requirements may, however, vary slightly.

Are there any disadvantages to an ABC as compared to a bankruptcy? The only disadvantage is that you lose the right to recover preferential payments made to a creditor. This would only be of interest to you when you want the creditor to repay the money into the estate, so there would be more money to pay taxes and other debts for which you have personal liability.

How can you make an ABC for your company? I recommend *Creditor Recovery Services.* They are listed in the resource section in the back of the book. They handle assignments in every state and are well respected by the IRS, lenders and other creditors. They'll liquidate your business quickly, smoothly and usually without a fee to you. They also have a free report for you. Call them and ask for *How to Liquidate Your Insolvent Business Without Bankruptcy.* It's well worth reading.

☑CHECKPOINT

1. Do you understand that as a small business owner you have less than 10-percent chance of surviving a Chapter 11?

2. Is a Chapter 11 the remedy you need to stop bank foreclosure or tax seizure?

3. What efforts have you made to resolve your creditor problems without a Chapter 11?

4. Can a pre-packaged Chapter 11 work for you?

5. To what extent do you need a Chapter 11 to rebuild credit or obtain new financing? What about canceling unfavorable leases and contracts?

6. Would a Chapter 11 cause you to lose essential customers?

7. Do you understand the disadvantages of a Chapter 11?

8. If you are planning a Chapter 11, do you have the ingredients to survive and succeed?

9. If you are planning to close your business, have you considered an Assignment for the Benefit of Creditors instead of Chapter 7 bankruptcy?

14

DUMP-BUYBACKS:
THE FAST TRACK TO A
DEBT-FREE BUSINESS

Years of handling troubled companies have led me to the fastest route to a debt-free business. Simply dump your company and then buy back its assets at a bargain price. The net result? You are back in business, and your pressing debts are gone.

It may sound too simple and too devious, but believe me, if you want to dump your debts quickly and with the least amount of aggravation, it can be your most practical strategy. I know. I have orchestrated this maneuver hundreds of times for troubled businesses!

It's not overly complicated. You "dump" your business by voluntarily liquidating it in any type of insolvency proceeding. For the "buyback," you set up a new corporation and have the liquidator sell your new company those assets you need to restart your business. The end result is that you're back in business, at the same location, with your same assets, but without the debts that once haunted you.

Sound tempting? It did to Henry. When his Cincinnati electronics distributorship went into receivership, Henry's $60,000 bid won him the $400,000 in inventory and equipment owned by his defunct company. It was a steal. Henry was quickly back in business for only $60,000. Gone was the $260,000 owed his bank, the $70,000 due the IRS and the $500,000 owed to his trade suppliers.

Henry now pockets more than $200,000 a year from his resurrected, revived and restarted enterprise. Not only is Henry still in business, but he walked away from more than $800,000 in liabilities with the drop of an auctioneer's hammer!

Barbara also "dumped" her way to a debt-free business. Barbara was tired of jostling with creditors that were pressing to collect more than

$600,000 in long overdue bills. With the stroke of her pen, she made a voluntary assignment of her home-accessory store for the benefit of creditors. Several days later, the assignee sold Barbara's newly formed corporation the assets from her former business, completely free of all creditor claims. It cost Barbara only $45,000 to buy from the assignee her old inventory and fixtures worth more than $150,000 at wholesale. A bargain! Armed with a new lease for her new corporation, Barbara again opened her doors for business. Six-hundred thousand in nagging bills were gone forever!

Ken had a similar story, except that he restarted his business without investing one dime.

Ken's Furniture Outlet owed a local bank about $200,000. The loan was manageable, but not the $1 million he owed suppliers. So Ken coaxed the bank to foreclose on its long-overdue loan. Then the bank sold Ken's newly-formed corporation more than $350,000 worth of merchandise and fixtures from his foreclosed business in exchange for the $200,000 debt due the bank. Of course, the bank agreed to finance the entire $200,000.

Here, a simple foreclosure wiped out $1 million in trade liabilities owed by the business. It also was a smart deal for Ken's bank, because Ken gave the bank a mortgage on his home as additional collateral. The bank now had a safer, more securely collateralized loan, and Ken had a business that was debt-free except for the bank loan.

Unusual stories?

Nope.

Dump-buybacks save businesses like yours every day. You too may find it the easiest, most practical way to save your business from its killer debts!

THE PERFECT SOLUTION?

A dump-buyback is the perfect solution for any business with relatively few assets and tons of debt. Why waste time and effort hassling with creditors when it's so much easier, faster and cheaper simply to restart your business by buying back your assets from your creditors, with your liabilities left behind? It sounds cunning, but rest assured it's 100-percent legal. In fact, your creditors come out at least as well in a dump-buyback as in an out- of-court workout, a Chapter 11 or a straight Chapter 7 bankruptcy. It truly offers a win-win situation for you and your creditors.

It's the surest most practical way to escape your debts and stay in business, because you avoid the fanfare and risks of other debt-reduction strategies. And your creditors get as much or more money even faster than in bankruptcy. Several bankruptcy judges reviewed and approved my dump-buyback cases because the deals were fair and equitable to creditors and the best deal they could possibly get in the circumstances.

What type of businesses can use a dump-buyback? I have seen hundreds of dump-buyback cases that range from large manufacturing plants to small service firms. Big or small, in each case, I successfully convinced bankruptcy trustees, receivers, Assignees for the Benefit of Creditors, the IRS, state tax collectors, banks and finance companies to sell the assets of the defunct business back to my client for a bargain price. And because the deal was quickly orchestrated, these businesses never closed their doors, so employees and customers never discovered that the business failed. Continuing a business was necessary to preserve goodwill. Yes, business again at the same old stand.

Why may the dump-buyback be your best bet?

■ **A dump-buyback is far simpler and less costly than a Chapter 11 or an out-of-court workout.** Nothing more is needed than forming a new corporation and negotiating to buy back the assets of your failed business from the liquidator. A Chapter 11, on the other hand, costs thousands in professional fees. Don't feed your lawyer money you will need in your business.

■ **A dump-buyback is faster.** You can be back in business in a few days with your creditor headaches behind you. A Chapter 11 or an out-of-court workout can drag on for years. Why prolong your agony? Get rid of your business problems as quickly as possible so you can concentrate on making money.

■ **A dump-buyback gives you the greatest control in the disposition of your business.** This is because you control the timing and method of liquidation and choice of liquidator. A Chapter 11 places your assets under the total supervision and control of the bankruptcy court and your creditors. If your Chapter 11 fails, you have little say about the disposition of your assets. And even if you can buy your assets from the bankruptcy court, your business may have been closed for months, destroying goodwill.

■ **A dump-buyback avoids the need to resolve contested creditor claims.** In a the dump-buyback, the liquidator is responsible for paying each creditor the correct share of the proceeds and resolving disputed claims. You must resolve disputed claims in a Chapter 11 reorganization or an out-of-court workout. This is always a costly, complex and time-consuming process.

Look how practical a dump-buyback was for a small Pittsburgh health club struggling with $50,000 in new fitness equipment and loans of $30,000. To add to its woes, the club's former landlord sued the health club for $200,000, claiming breach of lease.

Jim, the club's owner and a former Pittsburgh athlete, argued that since his former landlord neglected the premises he could legally move on and ignore the lease. Jim's landlord had a strong case, but for Jim to fight, it would have cost thousands in legal fees. Even winning would ruin Jim financially.

Sinking the health club was the more practical alternative. The equipment-supply company that held the mortgage on the fitness center's equipment agreed to foreclose and sell the equipment back to Jim at public auction. Jim's new corporation was the high bidder at $30,000. The cooperative equipment-supply company then swapped its loan from Jim's former corporation to his new corporation. Jim restarted his health club without closing his doors for even one day. Jim was out of his scrape for less than $3,000 in fees.

Jim's old landlord eventually won a default judgment against Jim's former corporation, but can no more squeeze money from Jim's assetless corporation than blood from turnips.

What would you have done differently if you were Jim? With time and money, Jim could have fought the landlord, but had the landlord won, Jim would then have had to a settle or file Chapter 11. Between legal fees and a modest settlement on the $200,000 claim, Jim could have spent at least $40,000 for a tiny business with negligible assets.

Be practical when you try to save your business. As in so many cases, practicality is folding up one tent and setting up another.

Large, publicly owned corporations can't do a dump-buyback. Burdened with legions of stockholders, high visibility, complex financing and restrictive securities regulations, these bigger firms must instead solve their financial problems through Chapter 11, an out-of-court workout or another more traditional debt- restructuring method.

While very large companies can't easily vanish in one night and then open for business the next morning under a new corporate banner, small, closely held family corporations can, because they are simple, low-visibility and nimble organizations.

But dump-buybacks aren't the answer only for nickel-and-dime ventures. While few Fortune 500 corporations can try it, it also can work wonders for multimillion-dollar operations.

Just last year, a dump-buyback saved Hal, who owned a failing $3-million-a-year wallcovering manufacturer with $1 million in liabilities. Apex Wall System, his 20-year-old Bay State company, saw sales drop 30 percent with the loss of a major customer. Apex owed the bank $150,000 secured by a first mortgage against the business. The SBA, was owed another $500,000 and held a second mortgage. Unsecured creditors totalled another $350,000. Because Apex's manufacturing equipment and inventory were cumbersome and costly to move, they had negligible auction value. Moreover, Hal's receivables were factored.

A Chapter 11 may have reduced the SBA loan from $500,000 to $250,000, and the general creditors from $350,000 to $50,000. But Apex would still emerge from Chapter 11 owing about $450,000 with a small chance for survival. I knew a dump-buyback was the answer when the auctioneers estimated Apex's assets to be worth about $100,000 under the hammer.

To raise the $100,000, I struck a deal with Apex's landlord, who also was in a precarious position. If Apex failed, he would lose a $50,000-a-year tenant for his old, hard-to-rent building. The landlord agreed to loan Hal's new XYZ Corporation $150,000, secured by the assets it would soon acquire from Apex. The bank auctioned Apex's assets the following week, and Hal's XYZ Corporation was the high bidder at $115,000. Hal conveniently pocketed the extra $35,000 for working capital. In less than two weeks, Hal exchanged $1 million in strangling debt for a comfortable $150,000 long-term loan.

Even when Chapter 11 can produce a similar result, I prefer the dump-buyback to Chapter 11's long, costly court hearings and endless creditor negotiations. It takes too much of a toll. Financial problems evaporate more quickly, cheaply and easily with a dump-buyback. It's your fastest if not the most perfect route to a debt-free business.

THE DUMP-BUYBACK BLUEPRINT

The dump-buyback sounds easy, but it takes professional skill, creditor cooperation and some luck to work. It's tricky because you must walk a narrow line: On one hand, you must be scrupulously fair and honest with your creditors. On the other hand, you want your business back as cheaply as possible. Within these two conflicting goals you must accomplish two basic steps:

Step 1: Liquidate your business.

Step 2: Acquire the assets you need to start again – at the lowest possible price.

You can liquidate your business in several ways. As you have seen, a creditor or lender with a mortgage on your business assets can foreclose on the pledged assets and resell them at a foreclosure sale.

You also can make an Assignment for the Benefit of Creditors. Most states allow a debtor to assign or transfer assets to a representative of the creditors – the assignee – who then sells the assets and distributes the proceeds to creditors. An Assignment for the Benefit of Creditors seldom involves court proceedings, so it's quick and efficient. Assignees are often attorneys who represent one or more creditors, but you can appoint an independent attorney who will work cooperatively with you while protecting the creditors' interests.

You also can petition the court to appoint a receiver to liquidate your business. Or your creditors can request a receiver, who, like an assignee or bankruptcy trustee, liquidates your business, sells its assets and distributes the proceeds to creditors.

Finally, you may file for a Chapter 7 bankruptcy and have the bankruptcy court appoint a trustee to liquidate your business. This is least desirable, because a bankruptcy trustee must plow through a cumbersome court process to sell a bankrupt business. This delay destroys goodwill, as your business will be closed for weeks or even months. You need a fast liquidation, and bankruptcy works too slowly.

You also can file Chapter 11, and ask the bankruptcy court to approve the sale of your assets to your new corporation. This is a "liquidating Chapter 11," and is sometimes used on larger cases. But it can be as cumbersome and risky as a Chapter 7 liquidation.

A liquidating Chapter 11 can be a smart strategy when you have an overencumbered business and the mortgage holder won't cooperate with a dump-buyback that cancels part of their loan. The bankruptcy court can order a sale of assets free and clear of all creditor claims, including liens and mortgages, allowing you to buy the assets free of the mortgage.

If possible, stay out of bankruptcy court. You will lose control and be mired in endless red tape. Bankruptcy plummets the odds of a successful dump-buyback, although I have had numerous cases where a business was forced into bankruptcy and successfully reacquired its assets from the bankruptcy court to start again.

Whether your business is liquidated by a secured creditor, assignee, receiver or bankruptcy trustee, every liquidator has one function: Sell your assets quickly and for the best price possible.

Now to the second step. How do you buy back your assets for pennies on the dollar?

Your liquidator must sell your assets in a commercially reasonable manner, whether by public auction or private sale. Take advantage of the fact that assets under a distress sale sell for a small fraction of their cost. Attend a few business auctions and you will see how tiny a fraction:

- A fabric store, packed with $200,000 in quality fabrics, fetched only $38,000 at public auction.

- A refurbished Ohio printing plant with $200,000 in new equipment was peddled piecemeal for $60,000.

- An $800,000-a-year Florida restaurant was liquidated for only $26,000. What are a few chairs and tables worth?

- A Detroit variety shop with a bulging $70,000 inventory yielded only $28,000 for creditors on a private bid.

- A Georgia textile factory whose equipment and raw materials cost $300,000 attracted a $40,000 high bidder.

Each was another distressed business owner who successfully repurchased his own assets to start fresh. Collectively, they left behind millions in liabilities.

It's not what you paid for your assets that counts. It's what someone will pay for those assets under the auctioneer's hammer. And when you want to buy back your own business, you enjoy a distinct advantage over other bidders: You can afford to pay a premium to start again because you don't see odd lots of merchandise or equipment to be trucked away. You see a new and revitalized business emerging from the ruins of one that's been temporarily dismantled to shed a few creditors.

A well-planned dump-buyback avoids the guesswork about what it will cost to win your business back. An auctioneer can give you an estimate before you liquidate. This is important. Avoid surprises. My dump-buybacks succeed because I know in advance what it will take to buy back my client's business, and where that money will come from.

You can, in most instances, avoid a public auction. Most liquidators will sell you back your assets at private sale if the deal is unquestionably fair to your creditors. Make it a super-fair deal; offer your liquidator about 20 percent more than what creditors would get if the assets were auctioned, based on a professional appraisal. Your sale is then commercially reasonable and your creditors have little cause to squawk.

My firm is now finishing the paperwork on a small dump-buyback, a silk-flower business with assets valued at less than $20,000. We offered the assignee $24,000 for a quick, private sale, and he promptly agreed. The creditors will get about $4,000 more than they would get at a auction and saved $3,000 in auction fees. Professional liquidators seldom object to a private sale if they are convinced it's in the creditors' best interests.

I emphasize that your deal must be honest and fair in every respect. Avoid impropriety. Liquidators will rightfully refuse to sell privately to the principals of a distressed business unless the deal can withstand the closest scrutiny. This is understandable. Liquidators have a fiduciary obligation: Convert your assets into as much money as possible. But if your pockets are deepest, isn't it in the creditors' best interest to sell you back your assets? Don't hide in your new corporation. Your creditors will eventually find out that you're the buyer, so why raise suspicions that you acted improperly? In fact, you must disclose your personal interest in a buyer company when you buy through the bankruptcy court. Let your lawyer guide you on these technicalities so you avoid serious legal blunders.

A well-orchestrated dump-buyback is as fair to your creditors as it is practical and beneficial to you. I rarely liquidate businesses for creditor groups, but when I do, I ask their owners whether they want to bid for their business. I often put them right back into the businesses. It's not philanthropy, but a sensible way to get creditors the most money. Some owners jump at the chance to restart their business once they see how easily it can be done. It is everyone's ultimate win-win deal!

HOW TO ORCHESTRATE A FRIENDLY FORECLOSURE

The easiest dump-buybacks? When a friendly mortgagee forecloses on your business and sell its assets back to you-on no money-down terms.

You saw it early in this chapter with Ken's Furniture Outlet, but let's again go through the exercise:

Suppose your assets are worth only $40,000 at auction, and you owe $100,000 in liabilities. If you owe one friendly supplier $40,000, why not give that supplier a mortgage on your business? Your supplier is now in the position to foreclose and sell your assets at a foreclosure sale to your new corporation, should the road become rocky.

If your assets are worth less than $40,000, your supplier can sell you the assets privately, without auction, and refinance the entire deal with no money down. Your new business will owe this supplier $40,000, but you are otherwise debt-free!

Secured lenders commonly refinance buybacks of troubled businesses. It's smart business. If liquidating your business won't fully repay their debt, refinancing your new corporation may improve their chances to get fully paid, since you now have a healthier business without other creditors competing for your cash.

Susan, one feisty Californian, had her cake and ate it too. Susan's near-bankrupt bakery owed a bank $150,000 and unsecured creditors $200,000. Susan's bakery assets were worth about $80,000 at auction, which wouldn't even cover the bank loan. Susan confidently collared her banker to apologize for her problem loan and the substantial loss to the bank if she closed up shop. Susan followed with this proposition: "Foreclose and rewrite $100,000 of the loan to a new corporation I will form to buy back my business. Your bank will recover $100,000, which is $20,000 more than the $80,000 you would get at auction. But you must cancel the $100,000 balance, and extend the term of the loan."

The banker saw no better alternative, and agreed. Susan cautions that if you do finance your buyback, limit your "going-forward" debt to what your business can realistically support. A big loan against small assets is still a business in trouble.

HOW TO NEGOTIATE 100-PERCENT FINANCING

How can you buy back your business with 100-percent financing? Offer a premium for financing. A 20 percent financing bonus may convince your liquidator to bypass cash buyers and accept your no- cash-down deal. Those few extra dollars can make the difference between again owning a healthy business and punching a time clock.

A liquidator can only justify financing you if it puts more money in the creditors' pockets and your loan does not pose a high risk. So don't be shy. It's only business, and no-cash-down business deals are common. Smart liquidators invite leveraged financing deals if creditors will come out ahead and will incur little or no risk through financing.

That's how I won financing for a failing Philadelphia discount cosmetic store with more than $250,000 in unsecured debts. I could have filed Chapter 11 to cut the company's debts, but since the assets were worth only $40,000 at auction, I decided a dump-buyback would be smarter. Unfortunately, the owner, John, didn't have the $40,000 to bid for his assets. So instead, I proposed to the assignee for creditors that John would pay $60,000 over two years plus ten percent annual interest on the unpaid balance. The loan would be secured by the business assets and a second mortgage on John's home that had $30,000 in equity. The creditors would get a $20,000 bonus plus interest for financing the "no-risk" deal, and John would get his business back with no other debts. Another win-win deal!

Common cases? Sure. In another recent case, a major finance company foreclosed on its $3-million mortgage to wipe out $8 million in unsecured debt owed by a large machine-foundry client. Hap and Barry are now back in business, and owe only the $3 million to the finance company. That's far better then the $11 million debt load they had carried before. We are now renegotiating the $3 million due to the cooperative lender down to about $1.5 million, or what their assets are worth. A debt-free business sometimes happens in stages!

FORTIFY YOURSELF

In Chapter 10, you saw why it's so important to your survival to turn your business into a creditor-proof fortress. It's absolutely critical in dump-buyback cases, when your objective is to buy back your business as cheaply as possible. And to buy cheaply, you must control your business's key assets.

Your lease is a good example. When location is important, why let a competing buyer grab your lease so he can take your business as a going operation? Neutralize your competitors. Control your lease, and you force the liquidator to sell to either you or a competing bidder who can only cart away your assets piecemeal. Obviously by controlling your lease, you'll cement the deal for a far lower price.

The Cabots, a husband-wife team, own a small hardware store in my town and are a typical example. The Cabots owed their creditors more than $450,000, and made an Assignment for the Benefit of Creditors. Following my strategy, they wanted to buy back their inventory and fixtures, a value of $200,000, for pennies on the dollar, and restart their business. So I went to work!

Shortly before the assignment, I formed a new corporation that signed a new lease with the landlord. With the location secured, prospective bidders couldn't operate the business at that location and would offer less for the assets than if they could take over an operating hardware store. Wouldn't you pay more for a hardware store grossing $1.2 million a year than for a pile of inventory? With their location secured, the Cabots successfully bid to buy their business back for only $40,000.

Keep the lessons from Chapter 10 in mind. Use building blocks to creditor-proof your business. Transfer your valuable patents, trademarks, copyrights and other proprietary assets, as well as distributorship and licensing rights, to another corporation and license them back to your troubled business. These are assets you won't have to buy, and it will discourage a competitive buyer if these protected assets are essential to the business. Turn your business into a financial fortress. You may win yourself a debt-free business on a shoestring!

DIRECTLY SELL YOUR ASSETS DEBT-FREE

You may not have to transfer your assets through a liquidator to buy them back debt-free. One alternative is to sell the assets of your troubled business directly to your new corporation, free and clear of all liabilities. You do this with a "bulk transfer."

Every state has bulk sales laws, intended to prevent a business owner from selling his business assets outside of the ordinary course of business without paying his creditors. Should a business owner sell business assets outside of the ordinary course of business, all creditors must be notified of the intended transfer no fewer than ten days before the transfer. Creditors not notified can later reclaim the assets sold to the buyer, so buyers under a bulk transfer must make certain the seller's creditors are properly notified.

But the bulk sales laws do not require the seller's creditors to be fully paid. Creditors need only be advised whether they shall receive full payment from the sales proceeds. Creditors who won't be fully paid must receive detailed information concerning the intended sale so they can decide whether to contest the sale within the ten-day notice period. Creditors who do not object (usually through a lawsuit to prevent the sale) lose the right to later claim the assets sold to the buyer. Bulk-sales laws do not apply to sales by a secured party, assignee, receiver or trustee in bankruptcy.

Let's take a closer look at how the bulk sales laws can help you if your objective is to restart your business with a few less debts.

If you own Company A and want to transfer its assets to Company B free of Company A creditor claims, you must first notify Company A's creditors. If Company A's creditors do not stop the sale, then Company B receives clear title to the assets even though Company A's creditors receive less than what is owed to them.

My success with bulk transfers is rapidly improving because I've learned how to minimize creditor opposition. I sell creditors on the deal. You, too, must build a strong case for why the sale is in the creditors' best interests. Your bulk sales notice should include two or three professional appraisals that show a considerably lower auction value than what your new corporation will pay. This is the key. Creditors must get more than if your business were liquidated, and you must convince them that this is the case.

A bulk sale can be ideal if you only have unsecured creditors. Secured debts and tax liens automatically follow the assets to your new business, so you need a dump-buyback or Chapter 11 to shed these liabilities, if you can't negotiate an out-of-court settlement.

Debt restructuring can be full of zigs and zags. I may try a bulk sale when I expect no significant creditor resistance. I try to convince creditors the sales price is fair. But if creditors object, I may then attempt the transfer through an Assignment for the Benefit of Creditors, or some similar method. If that is blocked, we may file Chapter 11 and try to force the sale through the bankruptcy court. There are always ways! Map out your strategies in advance so you know your alternate routes to a debt- free business.

FADE OUTS AND WALKAWAYS

If you own a small business with few assets, then why even bother with a buyback? Your best bet may be to set up a new shop from scratch. This advice is particularly appropriate for service firms with few tangible assets.

Packing up and beginning again with a brand-new company makes much more sense than wrestling with creditors. A local landscaper, with about $10,000 in equipment and no receivables or other assets, consulted with me a few months ago. His lawyer advised him to file Chapter 11 to restructure $100,000 in secured bank loans, $90,000 owed the IRS and $160,000 due general creditors.

What ridiculous advice! I told the beleaguered gardener to buy back his equipment for a few bucks at auction, or better yet, replace his equipment with some new gear so he could start fresh. The gardener's many loyal customers would patronize his new landscape business. Why not walk away from a few thousand dollars in landscaping equipment when you also walk away from more than $300,000 in liabilities? That's practical advice. And it's yours if you own a small, easily restarted service firm.

Restarting your business gradually and on the installment plan is the "fade in/fade out." The strategy is to build up a new company while your defunct business winds down. The fade out gives you time to develop your startup when it's operationally impossible to simultaneously close one business and open another.

The fade in/fade out was certainly the right formula for a Tampa employment agency saddled with more than $200,000 in IRS liens. When the IRS breathed fire, Burt, the owner, simply opened another agency across town using a very similar name. Burt gradually weaned his many accounts to his new agency. With his oblivious customers safely channeled to his new agency, Burt handed the IRS the keys to his old agency. They finally auctioned two old desks, receiving $85 to apply to their $200,000 tax bill.

Admittedly, these practical, no-nonsense survival tactics aren't taught at Harvard Law School. Then again, I didn't go to Harvard Law School.

But even here, you can't be too cavalier. The fade in/fade out requires meticulous planning to avoid creditor claims that you misappropriated assets from your defunct business to start your new venture. Have your accountant and attorney guide you so you start clean, without angry creditors chasing you.

GUARANTEE YOUR SUCCESS WITH A BACKUP PLAN

Plan for the worst. Always! What would happen if your creditors threw your business into bankruptcy to prevent you from pulling one of these legal but nevertheless fast-footed maneuvers? That's an important question.

The answer: You don't rely on one strategy alone to save your business. You need backup strategies. When one tactic fails, you switch to another. Stay two steps ahead of the enemy. Develop a chess-player mindset.

My backup plans have backup plans. I'm no optimist; I can't afford to be. My clients expect me to keep them in business. So for starters, I may slap a friendly mortgage on the business as a setup for a later dump-buyback. Should that fail, my backup plan may be a dump-buyback through an Assignment for the Benefit of Creditors. If creditors dump the assigned business into bankruptcy, I am prepared to bid the business back from the bankruptcy trustee. With an uncooperative trustee, I would convert the case to a Chapter 11 reorganization so I could dump the trustee and regain control of the business. I would then try to transfer the assets to the new corporation with bankruptcy-court approval.

These are only a few of the many possibilities for ending up with your defunct company's assets for pennies on the dollar. There is never just one way to save a business.

To zig and zag to shed your creditors is like a snake shedding its old skin. You now know a few of the moves, but do your advisors? Have your advisors explained why they selected their one debt-busting strategy? What are their backup plays if their strategy is unsuccessful?

Develop a total game plan. Include every contingency. When you cover the bases, you get into the game more enthusiastically and optimistically, because you know exactly where you are heading and the many routes to get there.

☑CHECKPOINT

1. Can a dump-buyback be your ideal debt-busting strategy?

2. Have you well-fortified your business so it's defensively positioned for a dump-buyback?

3. Can a cooperative, secured creditor help you with a friendly foreclosure?

4. Would a bulk transfer of assets to a new corporation be workable?

5. Would a fade in/fade out or walk-away be the right strategy to solve your creditor problems?

6. Has your professional advisor reviewed these strategies with you?

7. What is your total game plan?

15

MAKING YOUR
MONEY MACHINE

Making money is the ultimate purpose of any business. It's great to have fun working, but if you can't make money, you have a hobby, not a business. If you lose money, you have an expensive hobby. I don't think you want an expensive hobby. You want a profitable business, one that is as profitable as you can possibly make it.

Everything you've read so far has brought you only to the point where you are well positioned to make money. Your business is stable. Your creditor problems are behind you or soon will be. But those accomplishments, although vital, remain wasted unless your business makes money.

Money! Money! Money! It not only makes the world go 'round, but keeps you in business!

How do you turn your business into a perpetual money machine? I offer no simple formula because there isn't one. Businesses and business strategies, like snowflakes, are never identical.

Whether on my *Business Doctor* radio show or at my seminars, I'm always asked, "How do I make money?" My (facetious) answer: "Take in more money than you pay out." "But how do I do that?" they invariably ask. "That's for you to answer," is my reply.

I wish I could find that one right formula for making money. I'd patent it as my very own money machine. But I've had enough of my own failures to teach me there are no surefire formulas. Thank goodness I've had more success than failure.

Running several businesses, from drug stores to publishing companies, also taught me that while there's no surefire success formula, you can rethink your business to turn more profits. That's the goal of this chapter: To help you rethink your business into the money machine it can be.

SET SOLID PROFIT GOALS

It's not enough to hope for profits. Set goals for the profits you should make and will make.

Think big! You seldom achieve more than you shoot for. Businesses are like people: Modest expectations and few demands create underachievers. Even if your business makes a few bucks, it's too easy to fall into a rut, content to let your little business chug along as long as it pays its bills and gives you a paycheck.

Complacency is always dangerous. No business can survive very long when its owner has limited vision. A business must adapt to an ever-changing world filled with great threats and great opportunities.

Profits prove your competitiveness. Profits, more than lining your pockets, allows your business to grow, attract better employees, develop new products and services, invest in a more efficient plant and equipment, and market more aggressively. Profits signify a healthy future; losses mark an ailing or dead enterprise.

What kind of profit goals should you shoot for?

■ **Profits that can let your business grow by 20 percent a year.** But this conservative number is only for the mature business in a stable industry. You want considerably higher profits if you operate a young, entrepreneurial venture with dynamic growth potential. Businesses must double in size every five years or they lack the momentum they need in today's fast-changing environment. Stagnant firms typically slide backward.

■ **Profits that can produce at least a 30-percent return on your existing equity.** Without this return on your equity, you would be smarter to sell your business and plunk your money into the stock market. A smaller return should only be acceptable when reasons other than making money motivate you to be in business.

■ **Profits that are 50 percent more than your competitors' profits.** This tests your efficiency and managerial effectiveness. When you can wring 15 cents in profits for every 10 cents your competitors wring from the same sales, you have earned your stripes as a super-manager. Outperform your competitors. This important goal will keep you on your toes.

■ **Profits at least 20 percent above last year's.** Accept the challenge to outperform your own prior performance, an always-tough race when you lack resources. Ask any sprinter how it feels to beat her best time around the track. She'll mop her brow, and give you a mile-wide smile. Making more money than before is your gold star!

Do these goals sound unachievable? Believe me, it can happen! I have seen company after company, with small profits and huge losses, become incredible profit-producing money machines that outstripped everyone's wildest expectations. How did they do it?

DOWN THE YELLOW BRICK ROAD

The Wizard of Oz had his yellow-brick road. You have your own yellow-brick road to profitability: A strategic and operational bottom-line strategy to bring in more income at less cost.

Now, that moneymaking formula is so obvious and basic that you're scratching your head and wondering why I even mention it. But is it so basic? Maybe you have lost sight of what making money is all about, and now, you must again make it central to your strategic-planning.

How can your business bring in more money than it pays out? Think about it, and you will agree that your options are indeed limitless. Maybe answers won't quickly appear. Problems hidden in years of company tradition don't easily see the light. Your problems and opportunities may be subtle or out in the open, known only to you or known by everyone but you.

So how do you find your yellow-brick road? I offer you nine yellow-brick roads. These are the routes most commonly traveled by losing companies that have become winners.

Profit Strategy #1: Back to the future

A step backward may propel you two steps forward to renewed profits. How did you make money two, three or five years ago? Why not make this your starting point for making money again today?

Of course, if your business has yet to earn its first dime, you must still invent your money-machine blueprint. But if you once made money, you have the blueprint. Perhaps you only have strayed too far, or in the wrong direction, or moved too rapidly away from what worked in the past.

Retrace your steps. What was your business like when it last made money? What changes caused profits to decline? How can or should you reshape your business?

Reversing direction seems contrary to goals of growth and progress. And maybe it is, in terms of sales. But coming out of your turnaround, you need profits more than you need ambitious expansion that causes more unaffordable losses.

Small losses today for bigger profits tomorrow is okay – if you can afford those temporary losses and are confident of those future profits. But can you really afford to lose even one more dime?

Your company may have landed in trouble because you went in the wrong direction. Maybe it was a bombed new product line or a new retail location. Reversing course erases those missteps that hurt you.

Returning to your past is seldom permanent. But it does give you a temporary but profitable foundation from which to re-direct your business toward another yellow-brick road - one hopefully paved with real gold.

Profit Strategy #2: Shrink

Downsizing or shrinking your business sounds remarkably like returning to your past, but there is a difference. A reshaped business doesn't necessarily produce a smaller business. It may mean changing the product mix or the pricing, or even expanding your business if it once operated more profitably as a larger company. Still, reshaping for most turnaround businesses means downsizing, a strategy that rids your company of everything that destroys profits!

- Which products/services do you sell that are unprofitable?

- Which of your retail locations, divisions or branches loses money for you?

- What marketing programs don't pay their way?

Common sense questions, of course, but when you don't constantly ask yourself these questions, you lose the way. And when you have the answers, you must act decisively and quickly. You can't wait months, because you can't afford to lose money for even one more day!

Downsizing usually requires radical surgery, not just shedding a layer of skin. To build muscle, you must sacrifice every flabby, unprofitable product, service, function, location or asset.

A Detroit machine-tooling firm now understands the profit power of downsizing. When I started helping them sort through their problems, they were grossing $22 million and losing $3 million. We quickly stopped production on 35 unprofitable items. Two years later, the company grossed only $10 million, but earned more than $1 million in profits. Profits improved by $4 million while sales dropped 60 percent. A too common story!

Fast-growth companies must frequently downsize to shed their losers. They can be invigorated by their winners, but must never be blind to the fact that they also picked up a few losers. That's what a dynamic business is all about. You grow with the winners and periodically pause to dump your losers.

Profit Strategy #3: Atomize and synthesize

Never made a dime? No proven profit center to downsize to? Your answer may be to atomize and synthesize!

You atomize by tearing your business apart. You synthesize by building a new business from your assets.

Fed up with Connecticut's low Medicaid reimbursement, Bill and Martha Simon turned their failing nursing home into an alcohol-dependency treatment center. Same building, same beds, but a very different business. That's atomizing and synthesizing. Bill and Martha now earn $200,000 a year in profits from their new venture, in sharp contrast to the $120,000 they lost operating a nursing home.

Synthesize and atomize? It also worked wonders for Henry Wybel, whose Fort Lauderdale boat dealership got stuck on the shoals when stiff competition, a recession and a luxury tax on boats all rocked the boating industry in the early 1990s. What could Henry do with his huge used boat inventory and boat yard on Florida's famed Intracoastal? Rent boats of course! Henry rents plenty of boats – quite profitably, thank you – and also operates a growing water-taxi business for sightseeing and ferrying hungry tourists to popular waterside restaurants.

This is what I mean by rethinking your business. It forces you to think less about the business you're in and more about the business you should be in.

If you think your business is a born loser that can never be turned into a winner, meet Charlie Silberling, a Connecticut street-smart entrepreneur. Charlie's life centered on his old movie theater, a big loser when he bought it and still a big loser when I met him. The place featured old reruns and empty seats. "Dump it," I counseled. "The damn business loses more than $40,000 every year and will never be profitable. Face it, Charlie, you've got a loser on your hands."

Charlie disagreed. "True," he admitted, "as a theater, it's a loser." But old Charlie could see beyond what I could see. Three weeks later, Charlie had the seats ripped out, sold his projection equipment and was cleverly converting the tired, old theater into a beautiful new consignment-art gallery.

Charlie's "Wintergate Art Galleries" exhibit more than 800 paintings from local artists, and it's always swamped with art lovers. Charlie not only makes plenty of money, but he couldn't be happier; he always fancied himself an amateur artist.

Charlie never lets me forget my "good" advice. Every year he sends me his tax returns, not to impress me, but to make sure I learned a big lesson. Any business can make money!

Profit Strategy #4: Fast-forward

How do you make a near-bankrupt chain of sunglasses kiosks profitable? When Jim Whyke and Harry Robard asked me, I surprised them with my answer. "Quickly expand your eight kiosks to 20 or more."

I had two good reasons for this strange-sounding advice. First, with only eight outlets, I knew Jim and Harry could never buy sunglasses as competitively as the large chains could. Buying through middlemen cost them 20 percent more than if they had bought directly from the manufacturers. And the most fashionable manufacturers only sold directly to the volume retailers. I knew that with about 20 stores, Jim and Harry would have the volume and buying power they needed. Jim and Harry also each needed to draw $40,000 a year for living expenses, which was about twice what their fledgling chain could afford.

Throwing the organization into fast-forward, Jim and Harry now have 23 stores. They buy their sunglasses at rock-bottom prices from all the best manufacturers. More importantly, they have the clout to win locations for their attractive and profitable kiosks in the more successful shopping malls. And because their chain generates big sales, Jim and Harry each draw $75,000 a year!

Consider fast-forwarding your strategy when your basic business is sound, and you need more income to gain scale economies unobtainable in your present operation. How do you fast-forward? You have three options: Grow internally, acquire other businesses or merge.

Most fast-forward companies simply expand. A retailer multiplies its outlets. A manufacturer produces more products. A publisher publishes more books. But this growth may be achieved even faster through acquisition. And merging two businesses to achieve these scale economies can produce enormous profits.

When it comes to scale economies, big isn't always more beautiful, but it can be more profitable!

Profit Strategy #5: Focus

More businesses would make more money if they would no longer be all things to all people and instead select and focus upon one good target market.

Niche marketing is hardly a new idea, but only within the past decade or so have we recognized that businesses usually do best as big fish in small ponds, not as small fish in big ponds.

Wherever I go, I see businesses monopolizing small, profitable and less competitive niches. And they are thriving! Even the biggies now niche market and chase after small-market segments that were once beneath them.

But while the Fortune 500 companies have plenty of clout, they lack the entrepreneurial spirit, operational flexibility and love for the field that ensures true success as a niche marketer. These attributes belong to the rugged individual.

Is niche marketing for you?

- What market segments or prospective customer groups should you focus on?

- How can you best bundle your products or services to target this market?

Look around. I bet plenty of niche markets are available for you to tap. Whether you sell shoes, publish books or operate a dental clinic, why be a stumbling generalist when you can be a successful specialist?

Focusing on a niche is critical when your resources are too few to scatter in all directions. But focusing is more than downsizing. Even a downsized company can be unfocused, while a large firm may be tightly focused.

Profit Strategy #6: Knock on doors

Not everyone profits from retrenching, downsizing, reshaping or refocusing. Some need only knock on a few more doors to get new customers.

Maybe you never had to hustle customers to survive and prosper. Or maybe you opened your doors but never quite figured out how to get the prospect to walk through. Or maybe your marketing was too sporadic, too unprofessional or too ineffective.

There are hundreds of books that will tell you how to market and sell. And you should read some. But for now, just answer these four easy questions:

- How much more sales do you need to become profitable?

- How many new customers do you need to generate these sales?

- What effort have you made to get these customers?

- What more can you do to get these customers?

Come up with the right answers, and you'll come up with profits.

If you traveled with me, you too would be amazed by the number of fundamentally sound businesses that go bust only because they can't push their sales above the break-even point. They seem to have the right product, right market, right prices and right location. They have everything but the ability to get more buyers for whatever they are selling. It may be poor overall marketing, a fatal weakness in sales organization or just lousy salesmanship. Business people don't always know how to promote and sell.

But the right techniques can be taught. The person we can't help is the lazy individual who won't make the effort necessary to haul the customer in. You must go after customers aggressively, no matter what business you're in. If you believe they will automatically come to you, you will never enjoy the success those few extra knocks on the door can bring.

Profit Strategy #7: Hike prices

Clients howl when I tell them to hike their prices. "How can I? My competitors will kill me!"

You probably never realized that even insignificant price hikes can produce significant profits. See for yourself. Add 5 percent more income to your income statement without changing any other number. How much more profitable would you be if you had raised your prices only 5 percent?

Sure, you may lose a few customers with higher prices. But handled correctly, it seldom happens to the degree you think. Realistically, an overall 5-percent price hike may give you a 3- percent sales increase. Even if you lose a few customers, it puts you well ahead in the game.

Of course, pricing strategy must largely depend on your product, your service and your competition. And each must be carefully considered. But I say many businesses are in trouble only because their prices are far too low.

You have many ways to increase prices so your customers will love you, not leave you. Improved service, add-ons, bundling products and services and similar tactics build perceived value, reduce price resistance and, most importantly, add those few extra pennies per sale that you need to turn a profit.

About one-third of all manufacturing firms lose money only because they blindly price their products to match a competitor's prices. When their competitors are larger, more efficient and can produce the product much more cheaply, these firms must learn to outflank their competitors through product differentiation, superior service or both. You can charge higher prices and get away with it if you learn to be different. And when you need those few extra pennies per widget, you must make sure your customer will happily pay it!

Maybe you can change the customer's perception of what you are selling without changing the product. Gino Paulucci, the founder of Papa Gino's, tells a great story of how he unloaded a truckload of discolored bananas for twice the price of unblemished bananas. Gino, then a kid working in a Duluth, Minnesota supermarket, was told by the boss to stack the speckled and discolored (but perfectly edible) bananas in front of the store and close them out for 15 cents a pound, or half the usual 29-cent price. Instead, the bright Gino hung a sign announcing the arrival of the famed "Argentine banana." In two hours, he sold the entire lot for 49 cents a pound!

Profit Strategy #8: Cut-costs

Juggle numbers again. Look to your expenses. We hit costs in Chapter 8 because we wanted to conserve cash. Now look at ways to cut costs to build profits

Again, with your income statement in hand, hold your sales steady and cut total expenses by 5 percent. What are your new profits?

What's that I hear? You don't think there's a 5-percent fat factor in your expenses? You're kidding yourself. I never once found a business - even one run by the tightest skinflint - where I couldn't squeeze another 5 percent from the cost column. Even businesses once squeezed can be squeezed again for another 5 percent. There's no end to what you can cut when you are desperate to make a buck!

Nickels and dimes. Those are your profit builders. Two cents more per widget and 5 cents less on production and overhead costs, and *voila*, you now have 7 cents more profit per widget! Sell enough widgets, and you'll have one profitable little widget factory. Watch those nickels and dimes!

High overhead costs are the big profit destroyers in at least 40 percent of my cases. Right down the line, their expenses are too high. Sales may be okay, but the business still slowly chokes to death on operating expenses that constantly creep a little too high.

Remember my publisher friend with the swank offices in Boston? This almost happened to him. His operation was perched in the penthouse of one of Boston's plushest office buildings. A swank receptionist adorned an equally swank reception area; the place reeked of success. Their financial statements told a far different story. I developed a friendship with the publisher, who was a member of my Masonic Lodge, and after several visits he confided that his business had lost more than $100,000 a year for the past several years.

I am happy to tell you that that same publisher today operates from a 12,000-square-foot supermarket basement. How did it happen? Day and night, I hit him with the tough questions. Why did a newspaper publisher need an expensive office suite? Who was he trying to impress? Did his subscribers care what his operation looked like or where it was located? Only when he came up with objective answers could I produce big annual savings!

$ 96,000   on rent
     57,000   in reduced payroll
     18,000   on expensive office furniture leases
     12,000   in fringe benefits
_____

$ 183,000 total annual savings.

If you want to own a money machine, radical surgery on unnecessary overhead costs can make it happens faster than anything else. Cut, cut and cut again. Let nothing escape your scalpel.

Profit Strategy #9: Build mile-high sandwiches

Build a mile-high sandwich? No, it doesn't sound like something from the Harvard Business School. And it isn't. That good advice came from my dad, who never went to Harvard or any other college.

But for my dad, "the mile-high sandwich strategy" was the only profit strategy! You see, after World War II, my dad scraped together $500 to open a tiny delicatessen in the Roxbury section of Boston. He twice expanded within two years and soon had 40 bustling employees and legions of salivating customers crowding his small deli. Starting with almost nothing, my dad managed to build the second largest delicatessen in New England!

As a youngster, I became his chief busboy and observed customer after customer eat only half their sandwiches and "bag" the other half to take home. Of course, dad's sandwiches were about a mile thick, so customers with only one stomach could never finish one, no matter how tempting the challenge.

I asked my dad one day why he didn't put less meat in the sandwich. My dad then taught me my most valuable business lesson. "Son," he said, "Always give your customers more than they expect and more than your competitors will give them. When you do, they will come back again and again - and bring new customers with them! My sandwiches are the thickest in town because it's my way of giving my customers more!"

No business professor, no business book and no high-priced consultant ever summed it up better for me than my dad did that chilly day in 1949. My dad was right. The best and most enduring path to profits is through a thicker sandwich. Give your customer more!

That's my philosophy with clients. What more can I do for them? What more can I put into this book than what you expect?

It's your turn. Rethink your product quality. Rethink your service. Do your customers get more than they expect? Listen to my dad. Building your profitable business may be as easy as slapping a few more slices of corned beef between the rye.

EIGHT PROFIT-PLANNING TIPS

The ability to turn your profit strategy into actual profits is the heart of the turnaround. No matter how brilliant the scheme, you must start with an overall objective or profit concept, followed by sub-objectives and, finally, an action plan. This complex process becomes appreciably easier with these eight tips:

Tip #1: Get a sense of what is going on.

Sometimes those who know the least about what's happening within an industry are those within the industry.

You can become so immersed in your day-to-day events that you lose touch with new trends within your industry – trends that nevertheless pinpoint possible opportunities and directions your business may take for long-term profitability.

So get your head out of the sand. Read your trade journals. Visit or spy on the success stories in your industry who are spearheading change. Analyze. Ask questions. Steal ideas!

Tip #2: Brainstorm.

Make profit-planning a group sport. I enjoy brainstorming. Bouncing ideas back and forth synergizes the process, and you then have a sounding board – a particularly valuable ingredient when you have free thinkers, not yes men, in the group. Encourage a free and open flow of ideas and suggestions. Let ideas run wild. Review not only the possibilities but the potential of each idea. My best advice: Involve those within your organization who must implement your plans.

Tip #3: Prioritize strategies.

We talked about only a few possible profit strategies. There are many others, and you should consider them all. Few successful turnarounds employ only one or two profit strategies. You may have one or two primary strategies and many secondary strategies. Prioritize each so you know the resources and attention each deserves.

Try to concentrate first on business changes that can occur most rapidly and produce the most definite, significant and immediate profits.

Especially clamp down quickly on your big losers. We generally start with a cost-cutting program and then define product lines or operating divisions that are constant money- losers. But we always follow a concentric pattern of hitting hardest and fastest at those areas that will bring the most immediate results.

Pay attention not only to changes that will increase profits, but also will increase the all-important cash flow. You still have a cash-hungry business. Always increase cash today, profits tomorrow.

Tip #4: Set realistic profit goals.

You want a profit plan that works. Pie-in-the-sky plans only distract you from making the practical operational changes you need.

A realistic plan has detail, hard numbers, and shows how each change will increase profits.

Short-term profit strategies can be more precise. However, long-term planning, while less precise and predictable, must still be measurable.

Lack of reality can be your major stumbling block when you fight for profits. Your idea may sound intriguing but lack operational practicality. You cannot afford more mistakes; you have already had your share of managerial blunders. Your future plans must work. Elect a safer course that may generate more modest profits than a big-potential, big-gamble plan. Make safety part of reality.

Does your plan fit your financial, organizational and logistical capabilities? Do you have the money and other resources to implement the plan? Many owners develop perfect plans but lack the resources to put the plan into action. So they don't. You too must work with what you have or can obtain. A plan that goes beyond what you can accomplish is nothing more than an idle and costly dream.

Tip #5: Stay flexible.

Few plans follow a straight line. Most zig and zag along the way as new, unexpected opportunities and roadblocks enter the picture.

When your initial tactics don't achieve results, you too will switch to alternate strategies. You can look only so far ahead, and the path to profitability can be a long one. So proceed step by step. Never look too far ahead; the path will seem discouragingly long. Measure the impact of each step. Then step again.

In most of my cases, I've found profits at the end of a path I never originally intended to travel. What seemed logical at first took us to alternate routes discovered only once the process actually began. Watch for your bends in the road. Don't be afraid to follow them – if they make sense.

Tip #6: Act quickly.

Never forget that initial efforts in the turnaround must cure serious operational problems and fend off creditors. Building cash flow and protecting what's left of your business must take priority. Profitability is deferred, but not forgotten. Pull the profit file from the drawer when your firm is beyond the emergency stage, and you have operational matters under control. Only then can you step back, catch your breath and take a hard, decisive look at your business - where it's heading, and where it should go!

Long-range profit planning is all but impossible early in the turnaround, because you have no idea what your firm will look like once the turnaround is completed.

Nevertheless, do formulate profit plans as quickly as possible, if only to gain the confidence of creditors and employees. I always walk into a meeting with creditors or employees with some type of profit plan

Tip #7: Implement decisively.

What is profit planning without good implementation? Only a gesture in the right direction. You planned to stabilize your business, and you implemented it. You planned to restructure your debt, and you implemented it. Now you must implement your profit plan, which will be considerably more complicated when you must essentially change how you do business. Of course, some profit plans are less ambitious than others, but even modest business overhauls consume a considerable amount of time, effort and resources. Take it in small bites:

What will you do first? How will you implement each objective? Who will be responsible for each task? What is your timetable for implementation? What are the overall costs and costs per activity? How do you know whether your profit strategy is working?

This last point bears a message! Even the best plans may not improve profits or improve them sufficiently. But bad plans can produce even greater losses! So good financial monitoring is essential so you know quickly whether your plans are working. Also stay open to new ideas and modifications to your present plans because profit planning is a never-ending effort to increase sales and lower costs. You have constantly changing variables to play with.

Tip #8: Produce enough profits.

Some businesses never produce the profits they need. They may have become profitable but not profitable enough to handle their commitments.

The bankruptcy courts are loaded with profitable companies who make money, but not enough money to cover their checks.

Profitability is a meaningless objective when your cash flow is still a dollar short. Earning those few extra dollars may put you on the right side of the financial ledger, but many more dollars may be needed to keep you there.

☑CHECKPOINT

1. *Can your business make the money you need? The money you want?*

2. *What are your profit goals?*

3. *What is your vision for your business? How can it be changed to produce a profit?*

4. *Was your business once profitable? Can it be made profitable again by reshaping it to what it was?*

5. *Can your business become profitable by increasing prices, cutting costs or selling more effectively?*

6. *Are you giving your customers real value for their money or are they shopping elsewhere, where they find more value?*

7. *What is your plan for achieving profitability? Is it realistic? Attainable?*

8. *Can you earn sufficient profits to cover all your obligations?*

16

SECRETS OF
SECOND-CHANCE FINANCING

"Successful companies live within their incomes, even if they have to borrow to do it." These words from humorist Josh Billings also apply to unsuccessful companies.

Your troubled company may need more than financial first aid to survive. You may need new financing to muscle your way through the turnaround so cash-flow shortfalls won't force you to shut down. You later may need financing to recapitalize your business or to grow. Many failed businesses could have found the money they needed to survive and grow with a more assertive and savvy refinancing strategy, but as the saying goes, "They were a dime short and a day late."

Is your business hard pressed for money? Your thoughts are probably running in a hundred different directions. Can you get more money from present lenders? Can you borrow from long-standing customers who depend upon you? What new money sources can you tap? What assets can you pledge for additional loans? Will the government bail you out? Should you throw more of your own money into the business? It's so perplexing!

Answers to these questions rest on many factors: The size and type of company you own, your relations with lenders and creditors, whether your problems are behind or ahead of you, and what you can offer a financier. You'll find answers to these questions in this chapter, and hopefully a road map to your pot of gold.

But regardless of your business or who you are, fresh financing for your stricken business will never come easily or cheaply, not when you're competing for money against bright-eyed entrepreneurs with slick business plans for another Apple Computer or McDonalds. Also on the prowl for money from these same lenders are about 12 million healthy, established companies with solid track records for paying their bills. So why should a lender give money to your tarnished and faltering company, which may present neither a spectacular future nor a successful past? You see the problem.

A hustler stepping from the train in a striped suit has more chance of raising money for a gold mine in Manhattan than does the sick and stumbling firm. That's fact. I have known what it is like to have lenders ask me to close the door quietly on my way out as they sprayed their offices with Lysol. Borrowing money for the troubled company is never easy.

But not all is gloom and doom. The good news is that turnaround companies do get refinanced. You can too if you keep in mind the two key secrets: **1)** You must forget conventional financing strategies which work for startups and stable enterprises but not for sick companies. **2)** You will need considerably more patience, perseverance and old-fashioned shoe leather before you find someone who will open his pocketbook. Financing a troubled business won't be easy. I only say it's possible!

HOW MUCH MONEY DO YOU NEED?

Conservatively calculate the money you need. Set a minimum and a maximum range of what you can reasonably use and pay back. Overreaching is seldom fatal because few lenders will overfinance you. Setting a minimum is the greater problem. You can easily underestimate what it will cost to put your business together again. Borrow as much money as you need to stabilize the business, and position it to make money! Anything less is still a dime short.

Don't refinance in stages. You can't logically refinance more frequently than every two or three years. Many turnarounds try two- step financing. The first round of borrowing is to pay creditors. Only then do they worry about finding the money to recapitalize their businesses so they can make money! These short-sighted financing strategies seldom succeed because all available collateral has been pledged in the first financing round, and there's no borrowing power left to refinance for growth.

Most lenders prefer to cautiously advance a few dollars to nurse the company through the turnaround, and then advance more as the company progresses. But arrange these loans so you know what your lender will do for you in the future. Only then can you be sure you will have the money to both turn around and rebuild your business on agreed benchmarks set by you and your lender.

When projecting your financing needs, prepare a business plan that shows precisely how your loan will be used. Do you need money to:

- Pay creditors?

- Reinventory your business?

- Buy or refurbish equipment?

- Undertake new marketing?

- Finance receivables?

- Replenish working capital?

How much will you need for each? What are your minimum and maximum needs per category? When will you need the financing? Can financing come in stages? What will you pledge for collateral? How do you propose to repay the loan?

Turnarounds, like startup ventures, must be projected cautiously and carefully. Extravagant, grandiose plans won't win financing. Faulty financing plans – like faulty turnaround plans – don't add up to success.

Frugality and a tightwad mentality are the keys to good planning. Plan to work on a shoestring, because a shoestring is about all you will get. But a shoestring mentality is healthy. It forces innovation. You then question every purchase, slash every cost and pare the dollars you thought you needed into the dimes you do need. That drill builds self-discipline and the right perspective on financing. Second-chance financing is only another name for a shoestring loan.

CLOSE-TO-THE-VEST FINANCING

So where do you find money? Don't hop into your car, and head for the bank quite yet. Most turnarounds are bankrolled by what I call close-to-the-vest financing. That's money that comes from your own pocket!

Before you even think of financing your business, make sure you exhaust your businesses resources. Convert every idle asset into hard-working dollars. What can Chapter 8 teach you? What excess inventory or sluggish equipment can you turn to cash? Lenders will want to see that you have exploited every internal resource before they finance you – and you shouldn't reach into your own pocket if money can be found within the business.

Cash that your business cannot produce may have to come from you. Business owners are usually the only ones with sufficient interest and confidence in their business to dig deep enough into their pockets to keep it alive.

Even parent companies nursing sick divisions or ailing subsidiaries finance for only so long, and know when to stop throwing good money after bad. No company can forever feed its losing ventures. The corporate graveyards are littered with the bones of broken companies too slow to cut their losses, and shed their poor performers.

You too must be objective. But as a small-business owner, it's very easy to lose objectivity and make unsound investment decisions concerning your troubled business. Unlike a corporate executive, you are emotionally involved in your enterprise. Emotion can be dangerous to your pocketbook!

There's no hard-and-fast rule that dictates when you should throw more of your own money into a venture. But you will make a sounder decision if you first ask yourself four key questions:

1. How much **can** you invest?

2. How much **should** you invest?

3. How much **will** you invest?

4. **When** will you invest more?

The first question establishes the additional financial risk you and your family can safely absorb without jeopardizing your financial security. What you should invest, however, is determined by what your business can justify as an investment. This, of course, assumes it can be turned around. Any business can consume massive capital, but does the profit potential of your business measure up to the investment you must make?

The amount you invest must always be limited to what you cannot internally finance or get from other loan sources. Use your own money only after you exhaust all other possible financing sources. The final question challenges you to set performance standards and benchmarks to measure your recovery. You can then objectively advance more funds only when you pass each benchmark.

It takes tremendous discipline to deprive your struggling business of those few extra dollars from your own pocket when it is desperate for those dollars. But throwing money at your business doesn't solve problems. And don't throw fresh money into the business until you first have your turnaround plan under way. Only then do you know how your investment can best be utilized. Feed your business slowly so you'll have funds in reserve for contingencies and growth. You want a safe investment, not a good- money-after-bad situation. So advance those few extra dollars only when the indicators say your turnaround is right on target.

Remember that borrowing from a bank by mortgaging your house is not a bank loan. It's your loan. If the business fails, the bank simply takes your house. Every day, I stumble across business people foolishly mortgaged to the hilt to keep their businesses alive. These are the entrepreneurs who first empty their savings, then cash in their life insurance and then finally rob their kids' piggy banks in the blind pursuit of survival. These people eventually find that more money is not the cure, but only after they have nothing left to throw into their business. It's expensive medicine.

Deciding whether, when, and how much to feed your business is difficult. But unless you are confident your company is poised for a rebound, your business doesn't deserve that second-chance financing.

LOANSMANSHIP 101

So zip shut your pocketbook, and put on your walking shoes. While it is easiest to throw more of your own money into the business, it is smartest to throw in someone else's money. How successful will you be in finding that money? The answer depends on three factors: How long you look, how much you look for, and where you look.

1. How long you look:

Check your staying power. You need perseverance when you shop for money to jumpstart a recovering business. You may have to knock on 100 doors before one finally opens. So you can't get discouraged. I have hunted financing for months for several clients who are good financing candidates, and I have been turned down at least a hundred times. Discouraged? Sure. But I m not ready to throw in the towel. And I know I will eventually find the money because the loan proposals are sound. But it may take time – and it can take you more time and effort than you expect to win your refinancing. So start early, and knock on those doors. Yours also will open!

The big reason you may strike out? You may be looking for permanent financing too soon. Go for permanent financing only when your company is stable, and you can show you have the profits to repay the loan. Financing too soon also may force you to give part ownership in the business, a step that could be avoided by waiting until you have a stronger track record and greater borrowing power.

2. What you look for:

Deal making. Forget conventional financing terms when you are in a turnaround. Your deal is what you can bargain for. And to succeed you may have to be a bit of a wheeler-dealer. Every lender has his own motivations and expectations, so you must talk and think in his terms to cement a deal.

Turnarounds mean shaky loans, so unless the loans are backed by solid collateral you will pay a very stiff price. Some lenders and private backers demand two or three times the interest charge for safer investments. Usually, they also will demand a piece of your business as a bonus. Your suppliers, for example, may give a cash or a credit transfusion only because they want your business. For them, interest is secondary. Friends and relatives? You never know what will make them happy. No matter who you talk to, anticipate what will make them open their wallets.

3. Where you can look:

Matching your deal to the right financial backer is half the battle. There are plenty of capitalists in the crowd without pinstripe suits.

You can't stop with banks, the SBA and other conventional lenders. It usually wastes time to even start there.

So where do you look? Here are your best money sources.

START WITH YOUR PRESENT LENDERS

Start with a tap on the shoulders of your present lenders. They may rewrite your loan, and lend you even more money, if you can convince them it is the best way to salvage their present loan.

Lenders may make additional advances if they believe your troubles are behind you, and you won't keep pestering them for more money. The lender's primary concern is whether the additional loan will improve their odds for a total loan recovery. This decision is seldom intuitive. "Essentially, we ask ourselves if we would be throwing good money after bad, or whether it is reasonable bridge financing to rescue the company so it can eventually repay the entire loan," explains one Midwest banker.

Any rescue loan must be reasonable in relationship to the loan at risk. But how much more should be risked to protect a $500,000 loan? Is $25,000 reasonable? Perhaps, but is $250,000? The risk/benefit ratio is judgmental and can vary greatly between lenders. Still, the key to negotiating a rescue loan is to assure your lender that the new money will help the old money come back.

You will get refinanced more quickly if you give your lender additional collateral, subordinations or other protections to help ensure repayment. But remember, if the additional collateral is a mortgage on your own home, then it is your money going into the business, not the bank's.

Lenders can get into a troubled business so deeply that they cannot pull the plug without endangering their loans. This forces them to provide reasonable bridge financing for the turnaround. Even the government refinances its problem borrowers in hopes that a new round of financing will move the business closer to the day the loan can be stamped "paid in full."

LOOK TO ASSET-BASED LENDERS

Asset-based lenders frequently finance turnaround companies. Because they want to be solidly collateralized by hard assets, they worry less about your profits or your ability to repay from earnings. For them, hard collateral is aces over soft promises. Asset-based financing can be used to replace your existing, more conventional lenders, such as banks, which may compromise their loan for a quick cash payment.

New lenders, whoever they are, are reluctant to step into the uncomfortable shoes of another lender in jeopardy. Most new lenders, even asset-based financiers, want several quarters of satisfactory performance to prove your company can perform on its loan before they jump in. New lenders more willingly loan new funds to build the business, rather than to replace old lenders. Finance companies or other higher-risk, asset-based lenders often obtain a priority position on collateral over the existing lenders. The existing lenders agree to subordinate their position because the new financing gives them the best chance to escape the situation with the least possible loss, or often no loss!

A new lender, particularly an asset-based lender, can teach you good cash management. Since these lenders are well-experienced with troubled companies, they are geared to provide specialized audits to monitor assets and to control cash flow more closely than are institutional lenders, who deal mostly with healthy firms.

Conservative banks and institutional lenders want to see a two- or three-year recovery for the turnaround company, so your asset-based lender will probably be a finance company. The more aggressive asset-based lenders will demand higher interest rates, tighter controls over the collateral, hair-trigger default provisions and strong personal guarantees, coupled with additional collateral from outside the company. Your personal guarantees or collateral may have little value and be inconsequential to the overall loan security, but they can commit you more firmly to the future of your company so you don't walk away too easily.

FIND A FACTOR

Do you have accounts receivable? Then factoring may be your answer. Many industries routinely factor their receivables. But factoring can be a costly financing source, as a factor accepts your receivables at a discount of 5 to 10 percent. For the unprofitable or marginally profitable business, a factor's discount can create totally unacceptable losses.

If your company generates sizable receivables and less costly lenders refuse financing, you may have little choice but to turn to factors. Your financial history will not be a problem. Larger factors, such as New York's Access Capital, look primarily to the quality of the receivables, not the creditworthiness of the company. Accounts-receivable factors are an expensive but smart temporary measure until your company gains the financial strength needed to win less costly accounts receivable financing. Even then many companies will remain permanently with factoring arrangements; they prefer the factor's fast cash and are willing to pay a few extra points for it.

ATTRACT VENTURE CAPITALISTS

The $1 million to $20 million firm with fast growth potential following the turnaround may find venture capital the answer.

Venture capitalists, disillusioned with the hi-tech startups that caught their fancy in the '70s and '80s, now invest much of their considerable portfolios in turnaround companies. Savvy venture capitalists appreciate that turnarounds can offer them even higher returns and richer rewards than do rosy-cheeked startups, where fewer than one in 10 become winners. Turnaround companies, with all their blemishes, do considerably better in the long run.

Another attractive feature of the turnaround company: It allows venture capitalists greater involvement in managing the firm, an intrusion not usually welcomed by startup entrepreneurs. Most venture capitalists love to roll up their sleeves and straighten out a corporate cripple.

One venture-capital firm I've worked with on several deals routinely has its own management team orchestrate the turnarounds they finance. The management team stays with the troubled firm for two to five years, departing only when the company is fully stabilized.

Not all venture capitalists succeed with their problem ventures. Some venture capitalists mistakenly believe that having money automatically imparts management smarts. This is not always true. One considerably poorer but now wiser owner who lost his hi- tech firm to a venture-capital group's blunders now admits, "You probably wouldn't hire the venture capitalist as a management consultant, but for some reason when he shows up with money you gladly hand him the helm."

Whether or not venture capitalists have the capability for the job, their motivation is always the enormous financial rewards a fast-growth turnaround can produce. Venture capitalists or "vulture capitalists," as they are sometimes called, will unabashedly bargain for a majority ownership in your company and then advance most of their money as a secured loan. The venture capitalists also are enormously well paid for their management efforts, with attractive options to buy even more of your company based on their making something from nothing.

GO PUBLIC

Several intriguing books have been published in recent years that reveal how to become wealthy by investing in financially troubled companies. Their message: The near-bankrupt company can be a terrific investment for those who understand that the selling price of the ailing company can be much lower than the company's actual worth.

Troubled companies can creatively package a combination of tax benefits, a cleaned-up balance sheet and a hope for a brighter future into an attractive cash-raising public offering.

Whether the turnaround sells common stock, convertible preferred, convertible debentures or debt with warrants, underwriters accept the issue only on a "best-efforts" basis. One major advantage of going public: You'll give up less ownership than with private placement or venture capital.

Surprisingly, some very small companies have financed their future by going public. Often they use a Chapter 11 reorganization, in which it is appreciably easier to sell stock because you bypass most SEC registration requirements when stock is issued as part of a reorganization plan. Nowadays, even small corporations can go public with a minimum of red tape thanks to IPOs or "Initial Public Offerings."

Is your company a good candidate for going public? You are if you have market appeal and growth potential. And if you can attract a venture capitalist, you may as easily attract many individual investors and come out with a much better deal.

ROMANCE AN ANGEL

Perhaps the idea of a bevy of stockholders and venture capitalists doesn't intrigue you. Maybe one working (or silent) partner with cash may do the trick. There are more people looking for good investments than there are good investment opportunities. The trick is to plant your honey pot of a deal outside the right bear caves.

When you look for a working partner with capital, your personal compatibility with the individual is much more important than his or her cash.

Silent partners are generally high-income individuals seeking business deals that can greatly outdistance the potential returns of conventional investments. Doctors, lawyers, executors and other professionals are your best candidates.

Also hunt for candidates experienced in your type of business. They will invest faster because their familiarity with the industry bolsters their confidence. And don't ignore those who can benefit from doing business with you, such as present or prospective suppliers.

Turn your accountant and lawyer into bloodhounds. They probably have clients with investment capital who will heed their recommendations.

Avoid taking money from close relatives or friends. If you lose their money, you lose a valuable relationship. Money turns father against son and brother against brother. Keep relatives and friends out of it. If your business goes bust, you still want to show up at family gatherings and at the poker game with your old pals.

TRY TRADE SUPPLIERS

No company can do business from an empty wagon. Empty shelves mean a silent cash register.

Can trade credit solve your refinancing needs? Low inventories can be rebuilt through trade credit, and that's as good as cash!

Owing heavy accounts payable locks in your trade creditors. Heavily exposed trade creditors are forced to further support you, just like undersecured lenders. They will cooperate with more credit if their risk is small, and if it improves the odds for collecting all that's owed them.

Some trade creditors cling to the old axiom that the first loss is the best loss. You won't sway these creditors. Nor should you cavalierly lose more money for your trade suppliers by accepting credit when you have no realistic chance for repayment. But when the unpleasant reality is that you must have more credit to survive, you and your supplier have various options.

One common solution is to personally guarantee the future credit. Your banks may provide letters of credit or guarantees or subordinate their security interest on collateral to trade creditors. W.T. Grant's banks guaranteed more than $100 million in new shipments of merchandise to restock the troubled retailer. Limit your exposure to what is reasonable under the circumstances. Because a guarantee is the same as a personal investment, watch your exposure.

Even highly encumbered businesses can secure new shipments of goods. If the goods are identifiable, a purchase-money-security interest, a trust receipt or a field warehouse receipt can secure the supplier. I have used consignment agreements to remerchandise quite a few retail businesses. Many manufacturers are anxious to open new outlets, and stock them on a consignment basis. Retailers often discover new and more profitable merchandise lines once they scout consignment sources. A three-store Boston ladies-apparel chain accepted on consignment a new line of artificial furs to augment its skimpy dress inventory. The small chain soon discontinued dresses in favor of its new fur line. Now revitalized, the chain has 20 artificial fur salons, another example of how companies find opportunity from adversity.

The urgent demand for merchandise can forge strong relationships between supplier and customer and often creates a partnership. The supplier sees the takeover of a troubled distributor or retailer as an innovative, potentially profitable opportunity to sell more goods. The inventory-poor business sees the supplier as its lifeline to essential merchandise. Business-school professors call it vertical integration, but marriages between supplier and customer may be a common-sense way to revitalize a business.

Not having the money to restock your business can bring you to new levels of creativity.

I like to tell the story of what happened in my town when a local supermarket failed, and two young chaps took control of the lease. Desperate and penniless, the entrepreneurial pair had neither the money nor the credit to inventory the store. Nor did they intend to. Instead, they shrewdly leased the various food departments to established local merchants. A nearby butcher set up a meat boutique, a local produce distributor became the "greengrocer," and a bakery chain grabbed at the chance to add its tempting baked goods, all surrounding fully stocked shelves rack- jobbed by a food wholesaler. The young owners, for their part, coordinate the advertising and operate the checkout registers, but each pockets more than $80,000 a year in profits without investing one nickel in inventory! Innovation and imagination is more valuable than cash.

MONEY, MONEY EVERYWHERE

Money. Money. Money. There's no end to where you can find some.

■ How about the SBA? Yes, they make loans even to stumbling companies – if the loan won't be used to pay unsecured creditors. When your bank says no, the SBA may be your next step.

■ How about your customers? If you supply an essential or hard-to-find service, they may bankroll you rather than lose you.

■ Can your business be converted into one of the thousands of successful franchised outlets that dot America? A franchisor in your industry might finance your recovery if he or she thinks that your business would make a good franchised outlet.

■ Do you deal with the government? Call the Chamber of Commerce, which can tell you about loan programs available for your type of business.

■ What about your employees? Do they have enough confidence to buy a piece of your business? Maybe they only have to loan you those few dollars to pay the rent so you can give them their next paycheck.

Where will you find your money? Whether it's a dribble or several million, the money is out there. Be an optimist, like old Casey Stengel, who simply announced when his New York Yankees returned from a 0-12 road trip, "You can't win them all."

That message should ring loud and clear in this chapter. You may not find cash on your first try. You may have to beat the pavement, and accept terms that will make your life somewhat harder. But regardless of how you borrow, or from whom you borrow, when your business needs cash to survive, you go and get it!

NEGOTIATING YOUR BEST DEAL

Whether your new financiers are commercial banks, asset-based finance companies or venture capitalists, keep certain realities in mind.

First, your financier has the negotiating power, whether he is a lender or investor. There are generally many more companies in search of funds than there are capital sources looking to throw money into ailing enterprises. You need not beg, but a dose of humility can't hurt.

That warning doesn't mean you should cave in and reach for the first financing deal you're offered. Desperate, anxious companies give away too much. You will strike your very best financing deal if you can finance yourself in the turnaround as much as possible. Delay refinancing until your company is stabilized, and you have more bargaining power. But put out your feelers as early as possible. As your workout progresses, continuously contact your potential finance sources so you know what financing is available when you are ready.

Nor should you count on new financing to bail out your unsecured debts. This is particularly true with investors. Investors don't invest to save a businesses, but to a build businesses. Clean up your balance sheet before you search for permanent financing. If your new financing is to replace existing loans, have your "takeout" agreements ready with your existing lenders.

Know how your prospective lender operates. Check whether your prospective lender will support your future growth with the same fervor he protects himself from your failure. Many turnaround lenders are too preoccupied with complex protective mechanisms, such as loan covenants, board representation and the accelerated conversion of warrants. They also may ignore their loan commitments to finance your company's growth. How your prospective lender responds to your opportunities is as important as what it will do in rough weather.

A mismatch between lender and borrower occurs when neither knows enough about the other. Your lenders should look beyond your collateral and cash flows and talk to your key managers, employees, suppliers, customers and competitors.

You, in turn, must investigate the lender's relationship with other borrowers. Is the lender flexible or rigid? How long a relationship has the lender had with its borrowers? Are there signs of overreaching or coercive or slippery practices by the lender?

You both must clearly understand the financier's role in the workout plan. Not only must you and your lender agree on the basic turnaround strategy and future direction for your company, but you also must review the possible contingencies and alternatives and candidly discuss what would happen should these contingencies materialize. You also must set performance benchmarks, the timetable to review performance, the rewards for success and the penalties for poor performance.

You and your lender also must understand in advance the lender's managerial or financial control. Companies entering into major financing frequently lose the managerial and financial autonomy they once enjoyed, as the lender constantly peers over their shoulders.

Venture capitalists, for instance, will pressure you for fast growth as they inevitably want fast, if not spectacular, returns. This may be beyond the reach of your company, or not what you want for your business. Few turnaround companies burst into full bloom quickly. Financiers with an equity position in your company may have unrealistic expectations for the company – expectations you may encourage when you are anxious to attract funds.

HOW TO ZERO IN ON THE MONEY

There are literally millions of banks, finance companies, venture capitalists and other financiers who want to talk to you about your opportunities. The trouble is that each has its own niche – the amount they will loan, the type of business they lend to, repayment terms and equity participation. That's why financing is so hard to land. While there are plenty of doors, the odds of knocking on the right door can be absolutely staggering.

Well, here's one solution: Subscribe to a valuable service called the *Turnaround Loan Locator.* For a nominal fee, they will send you a database of hundreds of potential loan sources, matched to your company and your precise needs. This program lets you target the finance sources that most want to hear from you. The *Turnaround Loan Locator* is listed in the appendix.

Do your homework before you call. You will need a detailed loan proposal showing six points:

1. The loan amount you request

2. The minimum loan you will accept

3. What you will do with the money

4. Who else you will borrow from

5. How you propose to repay

6. What collateral you offer

Since these same questions will be asked by any lender, it will pay to get started today.

WHEN YOU STRIKE OUT

You may still strike out no matter how many doors you knock on. This can be helpful if it pinpoints a serious weakness in either your business or your proposal. So don't stroll on to your next prospect until you find out why you were rejected. Lenders may not answer candidly because they want neither to offend nor to engage in prolonged discussion on an unmade deal. But push for a reason.

Your lender may point out weaknesses you overlooked or raise unanswered questions other lenders also will ask. Listen closely. Pick a brain.

You may strike out because your company's long-term prospects remain poor. Your case for refinancing is strongest if your business suffered that one definable catastrophe. Your prospects are nil when your company suffers from obvious mismanagement, prolonged losses or a pattern of fraud or creditor abuse.

Even when circumstances favor financing, your lenders will want to see that you first exhausted your internal sources of cash. And tapping your internal resources is important because negotiating outside financing takes time. You must inevitably live off your assets until then. So finance only after you've harvested your internal resources. Maximize what you already have, and you have your cheapest and quickest source of capital.

☑CHECKPOINT

1. How much money do you need for your business?

2. Have you tapped your internal resources to the fullest extent possible?

3. Who are your best loan sources?

4. Have you zipped shut your pocketbook?

5. What are you prepared to give a lender?

6. Have you been turned down for a loan? Why?

17

ON YOUR WAY

If you glance back on the stories of America's Fortune 500 companies, you will see that most stumbled on the climb up. And a good many continuously stumble and are still stumbling. Somehow each lifted itself up, dusted itself off and started again.

The business world is a lot like the tune: ups and downs, pauses and spurts. When you make money and put your problems behind you, your momentum builds again. Once again, cash flow and trade credit are yours because you promptly pay your suppliers. Banks and other lenders know that you don't have merely an idea, but a winning venture in the making.

Prospective partners now will see opportunity, not risk. You are finally poised to expand and grow. You have marshalled assets, power and influence. Your future comes from trading on what you have done, not on what you might do! Sickly acorns do grow mighty oaks. Some examples:

- *Derwood Creamery was mired in Chapter 11 bankruptcy in 1984 and failing badly with anemic, $400,000-a-year sales. Today, this fast-growth company operates 42 humming ice cream shops generating more than $20 million in revenue every year.*

- *Alpha-Tectronics couldn't even pay its 14 employees in 1982. Now, perched on Boston's busy Route 128, Alpha owns 16 computer software-related firms that dot New England. Alpha's profits this year are more than 20 times its total 1982 sales!*

- *In 1988, Pilgrim Press was just another tired Detroit printing company barely able to stay ahead of its creditors. By switching from the printing industry to publishing newsletters and other niche publications, Pilgrim quintupled its sales and profits in only a few short years.*

Derwood, Alpha and Pilgrim are everyday humdrum businesses compared to the skyrocketing mega-corporations featured in business books and magazines. But these are the businesses that probably are most like yours – small companies, that in their own unique way, stuck their necks out of one trench and ran like hell for the next. Who knows? If you keep running, you may someday head a mega-corporation.

Then again, maybe you won't make it to the next trench. The most dangerous phase of the turnaround is when you think you're on firm footing and can once again venture forward. We have all seen companies with the ink barely dry on their Chapter 11 bankruptcy confirmation go on a binge buying other companies, or racing to grow at breakneck speed.

This daredevil growth on a still shaky foundation explains why four out of five companies that make it through Chapter 11 bankruptcy won't last more than two years. Most of these companies never really resolved their problems. And yet others that transformed themselves into reasonably profitable and solvent enterprises, fatally overestimated their strength and bit off more than they could chew.

A successful turnaround is like an aphrodisiac. You suddenly feel omnipotent. You catch a second breath, and forget where you were two years before.

So when and how do you grow? When is it smarter to stand pat? What are the booby traps as you shake off your past and begin to move forward?

EMPIRE BUILDING

Who needs an empire? A rhetorical question? Hardly. Your venture will someday fly high and be ready to grow. Will you be the one holding it back?

You will if you are a "who needs it?" type. You work your fingers to the bone to build a successful business that gives you a comfortable income. Ambition then runs out, and your business is stalled in a holding pattern. You rationalize, "How many steaks a day can I eat?"

I won't preach on how you should live your life. That's for you to decide. Plenty of people are happiest running a small, steady business. Wheeling and dealing and collecting businesses like squirrels collect nuts is not for them. And it may not be for you.

Still, no business remains absolutely static. You either move forward or move back, however gradually. So you must necessarily nudge your business one notch higher, even if it is a tiny notch. Only growth keeps you from sliding back.

A quiet, complacent life may not be your cup of tea. More than a few of my more entrepreneurial clients have striven to grow their acorn businesses into mighty oaks. I know I have. That's why a few of my clients and friends get together with me and like war veterans at a reunion exchange business experiences. They tell fascinating stories on how they launched and built their businesses. There's a thrill in their voices. Most admit that building the business, not running the business, was the fun part.

"It's easy to sit back, rest on your laurels and let the business take you where it wants to go," counsels one chap who started with a tiny bicycle rental shop in a Cape Cod resort town and ended with 15 thriving businesses, ranging from a car dealership to a partnership in a large restaurant.

You rarely build for the money alone. You build for the thrill and challenge. Ego. Power. Drive. Satisfaction. Whatever it is, some itch drives you to build a business. Feel itchy?

BIGGER CAN BE BETTER

Growth invigorates. Growth creates energy, excitement and a sense of accomplishment. But running a bigger business need not interfere with your leisurely lifestyle or make you a workaholic. In fact, I found that running a larger business is considerably easier than running a smaller venture for four powerful reasons:

1. You gain staying power.

One small business spells vulnerability. Blow your business, and you're out of business. A well-organized larger business stays alive when one or two of its parts die.

Speaking as an entrepreneur, I made this reality my driving force. Can you afford to put all your eggs in one basket? A thousand and one things can quickly kill one business – even a successful business. It may be a devastating competitor, a landlord who won't renew your lease, or a fatal labor strike. That's why I always spread my risk and opportunities by operating several independent businesses. You, too, are secure only as long as you are in business. But with millions of ventures closing each year, owning one business isn't much security. Can you predict how long your one business will last?

Imagine beginning your day at your appliance stores, taking lunch at your car dealership, mid-afternoon tea at your sporting- goods chain, and finally checking sales at your movie theater before heading home.

Now that entrepreneur is Ken Volpi, a Seattle daredevil eager to tackle any business. Ken finds the right people to operate his businesses, and then sits back and watches the money roll in. Ken grew up poor in Cincinnati and watched as his father's garment business was wiped out during the Depression. Ken learned about vulnerability from his father's bitter experience, and decided his only security was operating several very different businesses.

"If one industry is down, another is bound to be up," Ken theorizes. "Besides, I enjoy the variety of challenges, problems, and opportunities that comes from a spicy mix of ventures," he says. Would you?

2. You gain cash-flow power.

Cash-flow power is staying power. Cash flow from multi- operations can cover the slumps of any one business. Peaks balance valleys. Every business has ups and downs. But where do you get cash to survive when your one business goes into a long sales slump or suffers severe losses? Multi-operations mean each business has a sister business to turn to if money ever gets tight.

For many businesses, growth creates a more stable cash flow. These businesses may operate in different areas to balance seasonal fluctuations, or they may use their cash-cow businesses to finance those burdened with slow receivables.

If you have been victimized by poor cash flow, taking on more businesses can smooth those rough spots.

3. You gain buying power.

Businesses are forced to expand because size alone allows them to compete with the chains and discounters. Retailing is very competitive. Small family-owned clothing, liquor, drug, food, hardware and toy stores, to name a few, fail primarily because of their weak-buying power. A small retailer in a competition-free location can survive. In a more competitive environment, you must match your competition on their terms. That means buying right because customers do watch prices.

Advertising power is equally important. Statistics of failed independent retailers show that poor marketing and weak advertising are two major causes of bankruptcy.

My neighbor and golf partner, Dick Safford, now owns a chain of twelve successful jewelry stores. For the first time, Dick can afford large space ads in the major newspapers. Since Dick began his aggressive ad campaign, his sales have grown more than 30 percent. Can you afford to reach your customers? If not, it's time to grow!

4. You gain management power.

The opportunity to build a talent-rich organization is, in my opinion, the best reason to expand. Growing into a larger business is the best way to support the solid management team you need to succeed. Running a small one-person show makes you a generalist in an era of specialists. And your life becomes easier when you have a few specialists aboard.

It takes no more time or effort to run a larger operation than a smaller one. With a large operation, you spend your time on more important decisions. A strong team to help you manage your business may free you from the chains of running your one-person show.

None of these arguments to grow may make sense to you. Maybe Joe Tevald, the only mechanic I know who drives a Rolls Royce, says it more convincingly: "I need a Rolls to comfortably drive between my 68 gas stations. The real fun is owning 'em, not working 'em."

TEST THE TIMING

With your toe in the water with a business of your own, you have endured the hardest part: The cold water of doubt. You wondered whether you would make it. Since you haven't drowned, growing your business should be relatively easy. Why not? You not only have your feet wet, but you also are a good swimmer. Add a few more strokes, and you will soon be an Olympic champion!

But before you swim into deeper water, you must know your destination and whether you have the skill and stamina to reach it. Those are the essential questions. The next few pages will help you discover some answers, but for now don't try to look too far into the future. You cannot foresee events five or ten years from now. Look only to next year. Take one small step at a time, but make each step the right step!

When can you again grow? As with all management decisions, timing is critical. You can't grow if your business isn't strong enough to support growth. Eager-beaver entrepreneurs who grow too fast run the risk of a business tumbling around their feet. If you are too cautious, you stifle the progress your business needs and can safely undertake. You must walk the timing tightrope.

There are several ground rules to follow: First, you cannot grow until your business is running profitably and has the surplus cash it needs to finance its growth. Cash flow is all-important. A profitable business with a negative cash flow is not a growth candidate.

Growth must put your excess cash where it will do the most good. Don't grow if those same dollars can give you a better return by improving the performance of your present operation. Growth is a competitive process. Your existing business must compete with the growth opportunities for your limited capital and other scarce resources. But which investment offers you the best return? Weigh your decision carefully.

Second, estimate when your expanded operation will break even. Then cautiously estimate whether you can support it until the break-even point is reached. Few growing businesses become profitable rapidly. Most require considerable time. But there are exceptions.

I once consulted a small but fast-expanding chain of doughnut shops. Doughnuts are an incredible business. A well-located doughnut shop can be profitable a week after its doors open. Since each new doughnut shop drains very little cash, the chain's growth was limited only by its ability to find good locations, hire good help, raise financing and prepare each shop for opening.

Here was a business that could grow with amazing speed, provided each shop made money and its management team stayed strong. Most businesses have a less meteoric rise because their profitability is less certain, and you can consume considerable cash before you make your first dollar.

Play your own "what if" game. Ask: "What if my expansion plan fails? How will it affect my existing business?" Evaluating risk is a key part of the growth strategy. If you must risk what you have to finance expansion, then move slowly, very slowly! One misstep could kill your entire business and everything you fought to save.

In my younger, more entrepreneurial days, I quickly expanded my small drugstore chain. What did I do right? I set up the company so each store could stand on its own financially and legally. Some stores made money; others didn't. But with each store legally independent, one failure posed no financial threat to the others. This is how to grow – opportunity with little or no risk!

Growth can be push or pull. You "push" to expand because you have a solid foundation on which to grow and genuine opportunity through expansion. You are "pulled" to expand to save your present operation by building the business to a viable size.

You could see the "push-pull" theory at work with an appliance retailer who, barely able to run one business, found himself running three. His stores were losing a bundle. One look at his financials and we could see that our options were either to downsize quickly or expand. If we downsized to one store, my client could operate it, but would it have the buying power he needed? Would the profits be sufficient to make the venture worthwhile?

On the other hand, we could literally go for broke by opening a fourth or even fifth store. Their additional sales could support a stronger management staff. If these newer stores earned big profits, they could turn the entire chain into a winner!

Which way would you go?

It's a very common decision. Many businesses are now losing their shirts, and the more money they lose, the faster they want to grow. They chase cash flow to cover their losses. But this can be smart. As long as there is forward movement, there is the possibility the business can reach critical mass and be shaped into a profitmaker. This also is true when you downsize. Standing still when the business can't stand on its own feet is always fatal.

Perhaps you must grow to cover your fixed overhead (and your own big salary). A small Miami computer store tried to pay each of its three partners $500 a week. But you can't pay $75,000 a year for salaries when the business only grosses $120,000 and has many other expenses.

The choice was expansion or splitting up the partnership, leaving the business to one partner that the business could easily support. The young, enthusiastic partners enjoyed their close working and personal relationships and so they expanded into computer repairs. Their business soon had enough volume to cover the three-partner payroll, plus give each a big bonus!

UNLEASH YOUR GROWTH POWER

You say you have no money to grow? You may be right. Most just-turned-the-corner businesses fight to stay alive with precious few dollars. Then again, you may have plenty of growth power right in your business and just not realize it.

You learned a few tactics to squeeze cash out of your business to survive. Now learn how to wring out more money to grow. It shouldn't be difficult; you already mastered the basic lessons.

I frequently teach management courses at local colleges. My students are mostly seasoned business veterans looking for capital for a wide variety of reasons. But regardless of who they are, I ask them this one question, "What cash can each of you squeeze from your existing business?"

At their forlorn looks and sideways nods, I give my standard war cry: There **is** plenty of money to be found right under your feet!

Katie, a young super-charged retailer, waved her financial statements at me one week, obviously anxious to put me to the test. "Show me how I can get money out of my fabric shop so I can open another store," she challenged. I love challenges, especially when a small fee is involved. So our bargain was struck!

I first slashed Katie's inventory by deep-discounting her slow-moving overstocks, producing $60,000!

Katie foolishly paid C.O.D. for her merchandise, so I then negotiated 30-day credit terms with her suppliers. This gave us another $30,000. Some spare office furniture and equipment were sold for another $4,000.

Katie now nearly had $100,000 in her bank, and the fun was just starting. The big money came from a trip to Katie's bank for an $80,000 loan. The account now stood at $180,000. But how much money do you need to open a fabric shop? Katie estimated $100,000, but she never learned shoestring economics. A month later, Katie launched her second store in a nearby shopping center. Her $50,000 inventory ($40,000 purchased on lenient credit terms) and $12,000 in fixtures and equipment (leased for no cash down) looked magnificent.

Katie's empire grew from a paltry few thousand dollars. With plenty of money in the bank, Katie now had even more growth power. There's growth power in your business. Unleash it!

1. Check your new borrowing power.

You say your financial troubles ruined your credit? There are solutions. Even the recently troubled business can build borrowing power. What new equity does your business have since its turnaround? Are assets up and debts down? Have you demonstrated a good track record since your turnaround? This is always a bankable item. One banker recently confided to me, "The turnaround business is the best candidate for growth financing. These businesses are tempered by experience and weathered their financial storms. Balance sheets are clean and its troubles left behind. A new business, on the other hand, is untried and untested. Its problems lie ahead."

2. Make your assets work harder.

A business with excess or idle assets is a business whose growth power is on its shelves. So why did Heritage Crafts operate its one store with a hefty $140,000 inventory when a $70,000 inventory could nicely support its sales? Heritage wisely became two stores, and nearly doubled its sales with the same amount of inventory.

Trimming your inventory can release enormous amounts of cash. Suppliers may substitute new merchandise for returns of overstocks or a "fire sale" can turn inventory into cash. And what idle equipment or real estate do you now have that represents growth- power capital? Complete these exercises before your turnaround and not afterwards, when you should already be that lean and mean organization. Every company has fat to trim. Fat is growth power!

3. Use your credit clout.

The very same suppliers who chased you for payment yesterday may be thrilled to give you even more credit today. Of course, you may not believe it because you vividly recall those nasty phone calls and glaring stares from the rear of the bankruptcy court. Still, memories fade. Once you rebuild a good payment record with your suppliers, there's no reason to be bashful about credit. You should demand reasonable credit – even if it's a small amount that will increase as you prove yourself. Establish credit, even if you prefer to operate without credit. You may need credit to cover temporary or unexpected cash-flow problems. And credit is critical for growth power because it does free up cash. Growing without credit is growing half as fast!

Leverage is the game of business, and you lose leverage unless you prudently use every dime of credit that is available to you. I commonly encounter businesses with modest accounts payable that can easily and safely be increased to free growth capital.

Stretching your payments to suppliers from 30 days to 60 days gives you growth power equal to one month's purchases. Buy $500,000 a month, and you have a lot of money and growth power. Fortune-500 companies pay more sluggishly than smaller businesses because they learned to wheel and deal their way to an empire using their creditors' money. You can, too – but do it cautiously so you don't get into trouble again.

4. Prospect for big dollars.

Tapping your assets and inner resources can take you only so far, so fast. Fresh equity capital can help you grow much faster and more safely.

A partner may be your best financing source. You can strike a considerably better bargain with partners after the turnaround than before the turnaround. Taking on a partner or two may be a matter of timing.

It was for Cy Cunningham, who wanted to expand his medical billing firm in Akron, Ohio, to handle third-party billings for local dentists, physicians and pharmacies. Cy estimated $150,000 would be needed to fund this expansion, but Cy's best offer was $75,000 for a 50 percent interest in his growing business. Wisely, Cy turned down the offer. Instead, he borrowed $100,000 from the bank and ten of his largest physician accounts financed another $60,000. Cy is heavily leveraged, but he owns it all.

Within three years, Cy's enormously profitable business became debt-free. Cy decided to repeat his success story by opening branch offices in Cleveland, Cincinnati, and Toledo. Cy earnestly went after partners to raise the $800,000 in expansion capital.

Convinced that the business had a terrific future, a large computer firm invested the entire $800,000 for a 30 percent interest in the business. Best of all, the computer firm committed to loan the business another $1.5 million to expand further. Cy knew that if he had given away 50 percent of his business when he needed the small dollars to scrape by, he would have ended up with very little ownership in the company when it came time to chase those bigger dollars to grow.

Timing is critical when hunting equity capital. You may sell a piece of your business too soon, and in the process, give up too much. Others wait too long and fail. These firms couldn't sustain themselves or reach their profit potential without a cash transfusion. There is that perfect moment to pull in a partner or two, but for each business, it's a different moment. Watch for your perfect moment!

THE FIVE UNIVERSAL LAWS OF PERPETUAL SUCCESS

As we end our journey together, I offer parting advice as I send you on your way toward a brighter future: The five universal laws of perpetual success.

Law 1: Don't build on quicksand.

Make certain your business is solid, smooth-running and in good financial shape before you grow.

Connie and John Krasnow are like so many people who stumble on this point. The Krasnows ran two nursing homes in southern New Hampshire and prematurely opened their third. "We weren't ready for it; it was as simple as that," admits Connie. "Our two existing homes were too deeply in debt and losing money. Nor did we have a blueprint to correct the situation. We were probably running away from our two nightmares by thinking a third would somehow solve our problems."

Even when you operate on reasonably firm footing, your foundation may not be as firm as you think. Consider the strength of your business and what additional strain can be safely absorbed. Also consider stability. Any turnaround needs a solid year or two of good, steady performance before it can confidently undertake ambitious growth. Make growth your objective, but make it a lasting growth that results from cautious growth.

Law 2: Don't bite off more than you can chew.

Grow gradually and deliberatively, with each step a logical advance that is easily assimilated in terms of management, markets, money and know-how.

Allen Van Kamp, a management consultant with the firm by the same name, claims that the most common growth error is moving into new ventures that the existing organization isn't equipped to handle.

"And what a firm may not be able to handle covers a lot of territory," says Van Kamp. "The most dangerous error is venturing outside your field. The bankruptcy courts are loaded with such misplaced companies. Someone successfully operates four or five restaurants and suddenly buys a hotel. But what do they know about hotels? Size is another stumbling block. People with the management mentality for a $300,000-a-year business tackle a $3 million operation requiring considerably different skills. Don't bite off more than you can chew. Stay with what you know and what you can handle!

Law 3: Watch cash flow.

Acquisitions must stand on their own two feet and not drain cash from existing operations. Growth takes financial support. Make sure you know what the support payments will be and that you can afford them.

Deficit operations topple even the most stable company when there is too little cash to support the drain. "My best advice is to set firm limits on the money you will pour into a new venture," offers Paul Pellini, who, refusing to admit defeat, drained $240,000 from his once successful Pellini Bakery to keep his second bakery afloat. And it floated just long enough to sink both of Pellini's businesses.

My personal postscript is that whenever I set up a new business, I create a set-cash reserve. That's it. If the reserve won't see the business through the survival stage, the business simply doesn't survive. You must determine ahead of time when to turn off the spigot, or you may work on blind emotion and throw caution to the wind in a desperate struggle to keep going.

Law 4: Protect yourself.

Chapter 10 taught you how to transform your business into a creditor-proof fortress. Damage control is no less important when you expand and grow. Adopt the same strategies to protect what you now have – if your expanding empire topples. For starters, incorporate each business separately. If one goes sour, it won't destroy your good businesses.

"Correct legal organization is critical when expanding," counsel Frank Lainer and Keith McCarthy, who once owned a prosperous greeting card and gift shop in a Chicago mall. "We foolishly used our original corporation for our second store in a suburban mall. The mall turned out to be a dud, and we lost $120,000, which our corporation couldn't absorb even with one healthy store. So we filed bankruptcy and lost everything. With foresight, we would have separately incorporated our second store to protect our first."

Never ignore these business-protection strategies: Titling valuable assets outside your operating company? Friendly mortgages? Controlling your lease? Remember, the bigger you are, the harder you fall – unless you follow my good advice!

Law 5: Never forget your humble past.

Growth dims memories. And when you grow helter-skelter, you see only the future and too easily forget your past.

Now take my final advice. Through your past you gained your winning formula. You scrounged for pennies and wrung a dollar from each dime. You fought the odds, gambled on the risks, and won your own way. You've battled everyone and everything to survive. You've reached the point where there's an extra buck in the bank.

You have undoubtedly changed, just as your business has changed. And you'll change even more before you hit the finish line. But you do have a heritage – and a mighty proud heritage. Not everyone ends a survivor. But once a survivor, always a survivor!

☑CHECKPOINT

1. *What are your growth objectives? Do you really want to grow your business? Why?*

2. *How can growth benefit your business? How can it hurt it?*

3. *When will the time be right for your business to expand? Are your benchmarks realistic?*

4. *What is your growth power? How much expansion cash is available to you?*

5. *When would be the best time to take in partners? What would be your best deal?*

6. *What is your growth strategy? What are its potential pitfalls?*

18

PSSST!
WANNA BUY A BUSINESS?

There is a time to be born and a time to die, a time to laugh and a time to cry. So says the Bible. And there's a time to sell if your business is rock-bound. So says common sense!

To sell or not to sell? The trick is to assess the pros and cons realistically.

THE "WHAT IF" FACTOR

What if...

- You or an associate has a brilliant idea for breathing productive new life into your enterprise?

  Hang on **if** you have unshakable faith in the brainstorm!

- Lenders and creditors are pressuring you to sell?

  Hang on **if,** despite the pressures, you believe it's in your best interests to persist!

- Your business may still have a good profit potential, but you're not sure?

  Hang on **if** a consultant you believe in advises you to do so.

On the other hand, what if...

- Emotionally beaten and mentally exhausted from wrestling with constant problems and pressures, you feel your health may be at risk?
  Sell!

- You may lack the skills, energy, interest or resources needed for a successful turnaround?
  Sell!

- You fear that hanging on will mean throwing good money after bad, and you will incur further losses?
  Sell!

- A realistic evaluation of your business's potential is dismal?
  Sell!

- Your business still has a spark of life, but you can't get along with your S.O.B of a partner?
  Sell the business to your partner or to somebody else if you can't agree on a deal. Or persuade your partner to sell the business to you.

- You are convinced your business is headed for bankruptcy?
  Sell before you go bankrupt, which would result in the minimum benefit for you and your creditors.

- Profitable or not, your business is tearing your marriage apart?
  Sell if your marriage is more important to you than your business.

TWO'S COMPANY

My old college pal, Bernie Kopel, is a matchmaker, always on the lookout for a healthy firm interested in marrying a sick business. As Bernie puts it, "They often produce profitable offspring."

Bernie recounts some of his latest corporate weddings:

Broadway Cadillac to Evans Leasing. "A marriage made in heaven," says Bernie. The Caddy dealer couldn't sell enough cars to stay alive, while Evans was buying about 800 Cadillacs a year to nourish its expanding fleet. So Evans bought 50 percent of Broadway. Evans now buys its cars at dealer's cost and Broadway has the volume to win lower prices from General Motors.

Cornwall Stationery and Hutton Paper Corporation also are on a blissful honeymoon, says Bernie. Cornwall, gasping in Chapter 11 without the funds to survive, had six valuable store leases. Hutton, on the prowl for high-traffic locations, wasted no time becoming the anxious suitor. Hutton bought Cornwall, bailed it out of Chapter 11 and added six more winning locations to its fast- growing chain.

Capital Wallpaper and Economy Paint made another stunning couple. Capital languished on one end of a struggling shopping center while Economy, with its dismal sales and exorbitant overhead, suffered several stores away. Romance was inevitable. Joining forces, they relocated to a busy thoroughfare and proudly announced the birth of Economy Paint and Wallpaper Co.

Bernie explains why he is so busy as a corporate matchmaker. "There are thousands of failing firms. My job is to discover their charms. When I find those hidden charms, I don't have to sell. It's love at first sight."

SHOULD YOU HEAR WEDDING BELLS?

Small business owners are do-or-die fanatics who often plunder everything they own to stay alive. Then their businesses die.

A marriage is the right alternative if your firm can't achieve a turnaround and become the business you want it to be. Many of my clients wisely bailed out by selling.

Carlton Sales found selling was the perfect solution to its problem. Carlton, a large Chicago housewares distributor, was hit hard when Macy's filed for Chapter 11.

"Macy's owed us $470,000, which we had to write off," recalls Carlton's Owner, Norman. "And Macy's represented two-thirds of our business. We worried about our own survival and filed our own Chapter 11 to buy time, although we were losing money steadily and couldn't cover expenses. Our creditors wanted us liquidated before our assets completely disappeared.

"Solutions? We knew we couldn't reorganize, but we thought our company could be valuable to someone. After all, we still had some inventory and several strong accounts. That's what attracted Hillsboro Housewares, our oldest competitor, which bought 60 percent of Carlton's shares. And Carlton's sales became profitable when added to their own.

"Selling to Hillsboro turned out to be our only alternative. I lost control of Carlton, but my interest in the company is worth something. We'll do $7 million this year, and I get a good salary as Carlton's sales manager. That's better than watching Carlton liquidated and ending up with nothing but an unemployment check."

I see it every day. Owners struggle to survive but never quite make it. When their businesses finally collapse, they lose everything. If only they'd called Bernie Kopel and said, "OK, I can't save my business, but my business must be worth something to somebody. Can you help me cut a deal that will get me something?"

Some owners hunt for a mate even when they can muster the resources to save their company. "Survival doesn't prompt every marriage," insists Bernie. "Some owners decide that combining with a stronger company can produce far greater profits." Several of my own cases prove he's right.

R&T Printing crept along for years with profitless sales. Their problems weren't dramatic, but they did have some nagging debts which we solved. When I forced the owners to consider their bleak future with the firm, they merged with another small printer. Consolidating their overhead, they now have a healthy profit.

"Selling was the smartest decision of my life," reports Marilyn, a young Philadelphia entrepreneur who started her Computer Carnival on a shoestring. "We were undercapitalized from the first day. We were growing, but we couldn't finance our growth. So I sold to a public corporation for shares worth $650,000. They had the money to exploit our ideas."

Today, Computer Carnival does $12 million annually. Held back by Marilyn's limited capital, it would only be undeveloped potential.

Some owners refuse marriage even when it's their only alternative. Mel spent every waking moment trying to save his troubled Lifeway Health Food chain, which needed at least $500,000 in fresh capital. Mel couldn't even afford the $150-a-month lease payments on his Honda Civic. Trying to help Mel before he lost everything, I proposed he sell to a health-food manufacturer who offered Mel $175,000 for his interest in Lifeway. Mel wouldn't budge. Lifeway was his baby; "Not for Sale" was his lullaby.

So I tried a different approach on another round with Mel. A vitamin manufacturer agreed to loan Lifeway $500,000 and acquire 40 percent ownership in the company for another $100,000. The vitamin manufacturer knew that Lifeway could sell tons of its vitamins.

Mel remained the unwilling bride. He didn't want my "deals." He was hanging tough and didn't need help.

Mel watched his pride and joy auctioned off to the vitamin manufacturer who picked up the business for a paltry $80,000. Two weeks earlier, Mel could have been handed $100,000 from the same buyer, and he would still have owned most of the company.

You must sense when it's time to get married. The right company can bail you out if it provides you essential:

- Capital or financing

- Inventory or product lines

- Added income or more profitable distribution

- Management to help you navigate your turnaround and grow.

It doesn't always pay to be that rugged individual. Hooking up with someone who has resources you need cannot only keep you alive, but also create the synergy for a new and enormously profitable business combo.

FLAUNT YOUR HIDDEN CHARMS

The big question is why would someone be interested in you? The answer: Assets that can be valuable to someone else are under your mountain of debts. You must learn to flaunt those assets as bargaining chips Here are four big selling pints you can easily overlook:

1. Leases:

Does your company hold valuable leases?
Remember Cornwall Stationery? When Cornwall filed Chapter 11, its tangible assets were worth less than $300,000 and its liabilities exceeded $800,000. Cornwall's owner didn't think his debt-ridden company would interest anyone, but he was sitting on a hidden gold mine. Cornwall held six long-term leases in the best shopping malls, and the leases were real bargains: Cornwall's rents averaged $10,000 below market per location.

Hutton Paper wanted those bargain leases, and that's why the company paid Cornwall $400,000. When Hutton took over, it paid creditors $250,000 on the $800,000 they were owed and went on to build Cornwall into a healthy 36-store company. Hutton made a smart move.

Cornwall never thought much about their leases. Maybe you haven't either.

2. Customers have a big value:

Can you channel your customers to another company in exchange for an interesting proposition?
When Harry's Chilton Produce Supply began to fail due to strong competition and poor sales, Harry was ready to throw his company into bankruptcy. But why let competitors grab 400 retail accounts for nothing? Instead, Harry approached Pathmark Food, one of his major competitors, and soon had a deal. Harry would refer his customers over to Pathmark and aggressively follow up to keep the accounts loyal. In turn, Pathmark paid Harry 3 percent of all sales made by Pathmark from Harry's accounts. Last year, sales amounted to $2 million, and Harry happily picked up a $60,000 commission check. "It's like an annuity," says Harry. "And more money than I made running Chilton."

And what are 600 landscaping accounts worth? Evergreen Landscaping Service will soon find out because its owner, Mario, wants to dump his unprofitable landscaping service and spend his time on his garden-supply outlet. Mario's best offer so far? $60,000. But Mario figures he will eventually find a buyer for $100,000.

Did you ever hear of the Body Works? When the Maryville police tried to drum the controversial massage parlor out of town, Mike, its flamboyant owner, struck a deal with Ecstasy Massage, operating nearby in a more liberal town. Mike's customers were soon enjoying their massages at Ecstasy where Mike is now a 30-percent partner.

3. Valuable franchise and distributor rights attract money like magnets:

Even in troubled companies, rights make might.

A case in point: Baby-time, a growing baby-goods wholesaler whose valuable Johnson & Johnson distributorship made Baby-time important to the area's discount outlets. Although profitable, Baby-time ran into serious cash-flow problems when the banks refused further loans.

Monarch Merchandising rushed to the rescue. Well-entrenched in the discount trade as a children's wear rack-jobber, Monarch saw instant value in Baby-time's customers and its Johnson & Johnson product line. It was Monarch's logical route for expansion, so it bargained to take control of Baby-time. But Baby-time's Jim Clancy shunned a complete sale and instead sold Monarch a half-interest in the business.

The marriage worked. Last year, Baby-time's sales doubled to more than $8 million; Jim Clancy expects to double sales again in the next two years. "When we became partners with Monarch," he says, "we were sure we would have all the expansion capital we needed. Our J&J distributorship sealed the deal. But without it, we would be just another starving wholesaler."

4. Established distribution channels catch interest:

Firms buy companies that can give them broader distribution.

Putnam Mills, for instance, searches for floundering men's clothing retailers that can feature Putnam's lines of fashionable but low-priced men's clothing. Putnam finances the turnaround, inventories the store on consignment and provides management support. Putnam takes a small-ownership interest in the retailer plus 10 percent of sales. But Putnam is mostly interested in the opportunity to sell more of the Putnam line. Some Putnam-affiliated stores quadrupled their sales and once unprofitable, now show healthy profits.

We see it in every industry.

A drug wholesaler acquired a small, failing 22-store drug chain. Injecting inventory and cash, the wholesaler expects the chain to produce a profit — and to sell its new subsidiary more than $5.5 million in merchandise this year.

Walden Stereo, a heavily indebted 10-store discounter, could neither raise capital to pacify creditors nor inventory its stores. A Hong Kong stereo manufacturer invested $1.2 million in the struggling chain; $300,000 came as long-term debt and $900,000 was paid for 30 percent ownership. Walden will retail more than $30 million of the investor's stereos this year.

Don't be shortsighted when you reach out in desperation for a marriage partner. Don't just look horizontally to those in your business. Sure, they're your best bet, but companies that can flow their merchandise through your business also are good marriage candidates.

Other deals come together for other reasons. You may represent the most valuable asset. Buyers do buy management and will buy someone's company to get good talent.

POCKETING THE CASH

At some point you must estimate what you can personally gain from a sale. Ask too low a price and you sell yourself short. Ask too much in hopes of paying off your creditors and pocketing a bundle, and you may be deluding yourself.

For example, you owe creditors $150,000. You reason that if you can come out with $50,000 for yourself, you'll laugh all the way to the bank. So you set the selling price at $200,000. Good thinking?

No way! You neglected to consider the critical question: Is your business worth $200,000? Unless you deal with this question realistically, you may waste your time!

The sad truth is that business brokers are swamped with near-bankrupt companies foolishly priced by sellers who think buyers will blithely pay for their mistakes. They view their businesses through blinders.

If you have too many debts, then you only have so many ways to come out with money in your pocket.

- Restructure your debt before you sell so you have some equity in the business that you can turn into cash.

- Cooperate so that a buyer gets your assets at a knock- down price; you then earn for yourself some compensation for your effort.

- Channel your goodwill and your customers to the buyer, and cut yourself in for a commission or some other compensation.

Pick the strategy you think will work best so you can best hunt for the buyer who will be most interested in the proposition you have in mind. Then know how you will package your proposition so it is attractive to the buyer and financially rewarding to you.

THE THREE MAGIC WORDS

In setting the terms of the sale, you need a clear idea of what you're selling, the price you're asking, and other major terms so business brokers and buyers will take you seriously. This means you need a selling plan that is

comprehensive, objective and **flexible**, three magic words that constitute the key to grinding out top dollar for your troubled company.

Comprehensive:

A comprehensive plan incorporates all the essential terms of the sale. Get your soldiers lined up at the outset.

- What assets do you plan to sell?

- What is your asking price? How firm is it?

- Are you shooting for a cash sale? Will you finance? If so, on what terms?

- If your business is incorporated, will you sell assets or shares?

- Is a lease available? On what terms?

- Is employment – for you or others – a factor? If so, on what terms?

- Will you agree not to compete? If so, on what terms?

- Must you sell by a specified date?

Objective:

The objective approach will ensure a realistic presentation and attainable goal. It will price your business by its values, not its debts. Remember: Focus is a key ingredient. While you can't disregard your business's weaknesses, never allow your liabilities to determine what your business is worth.

What's the best way to value your business? Test the market. Determine how much similar enterprises sell for. Keep in mind that your weaker bargaining power will place you at a clear disadvantage.

Flexible:

The distressed business needs a creative approach to yield the maximum return. Typically, you may start with one deal in mind and end up with a far different deal. On the one hand, you will have the best-case scenario, and on the other hand, the worst- case scenario. In between is the battleground. What's negotiable? What are your priorities? What are the possible trade-offs?

Given the realities of the marketplace, the more buyers you can get to kick the tires, the easier it will be to make the inevitable adjustments.

The sale of a troubled business rarely follows the conventional rules used by healthy companies. Still, however bizarre, the deal hammered out must be mutually beneficial for all parties concerned: Buyer, seller and creditors. If this can be achieved, nutty or not, it will work.

DOING THE DEAL

There are more ways to do deals than there are stripes on a zebra, some simple, some complex.

Small companies are usually sold outright. Most buyers want enrichment, not a partner. Large companies almost always insist on full takeover of a smaller acquisition. Small-business owners hoping to retain partial ownership should consider two simple facts: **1)** You're apt to do fare better with a complete sale. **2)** You're apt to find a buyer faster with a complete sale.

Ask yourself: Is my goal to stay on as part owner? Then ask yourself: If I achieve this goal what am I likely to get?

For the answer, turn to experience. What you're most likely to get is a small piece of the business and no control. OK, you may argue, a small piece is better than nothing. Says who? Again, turn to experience. Even if a piece is better than nothing, which is rare, it probably won't be enough to make the deal worthwhile.

Stock swaps are for the big-league merger-makers and takeover-artists, who fund the deal by issuing the acquired company's shares to stockholders. If you're not a member of that club, trying to play hard ball with the pros will probably cost you more in legal and consulting fees than you could ever make on the deal.

OK, so you are a hard-ball player. My apologies. Then it's no news to you that employee-stock ownership plans (ESOPs) are often used to buy out troubled companies, or that many rock-bound corporations have been thus acquired by employees.

Also popular is the stock-loan agreement. Here, the acquiring company finances the purchase through loans, doling out additional funds for part ownership. Partnerships with larger troubled companies usually require both equity and debt financing.

Does a stock-debt deal sound like your cup of tea? If so, the trick is to part with as little ownership as you can. But think twice about your ability to handle the debt. Excessive debt is self-defeating.

For example, Max, the beleaguered owner of a paperboard-manufacturing company, happily banked a $30,000 chunk of cash and received a $180,000 three-year secured loan in exchange for a 30-percent share of his business. A few months later the investor-lender foreclosed and sauntered off with the whole shooting match. How come? You guessed it: Max had defaulted – an all too common occurrence.

If retaining ownership is important to you, why not, rather than sell, affiliate with an "angel" willing to revitalize your company? That way you retain full ownership and enjoy a profitable alliance with the benefactor company.

This works best for companies with a good distributor network. Like Putnam Mills. Today several once-troubled retailers sell Putnam's menswear exclusively. Thanks to Putnam's survival tools – strong merchandising, promotion, and management, they now are doing well.

Like a franchise, the well-designed joint venture provides the distressed owner the best of two worlds: The strength and support of a large, strong company, and the rewards and benefits of running your own show.

MILKING THE MOST FROM THE LEAST

How to make the best deal? Selling is probably your last-ditch salvage attempt. Buyers know that. So face the harsh fact that this shoots holes in your bargaining power.

But wipe the sorrowful look from your face. In the past few years, I've put together deals for about 300 troubled companies. The objective was to come up with the best deal we could get. As often as not, the seller got more than expected.

Whatever the circumstances, we always beat the bushes for every possible buyer, presented our best case, tried to sweeten good offers through last-minute negotiations, and accepted the deal that made the most sense and yielded the seller the maximum dollar return.

With few deals to choose from, selection becomes surprisingly easy. Still several realities must be faced prior to making a deal:

- Many buyers have no intention of cutting a fair deal.

- Like vultures, some buyers may hover overhead, ready to swoop down on a bargain once your business goes bust.

- The vulture-buyer may be after confidential trade secrets, your choice location, valued customers, or your best employees.

- The vulture-buyer may be a prime competitor, hovering alone or behind a hired dummy surrogate. This buyer should be viewed most suspiciously. He's in the best position to exploit your troubles.

The vulture-buyer isn't always easily spotted, but there are telltale signs. Keep your eye on the prospect who appears preoccupied with one part of your operation: Technology, a particular employee, a special process or procedure. Be wary of delayed or unreasonably protracted negotiations. The vulture-buyer is a master at stalling, at ever-changing offers and nit-picking, until your business crumbles and he can get what he wants for pennies. It's a common ploy. If you can't cement the deal quickly, move on to other prospects.

The temptation for self-delusion is strong. Sellers are apt to reason that there's a better deal around the corner. They figure, if the business is worth X dollars to Buyer A, it may be worth X- plus dollars to Buyer B. Maybe so. But in my experience the excessively prolonged search can be self-defeating. Going beyond your point of no return could lose you that one solid deal.

Serious qualified buyers rarely assess the operation with the same set of evaluators. Corporate needs vary. Valuation standards differ from company to company. Every acquisition calls for its own tailored approach.

An insolvent enterprise acquired in bankruptcy, receivership, or foreclosure is priced by its liquidation value. Buyers know you're up against the wall. In such a case, only competition between buyers can boost the price. The trick is to find as many potential buyers as possible.

Will your business be dismantled and absorbed into the buyer's operations? It's an alternative the prospective buyer must consider. How will the acquisition affect bottom-line results? How will the selling price be affected if the two businesses continue to operate separately?

THE DIRTY DOZEN THAT MAY HELP YOU CLEAN UP

Here are 12 proven tips that have helped thousands of troubled business people become trouble-free sellers.

Tip #1. Define your objectives.

Are you after a complete sale? Or do you wish to become an employee or partner? Assess your personal needs realistically. Identify the type of buyer you seek. Visualize the ideal company to take control of your business. Track down the potential buyer best equipped to fill your needs. If you want to convert from owner to employee, pinpoint the suitor you would most like to work for. You may be better served dealing with such a company even if the price you get is a bit lower.

Tip #2. Test your timing.

Swift action becomes urgent if your business is slipping badly and needs a bailout in a hurry. Obviously, you'll command more during the initial stages of a downturn than in its terminal stages. Try to sell before you're in deep trouble. Buyers who sense imminent collapse develop the killer instinct. Wait too long, and you'll be forced to sell under pressure, with little time to consider the most favorable deal. Or clean up your balance sheet before putting your business on the block. Take every action you can to optimize your equity and staying power while you negotiate your best deal.

Tip #3. Add up your selling points.

What does your company offer? Translate its plus points into buyer benefits. Be prepared to persuade buyers they can make money with your business. Most important: Treat each asset as something of value if sold independently. Selling your business asset by asset may get you more than lumping them all together.

Tip #4. Solicit buyers aggressively.

Contact as many potentially interested buyers as possible. Don't play coy or try to conceal the fact that your business is for sale. You don't have time to play the field. Scores of contacts may have to be made before a worthwhile deal can be consummated. You need fast offers and lots of them. And you can't afford to box yourself in with one broker exclusively. Any number of places exist to advertise your financially plagued company. The Garrett Group maintains a database of thousands of potential buyers listed by state and industry. A call to Garrett at (305) 480-8543 will get you a no-charge ad in its *Buyer Alert*. If you own a large company, *The Wall Street Journal* and *New York Times* will yield hundreds of qualified buyers.

Tip #5. Stay flexible.

The deal you have in mind may not be the best deal you're offered. Each offer will trigger new ideas, new opportunities for a better financial yield. Keep an open mind. Listen to all propositions. Evaluate all possibilities. This prospect or that may come up with deal-making tricks that never occurred to you.

Tip #6. Avoid pie-in-the-sky propositions.

You're after hard cash, not soft promises. Too many eager sellers hand over their troubled businesses to sharpie buyers who promise a share of future profits or "earnouts." Speculation is risky unless the buyer enjoys a strong reputation for ethical behavior and turning losers into winners. Up-front cash is better than ending up behind the eight ball because of an earnout promise that fizzled. Buyers bail out fast when turnaround attempts flop. Experience proves that bird-in-the-hand deals usually pan out better than deals based on wishful thinking.

Tip #7. Evaluate personalities.

Too many business marriages end in divorce because of personality clashes. This is especially true if you plan to be part of the process of turning your company around. If your buyer has the upper hand legally and financially, you will lose in a fight. If the deal includes a place for you in the business, agree beforehand, specifically, and in writing on what the buyer's and your own expectations and goals are and how they will be reached.

Tip #8. Get your creditors in on the act.

Don't run yourself ragged tracking buyers and negotiating, only to find the deal blocked by creditors. There are a variety of ways to sell if you can't meet your debt obligations fully. If your deal is carefully structured by your attorney, you won't be stymied by creditor blockage. Legal wrinkles must be worked out before you put your troubled company on the market. Is your business franchised? Is the franchise assignable? Can the buyer get a new lease? Are special licenses transferable? Prepare a checklist and evaluate it item by item with your attorney.

Tip #9. Shine brightly as a survivor.

Act like a survivor and you'll be a survivor. Buyers know you're in trouble, but never let them think you are desperate. Buyers will view you as a survivor if you keep your cool, negotiate as an equal, and avoid take-it-or-leave-it ultimatums. Convince the other guy you have staying power. Selling a company is like a board game more exciting than Monopoly. Create phantom buyers. If buyers think they're your last resort, you'll never pass GO or collect $200. You need competing buyers for the best possible deal. Recruit friends or associates to play this role. It will make the game more interesting.

Tip #10. Dress up your business.

A small investment to make your business look sexy may pay a big dividend. Spend sparingly but strategically. A fresh coat of paint in your plant may change that rundown appearance.

Tip #11. Accentuate the positive.

The fact that you're in trouble needn't stop you from strutting your past triumphs and future potential. Convey the impression that the business rode high before and can do it again. To the extent legitimately possible, dramatize money-making opportunities. Help the buyer understand why the business went downhill and what tactics are needed to avoid past mistakes. If you level with the buyer regarding the negatives, you make the positives more credible.

Tip #12. Play square with your key people.

This is a touchy proposition. If you announce your plan to sell, it will create an insecure feeling among your employees, and they will start looking for other jobs. If you fail to reveal your plan, employees will feel betrayed and the damage may be worse. Use your best judgment. Often your best bet will be to confide in key employees only, and offer them attractive bonuses to stick it out with you.

IF NOT A SELLER, THAN A BUYER BE

Why not? It may sound a bit fruity, but it's my favorite troubled-company bailout strategy. The time to try it is when your business...

...has too few assets to survive...
...needs specific technology...
...needs a shored up distributor network...
...needs the cash flow...
...or anything else only another going enterprise can provide.

In short, what you need is an infusion – or transfusion. If the shoe fits, the skeleton of your insolvent company can help you expand your way out of the doghouse. Your creditors may even work with you if you can show them how an acquisition will result in a good payback. If you're going for broke, you might as well go big.

My last "buyer be" deal, Dorchester Printing & Graphics Plant, was on the brink of bankruptcy but its owner Bob never missed a beat when he got the opportunity to purchase three other troubled printing plants. Some minor cash was required since Bob took on considerable debt to finance each deal, but he managed to find the few dollars. With four printing operations in hand, Bob consolidated them into one company and filed Chapter 11. After shedding surplus equipment and debts, he emerged from Chapter 11 with a highly profitable, streamlined operation much larger than his original company. The moral of the story: When in trouble, you can look up as well as down.

☑CHECKPOINT

1. *Should you sell your business or hang on to it? Are you making an objective decision, or are you only reacting to your present situation?*

2. *What does your business have that could be of interest to a buyer?*

3. *How can you structure a deal so the sale of your business puts money in your pocket?*

4. *Is your game plan for selling your business comprehensive, objective and flexible?*

5. *Is this the right time to sell or would you cut a better deal later?*

6. *Do you know how you will resolve creditor claims if you cannot sell your business for enough to fully cover your debts?*

7. *Can you inexpensively dress up your business so it sells faster and for a better price?*

8. *Should you buy a business or two instead of selling your business?*

19

HOW TO BAIL OUT
FOR A SUPER-SOFT LANDING

Not every business can be saved, not every business can be sold. Your business, like so many others, may simply close its doors.

In Chapter 10, I showed you how to protect your business. It's no less important to protect yourself, if your business should fail.

You can lose your shirt if your business goes under. Test this proposition yourself by answering two key questions:

1. What personal liabilities do you face if your business fails?

2. What personal assets can you then lose?

Your answers to these two questions set you up for the big question: **What should you do right now to protect your personal wealth?**

Don't rationalize that your business **won't** fail. It may! Don't rationalize that you **won't** end up with a flock of creditors chasing you. You may! Don't rationalize that they **wouldn't** pluck you clean of everything you own. They would! So read carefully. This may be the most important chapter of this book.

Of course, you should have considered these questions **before** you started your business. But you probably didn't. Most entrepreneurs don't ask themselves what if: "What if the business fails? What will I lose? What can I do **now** to protect myself and limit my personal losses if I do fail?"

Entrepreneurs seldom ask these farsighted questions because entrepreneurs are optimists. After all, optimism is the fuel that launches new ventures.

The harsh realities of the rough-and-tough business world inevitably surface when you do fail. But by then it's usually too late to ask the question, too late to avoid personal liability and too late to protect your personal wealth.

Don't **you** make that mistake!

Buckle on your parachute as I show you how to bail out for a super-soft landing!

CORPORATE SHIELD OR SWISS CHEESE?

You may think your corporation will protect you from your business debts, but you may be wrong. Dead-duck wrong!

Your corporation will protect you from business debts only if it functions as a corporation and you treat it as a corporation. Only then do you force creditors to recognize your corporate protection. When you forget these rules, you lose your corporate protection.

Business creditors can ignore your corporate shield and grab your personal wealth if you commit any of these five common blunders:

Blunder #1:

You commingle assets. Maintaining a solid corporate shield requires you to operate your corporation as a separate entity in every respect. Keep corporate funds separate from your personal funds. Document all transactions between yourself and your corporation as well as all transactions between your different corporations.

Blunder #2:

You incorrectly sign documents. Sloppily signed documents spell trouble! When you operate as a corporation, all documents should clearly identify your corporation as the principal and you as its agent. Use your title when signing checks and other documents. Imprint the name of your corporation on all checks, correspondence, contracts, invoices and other documents.

Blunder #3:

You don't operate your corporation as a separate entity. Do you operate more than one corporation? If so, appoint separate, not duplicate or interlocking, boards of directors. Hold separate corporate meetings and keep separate corporate books. Make each corporation truly independent with the fewest possible legal, financial and administrative ties to your other businesses.

Blunder #4:

You don't keep adequate corporate records. Creditors can punch another hole in your corporate shield when your records are inadequate. You must document major corporate actions and keep up-to-date, accurate minutes of director and stockholder meetings. An inexpensive way to handle this is to buy *Corporate Secretary* from E-Z Legal Software, available at most stationery and software outlets.

Blunder #5:

You allow your corporation to be dissolved. A corporation dissolved by the state means no corporation and no corporate protection. Punctually pay all state taxes and corporate franchise fees required to keep your corporation in good standing. And never voluntarily dissolve your corporation if it has outstanding corporate debts, as these debts then become your personal obligations.

Check your corporate housekeeping. Put your affairs in order before your creditors can snoop around and find reasons to punch holes in your corporate shield. Have your attorney review this checklist with you and turn your swiss cheese shield into solid legal protection.

Creditors may try to claim that your corporation is nothing more than a sham or alter-ego, but they will have an uphill fight unless you ignore these basic rules for running your corporation. Make it more than an uphill fight so your creditors can chase only your corporation and not you.

SIDESTEP COSTLY PERSONAL GUARANTEES

Your biggest headaches will come from personally guaranteed corporate debts.

Most small-business owners guarantee a few corporate obligations. Some may be necessary, but most are foolish. Because guarantees increase your personal exposure, you must know how to avoid future guarantees and how to sidestep those you have already signed. How do you avoid those nasty personal guarantees?

Bluff!

One supplier may demand your guarantee, but not **every** prospective supplier will.

Your guarantee is only one bargaining point between you and a prospective supplier. Suppliers who want your business will give your corporation reasonable credit without your guarantee — if you bluff! Should they insist on your guarantee, then hunt for a more lenient supplier. But to win that credit, understand your suppliers' concerns and reduce their risks so they will forego personal guarantees.

A supplier may refuse to ship a $20,000 order without your guarantee, but gladly gamble on a $10,000 order. Or possibly you can secure credit through a mortgage on your business assets rather than on a personal guarantee. Or why not a limited guarantee instead of a full guarantee? This cuts your risk to an amount you can afford to gamble.

You see, there are alternatives! Observe this cardinal rule:

Never guarantee an existing debt!

What do you gain?

Creditors will plead, promise, threaten and cajole for your personal guarantee once your business shows signs of trouble. They will pursue almost anything to get you to sign personally on the dotted line. After all, this gives them the opportunity to chase you and your personal assets if your business goes bust. So why risk your personal assets to bail out your existing creditors? And don't naively think your business will pay these debts. Few troubled companies manage to. Very few!

Optimism is dangerous when you're in trouble. It's particularly dangerous when it encourages you to sign pieces of paper to keep you afloat temporarily.

You also will be sorely tempted to throw more of your own money into your business or to borrow money by pledging personal assets — all to keep supplies flowing and the rent paid. But you will soon run out of resources, and your business will run out. Period.

Banks and other lenders rarely finance a small business without its owner's personal guarantee. These guarantees can't be avoided. But if you must guarantee these loans, bargain for the greatest protection possible. Have your bank mortgage the assets of your business. This reduces your personal exposure only to the debt that remains after your business is liquidated. Assuming your business assets cover your loan, you avoid a deficiency should the lender liquidate.

Do you have partners? Did they also sign the guarantee? They enjoy the benefits of co-owning the business with you, so why not have them share the risk? But having your partners sign on the dotted line along with you is meaningless unless your partners match your financial strength. Creditors chase guarantors with the deepest pockets. It's consoling when your partners' pockets are deeper than yours. Such was the sad story of a part-owner in a bankrupt restaurant who had personally guaranteed more than $90,000 in supplier bills. "Why bother my partners?" he figured. You guessed it. His restaurant went bust, and he was stuck with a $90,000 headache, while his partners walked away.

How do you escape liability on your existing guarantees?

First, verify the obligations you have guaranteed. You may have unwittingly signed a guarantee as part of a credit application. Or you may have long-forgotten guarantees. Ask every creditor whether they hold your guarantee, and obtain copies.

Second, immediately and in writing revoke all guarantees for future credit. Why increase your liability when your goal is to decrease your exposure?

Third, try to liquidate guaranteed debts before your company folds. Frequently, my goal is to keep a failing business alive just long enough to pay the personally guaranteed debts. But this objective makes sense only when you have a fighting chance to fully pay your personally guaranteed debts and walk away clean. If you can't, then set aside whatever funds you can accumulate as a settlement-war chest. Your creditors may later settle for what you have set aside, or even less, rather than chase you.

Fourth, exploit the reality that cooperating with a creditor who holds your guarantees may be of greater value to your creditor. For instance, I convinced a Chicago bank that was owed $7 million by a failed health clinic that my client's willingness to process $7 million in outstanding receivables was worth considerably more to the bank than the paltry thousands they could squeeze from his personal assets. They wisely agreed. My client went to work collecting the receivables, and the bank ended up with millions more than they could have possibly collected on his guarantee.

Do **your** lenders need your cooperation to turn your collateral into more cash? Exchange your cooperation for a release on your guarantee. But negotiate when your creditors need your help, not later when you've lost your bargaining power! Once your business is gone, you may have precious little to negotiate with.

Negotiate creatively. What can you possibly dangle before your creditors in return for a canceled guarantee? A mortgage on your business? Returned goods? An immediate partial payment? You get the idea. Convince your creditors that what you offer from the business today is worth considerably more than what they can get from chasing you tomorrow. This is the key to a sidestepped guarantee.

What do you do with stubborn creditors who won't release your guarantee in exchange for your cooperation? Threaten to take even **more** money out of their pockets!

A prolonged Chapter 11, for example, may delay foreclosure and dissipate a lender's collateral. Do you have a good counterclaim? Have you paid back bills within the past 90 days to your creditors? Why not threaten bankruptcy to recover those preferential payments? Bees make honey **and** sting! Threats are an essential bargaining weapon when you confront uncooperative, unreasonable creditors. Still, the carrot-and-stick approach works best when you make it a tastier carrot and a bigger stick!

Years ago, as a young pup in law school, I learned from a cantankerous but wise professor that a guarantor was an "idiot with a fountain pen." Thirty years and 1,000 cases later makes me agree!

DON'T LET THE TAX COLLECTOR CHASE YOU!

You already know that as a corporate officer you are responsible for unpaid withholding taxes deducted from your employees' pay. Unpaid state withholding taxes, sales, meals, gas and similar taxes also can be your personal responsibility. Have your lawyer check the taxes that impose personal liability in your state so you know the specific taxes to pay.

With taxes, an ounce of prevention is worth ten pounds of cure because tax collectors have enormous powers to harass and collect from you compared to mere mortal creditors.

Avoid big tax troubles. If cash is tight, pay at least those taxes for which you are personally liable. Mark tax payments to be applied **only** to the trust taxes that impose personal liability. Unless you so specify, the IRS will apply them to the non-trust taxes so they can later collect the unpaid trust taxes from you personally.

These potential tax troubles are not necessarily yours alone. Others in your company who share your authority and responsibility to pay taxes also can be held liable. For instance, comptrollers and bookkeepers who sign checks should resign once taxes become delinquent because the IRS also can hold them personally liable. To protect them from liability, give your employees who write and sign checks an affidavit acknowledging their lack of authority and responsibility.

That's also why you should never make a spouse an officer of the corporation or a signatory to the corporate checking account. Limit the tax liability to yourself so that your spouse can be a safe haven for your personal assets. If the IRS goes after you and your spouse, your family wealth becomes highly vulnerable.

The IRS must first try to exhaust collection against the company before going after its officers, but in practice, the IRS moves quickly against responsible parties, even when the business is in operation. A business may seek refuge from the IRS by filing Chapter 11. This stops IRS collection against the business but does not stop personal collection attempts. Winning a six-year payment plan on back taxes under Chapter 11 has little value when the IRS is auctioning your home. The IRS may chase you much sooner than you think!

Failure to pay collected taxes is a criminal violation, but the IRS seldom prosecutes. Many states do routinely prosecute larger cases or chronically delinquent taxpayers, so it's important to know the penalties for each unpaid tax. Prioritize those taxes that can cause you the greatest grief.

If you do owe the IRS more than you can possibly repay, don't throw your scarce money at the problem. But do pay current taxes to show good faith, to avoid criminal liability and to encourage IRS leniency on any future settlement.

The IRS will initially send you a notice of proposed personal assessment (or 100 percent penalty assessment) for about 70 percent of the total tax owed, or the "trust" portion of the tax. Appeal this proposed assessment for two reasons:

1. You may have a valid defense. The IRS may not have credited payments, or you may not be legally responsible for the assessed taxes. Consider the possibilities with your lawyer or tax advisor. And never provide the IRS with financial or other information unless advised by someone experienced with IRS collection procedures.

2. An appeal may give you valuable time to protect your assets before they are encumbered with an IRS lien or seized. IRS assessment appeals can stall matters for as long as two years.

How can you permanently rid yourself of the IRS and other annoying tax collectors?

One way is to stay "paper poor" so that the IRS has nothing to grab. Once convinced you are truly collection-proof, the IRS will earmark you as uncollectible and stop pestering you. But you must stay "paper poor" for the entire ten-year collection period because the IRS will periodically investigate your finances.

Does the thought of perpetual poverty discourage you? It shouldn't. Many of my clients owe big money to the IRS — and yet live quite comfortably. They simply learned the asset protection secrets I'll soon reveal to you! And as mighty as the IRS may be, it can't squeeze blood from a turnip.

You also can settle with the IRS for a small fraction of what you owe if you can convince them that your offer is all you can afford and more than they could collect by seizing your assets.

My newest book, *How to Settle with the IRS for Pennies on the Dollar* (Garrett Publishing, 1994) discloses the key strategies and reveals how you can join the hundreds of thousands of Americans who benefit each year from the IRS's little-known "Offer in Compromise" program. Some recent examples from my files:

- *A restaurateur who settled his $300,000 IRS bill for $50,000, payable over five years.*

- *A jeweler who compromised his $80,000 tax bill for only $10,000.*

- *An elderly publisher who escaped a $92,000 tax claim for a tiny $3,000.*

I am presently negotiating to settle a $2 million tax liability owed by the owners of a bankrupt heavy-machine repair facility. The IRS has already agreed to accept $50,000, but I think I can settle for even less!

If you owe the IRS, get a copy of *How to Settle with the IRS for Pennies on the Dollar.* You'll see exactly how to end your tax troubles for far less than you ever thought possible.

MILES OF MINE FIELDS

Where-O-where does it all end? The problems that can follow you home after your business doors close are endless indeed.

To bail out for the softest landing, you must anticipate every potential problem before it becomes a problem. Will you miss stepping on these four commonly overlooked mines?

1. Bad checks:

Every state imposes criminal penalties for bad checks. Pay all your outstanding checks before you close your doors. Some states consider it a criminal offense only if the bad checks are for C.O.D. orders. And if you pay anything toward these checks, the creditor loses the right to press criminal charges. That's a valuable tip to remember.

2. Unpaid wages:

Unpaid employees also can create sticky civil or criminal problems in most states. You may even be personally liable for severance and vacation pay. Your safest bet is to pay all accrued wages before you close. Or ask your employees to waive accrued vacation and sick leave pay when you hand them their severance check. Surprisingly, most employees will sign away these benefits to get their final check.

3. Union liability:

If your business is unionized, you have bigger problems because owner-officers of a unionized business can be personally liable for "withdrawing" the business from its collective-bargaining agreement. If yours is a large company, this can mean significant liability and requires a good labor lawyer. If you don't know one, call me. I work closely with several labor lawyers quite skilled at resolving union-liability problems for owners of failed companies, and I would gladly refer you to one.

4. Fraud claims:

The mine field is booby trapped with two common types of fraud claims. First, creditors may claim that you gave them fraudulent financial statements to obtain credit. Creditors who press this claim may hope to coerce you into a payment. Was your credit information inaccurate? Did you try to make your situation appear brighter than it was? This is bad practice, but don't be coerced into a settlement too quickly. The accuracy of financial statements is neither easily challenged nor easily proven. Best advice: Don't hand out financial statements if you lack confidence in paying the bill.

Second, your creditors may claim you diverted or concealed assets. This, of course, is a most serious charge under the bankruptcy laws.

Why would creditors question your honesty?

You may have suspiciously transferred assets from your failing company. If you did transfer assets, be prepared to show that you received payment or to otherwise justify the transfer. For instance, if assets were shipped to an affiliated business, then have the affiliated corporation give your debtor corporation a promissory note to document the obligation. Even an uncollectible note documents the transaction.

Are there other potential mine fields? Absolutely! I constantly see lawsuits and claims of every variety and species aimed at hapless, penniless owners of belly-up businesses. Be careful, be honest and you can still find it tough to break clean from your busted business. Prepare for the worst because that's usually your fate.

EMPTY YOUR DEEP POCKETS

Think about the many ways your failed businesses can wipe you out personally, and you understand why savvy entrepreneurs completely protect their personal assets **before** they venture into business.

Believe me, in this world, you're a sitting duck unless you shelter your assets.

Business owners, oblivious to their impending problems, are usually the last to protect themselves. I know story after story of creditors that grabbed a home or of savings levied by the IRS. People in trouble do play ostrich.

That's why my neighbor was hit with an $80,000 tax lien and $200,000 in creditor attachments on his home and several income properties. Ostrichlike, he had left these valuable personal assets exposed long after it was obvious his hardware distributorship was failing.

Another ostrich, this one buried under a blizzard of lawsuits and tax claims from a failed Utah ski lodge, recently consulted with me. With his creditors ready to pluck clean more than $2 million in real estate, savings, cars, boats and annuities, I hastily devised an asset protection plan that saved some of his hard-earned wealth. I could have guaranteed 100 percent asset protection had he consulted with me earlier. He could then laugh at everyone chasing him, including the IRS. But he wouldn't listen.

Will you? I hope so, because protecting your assets may be your most important goal. How can you shield your personal assets legally and effectively?

■ **Take advantage of the homestead and exemption laws that automatically protect your home and other assets from creditors.** For instance, you can convert unprotected stocks and bonds into your pension account because your pension is protected. Or you can take cash and pay down your home mortgage if your home has adequate homestead protection.

■ **Give property to your children or relatives as part of your estate plan.** You can give up to $10,000 per year per donee without a gift tax, and you can make a one-time gift of $30,000. But don't transfer assets to your children unless you are confident that they will be a safe harbor for these assets. Gifts to your spouse will be more readily challenged by your creditors and leave you more vulnerable in the event of divorce.

■ **Harbor your assets in family-limited partnerships, corporations or certain trusts.** Although unfamiliar to most Americans, a family-limited partnership is perhaps the safest way to title your home and other assets and protect them from creditors. As the general partner, you continue to enjoy complete control over the partnership property while the partnership can be safely owned by other family members, trusts or a variety of other entities.

Trusts are effective asset protectors, but only if they are irrevocable trusts. Their downside is that you lose control of your assets. A revocable trust, such as a living trust, does **not** protect your assets from creditors.

■ **Taste the exotic and go offshore to shield your vulnerable cash.** It may be just the right move when you owe creditors big money and have big money to shelter. The Cayman Islands and Isle of Man are two havens whose principal industry is to safely shelter money from creditors. Offshore banking is perfectly legal, totally effective and neither as difficult nor as inconvenient as it sounds.

■ **Refinance the equity in your assets.** It can be the perfect way to discourage creditors who no longer have a net worth to chase. The cash proceeds can be used to buy exempt assets, pay "friendly" creditors, prepay expenses or give a gift. Or they can be deposited in offshore havens.

Are there other ways to protect your assets? Absolutely! There are literally hundreds of asset protection strategies.

In fact, I reveal no fewer than 233 proven strategies in my best-selling book, *Asset Protection Secrets* (Garrett, 1993). This is one book you must read now!

It was inevitable that I became an asset protection pro. Asset protection is a natural part of the business of handling troubled companies. Not only do I save businesses, but I also must make sure my clients have the parachute they need for a super-soft landing when they bail out.

What about you?

What is your personal exposure?

What personal assets are at risk?

Don't wait until the sheriff is at your door. Fraudulent conveyance laws allow creditors to recover last-minute transfers. The court will consider who received your property, what they paid, and when you transferred it. Transfers made before the liability arose are far safer than those made after the claim. But last- minute transfers **can** succeed against less-zealous creditors. For instance, the bureaucratically rigid IRS, despite its enormous collection powers, seldom chases transferred property.

Smaller creditors won't consider the chase worthwhile. So there may be nothing to lose by a last-minute transfer. But it's safer and more intelligent to protect what you own before you go into business. To bail out for a soft landing, pack your parachute before takeoff!

It's comforting to be 100 percent judgment-proof. Poverty **is** power. When you have nothing for your creditors to take, you have nothing to worry about.

That's why on paper, my clients are as poor as church mice. They sleep like babies once I construct a financial fortress around their wealth. Wouldn't you?

Are you **still** vulnerable? If so, find yourself a good asset protection lawyer quickly. If you can't find one in your area, give me a call. Chances are I can refer you to a nearby specialist. But first, learn a few of the tricks yourself with my *Asset Protection Secrets*. (An order form is in the back of this book.)

HOW TO GRAB THE CASH BEFORE THE CRASH!

Walking away from your defunct company with your personal wealth intact is a soft landing.

Walking away from the business with every dime you invested in the business is landing on feathers.

Bad businesses breed greed. Admit it: You hanker to grab some cash before the crash. But how do you do it legally?

Here are several tips!

■ Repay to yourself all loans owed to you from your company first and then fight to keep your business out of bankruptcy for at least one year. Because you are an insider, creditors can recover preferential payments made to you (or any other relative, officer, director or stockholder of your corporation) within the year preceding bankruptcy. Make certain you can prove that the debt was legitimately owed to you.

■ Take high wages. Excessive wages are a fraudulent transfer and a misappropriation of funds (as is excessive compensation to relatives or friends). Nevertheless, wage payments are less easily challenged than are loan repayments, which are recoverable as preferences. Your objective is to take the maximum wages you can reasonably justify.

■ Stagger your withdrawals. Large payments to yourself or family members are easily detected. Small payments to many different individuals are less easily noticed. And a bankruptcy trustee is less likely to sue to recover from numerous individuals paid for a variety of obligations, such as reimbursed expenses, wages, consulting fees, loans and royalties. A bankruptcy trustee usually investigates checks to principals or other family members, but less often questions checks made out to unfamiliar names. Assigning to a "friendly" third party the loans or other compensation due you from the business may be a way to avoid problems.

When you grab the cash **before** the crash, you have the financial ammunition you need to start again. Except for the ego- bruising, you're no worse off for your misadventure.

But do stay legal and aboveboard.

Grabbing the cash" only means recouping what is legitimately due you.

It does not mean you should rape your business of everything not nailed down.

It does not mean skimming mountains of cash to beat the IRS.

It does not mean fraudulent scams you'll later regret.

It only means looking out for #1... legitimately and honorably. And if paying yourself and not your creditors twinges your conscience, I leave that to your conscience.

What if you owe money to your business? Your company's books may show prior unpaid loans made to you or other family members. Did you forget an old $50,000 loan from your business? If the loan is carried on your books, the bankruptcy trustee must try to collect.

You have two ways to wipe the slate clean legally so you owe nothing to your business or its creditors. First, deduct from these loans any money the business owes you. Second, transfer some personal assets to the business as full repayment. Whichever strategy you follow, cancel the loan **before** you relinquish your books to the bankruptcy trustee. If you have personally guaranteed business debts, you also can cancel the loan as payment for your guarantee of the debts. This creates taxable income to you, but does cancel the loan.

Review each possibility with your accountant and attorney. Your accountant can structure your cash withdrawals with an eye toward tax advantages. Your lawyer can keep you legal.

A failing business with a good cash flow can put a sizeable investment back into its owner's pocket – if the owner knows how to properly channel the cash in that direction. I have helped numerous clients recover as much as six-figure investments before they finally collapsed their business. If you must fail, nothing obligates you to go home with empty pockets!

☑CHECKPOINT

1. *Will your corporation shield you from business debts?*

2. *What business debts have you personally guaranteed? How can you satisfy these guarantees before your business folds?*

3. *What tax liabilities are outstanding? How can these back taxes be repaid?*

4. *How deep are your pockets? What personal assets are exposed to creditors? How can they be protected?*

5. *What does your business owe you? How can you legally recoup this money from the business? How can you cancel what you owe your company so that you have no continuing liability?*

GLOSSARY

Adequate Protection – The standard of protection granted a creditor by the trustee or debtor-in-possession in order to avoid the court allowing the creditor to foreclose on its property.

Automatic Stay – An injunction, or court order, that takes effect when a bankruptcy petition is filed. An automatic stay prohibits all collection action against a debtor.

Avoidance Powers – The powers used by a trustee to reserve transfers of the debtor's property.

Balance Sheet – A statement of financial conditions as of a specific date. It is different from a cash-flow statement, which summarizes income and expenses.

Bankruptcy Code – The body of a federal statutory law that governs the bankruptcy process.

Bankruptcy Petition – The legal instrument filed with the bankruptcy court that commences a bankruptcy proceeding.

Bar Date – The last date for filing a proof of claim.

Chapter 7 – In a Chapter 7 proceeding the debtor's business is liquidated and its assets are distributed to creditors with allowed proofs of claims.

Chapter 11 – Normally, Chapter 11 proceeding is a reorganization proceeding. The debtor continues to operate its business after the bankruptcy is filed. Chapter 11 liquidations are not uncommon and usually are the results of an unsuccessful reorganization attempt.

Chapter 11 Plan – In a Chapter 11 proceeding, the reorganization plan sets forth the rights of all classes of creditors. It also may include various repayment schedules pertaining to the various creditors.

Chapter 13 – May only be filed by an individual debtor with limited debt. In essence, it allows a payment plan for an individual's financial an or business debts.

Closing – When a bankruptcy case is closed, it is no longer on the court's docket.

Collateral – Property of a debtor in which a creditor has a lien securing its debt.

Complaint – A pleading that is filed to initiate a lawsuit or an adversary proceeding.

Composition – Out-of-court agreement to pay a percentage of a debt in full settlement.

Consumer Credit Counseling Services – A non-profit

organization established to help debtors make payment arrangements with creditors.

Conversion – The conversion of a bankruptcy case from one chapter type to another.

Cram-Down – The confirmation of a plan to reorganize over the objection of a creditor or class of creditors by the votes of other creditors.

Creditor – One to whom you owe money.

Debtor – One who owes debts. In bankruptcy, the bankrupt business that is under the control and protection of the bankruptcy court is the debtor.

Debtor-in-Possession (DIP) – The business debtor in a Chapter 11 reorganization. In a Chapter 11, the debtor retaining possession of the assets involved in the bankruptcy.

Discharge – A discharge in bankruptcy relieves the debtor of the dischargeable debts incurred prior to filing. Discharge is the legal term for the elimination of debt through bankruptcy.

Dismissal – The dismissal of a bankruptcy case, for all intents and purposes, returns the debtor to the same place it was before bankruptcy was filed.

Examiner – An officer of the court sometimes appointed to investigate the financial affairs of the debtor.

Exemption or Exempt Property – Property of an individual debtor that the law protects from the actions of creditors, such as the debtor's residence or homestead, automobile, and the like.

Foreclosure – A debt-collection procedure whereby property of the debtor is sold on the courthouse steps to satisfy debts. Foreclosure often involves real estate of the debtor.

General, Unsecured Claim – A claim that is neither secured nor granted a priority by the Bankruptcy Code. Most trade debts are general, unsecured claims.

Involuntary Bankruptcy Proceeding – In an involuntary bankruptcy proceeding the debtor is forced into bankruptcy by creditors. Involuntary bankruptcies are relatively rare.

Judicial Lien – A lien created by the order of a court, such as the lien created by taking a judgment against a debtor.

Jurisdiction – The power and authority of a court to issue binding orders after hearing controversies.

Levy and Execution – A judicial debt-collection procedure in which the court orders the sheriff to seize the debtor's property found in the county to sell in satisfaction of the debtor's debt or debts.

Lien – An interest in property securing the repayment of a debt.

Motion – A request for the court to act. A motion may be filed within a lawsuit, adversary proceeding, or bankruptcy case.

Personal Property – Moveable property. Property that is not permanently attached to land is considered *personalty*.

Petition for Relief – The papers filed initiating a bankruptcy case.

Possessory Security Interest – A security interest or lien on property that requires the creditor to have possession of the property, such as a pawn or pledge.

Preference – A transfer of property of the debtor to a creditor made immediately prior to the debtor's bankruptcy that enables the creditor to receive more than it would have received from the bankruptcy. A preferential transfer must be made while the debtor was insolvent and as payment for a debt that existed prior to the transfer of the property.

Priority – Certain categories of claims are designated as priority claims by the Bankruptcy Code, such as clams for lost wages or taxes. Each classification of claims must be paid in order of priority (the claims in one class must be paid in full before the next class receives any payment).

Priority Proof of Claim or Priority Claim – A proof of claim of the type granted priority by the Bankruptcy Code.

Proof of Claim – The document filed in a bankruptcy case that establishes a creditor's claim for payment against the debtor.

Realty or Real Property – Immovable property, such as land and/or buildings attached to land.

Redemption – The right of a debtor in a bankruptcy to purchase certain real or personal property from a secured creditor by paying the current value of the property (regardless of the amount owed on the property).

Secured Creditor – A creditor whose debt is secured by a lien on property of the debtor.

Secured Proof of Claim – A proof of claim for a debt that is secured by a lien, a judgment, or other security interest.

Security Interest – A lien on the property in the possession of the debtor that acts as security for the debt owed to the creditor.

Statutory Lien – A lien created by operation of law, such as a mechanic's lien or a tax lien. A statutory lien does not require the consent of the parties or a court order.

Trustee – An officer of the court appointed to take custody of the assets of a bankruptcy estate.

Unsecured Creditor – A creditor without security for its debt.

SOURCES AND RESOURCES

U.S. Small Business Administration
Free management assistance publications and business development booklets are available from the U.S. Small Business Administration. Call your nearest SBA office, or write to 1725 I St., NW Room 408 Washington D.C. 20416. Phone: (800) 368-5851 or (202) 653-7561.

Small Business Development Centers
These centers are sponsored by the SBA and offer free counseling. To locate the center in your area, call (202) 653-6768.

U.S. Department of Commerce
Publishes the *Directory of Federal and State Business Assistance: A Guide for New and Growing Companies.* It includes descriptions of more than 182 federal and state programs and services. Call or write the U.S. Department of Commerce — National Technical Information Service, 5825 Port Royal Rd., Springfield, VA 22101. Phone: (703) 487-4650: Order number PB88-101977.

Dun & Bradstreet
D&B provides a variety of services for the business owner, including collection and credit-rating services. Write for their free brochure: Dun & Bradstreet Commercial Collection Division, 225 Broadway, New York, NY 10007.

The Small Business Service Bureau
A national organization for small-business owners that provides information, management advice and legislative advocacy for its members. Write 544 Main St., Worcester MA 01601.

Creditor Recovery Services
Provides business liquidation services nationwide. Call (305) 420-4991.

Garrett Group
Specializes in turnarounds for small- and mid-sized businesses of all types. 360 S. Military Trail, Deerfield Beach, Fl. 33442. Call (305) 480-8543.

Turnaround Loan Locator
A directory of lenders interested in financing or investing in financially troubled companies. Call (305) 480-8543.

INDEX

A

A&P, 135
Academy Awards, 5
Accountants, 71
Accounts receivable, 106
Advertising, 121
Affirmative action, 128
Alice in Wonderland, 43
American Society of Consulting
  Engineers, 63
Amex, 107
Anderson, Arthur, 62
Aristotle, 19
Asset-based lenders, 244-245
Assignment for the Benefit of
  Creditors (ABC), 141, 208-209,
  215
Atomize-and-Synthesize, 8
Attila the Hun, 55
Attitude, 13

B

Bad politics, 131
Baldwin-United Corporation, 132
Bankruptcy Code, 22
Bankruptcy spin, 41
Bankruptcy trustees, 63
Big Seven accounting firms, 71
Bill collectors, 146
Bloomingdale's, 59
Book stores, 6
Bootstrap business, 9
Booz-Hamilton, 62
Borrowed funds, 27
Bounced checks, 152, 288
Break-even projections, 71
Bulk sale ,221
Buried cash, 106
Business bailout, 281

Business brokers, 271
Business consultants, 66
Buyer-be deal, 278

C

C corporation, 141
Cash before the crash, 291-293
Cash-flow, 9
Cash-flow power, 256
Cash generation, 77
Certified Management Accountant
  (CMA), 72
Chamber of Commerce, 3
Chapter 7 bankruptcy, 216
Chapter 11 bankruptcy, 22, 169,
  177, 192, 195, 202-206
Chrysler, 40, 56, 127
Collection agencies, 152-153
Collection lawyer, 106
Combat fatigue, 11
Commercial Finance Association in
  New York, 107
Competitive, 25, 100
Comprehensive sale plan, 272
Computerized financial models, 95
Consumer rights, 32
Continental Airlines, 94
Contracts, 199
Corporate casualties, 20
Corporate comebacks, 91
Corporate dissolution, 283
Corporate doctors, 91
Corporate graveyards, 141
Corporate shield, 140, 282-283
Corporate transformations, 84
Corporate weddings, 266-279
Cost analysis, 71
Cost Control Consultants Corp., 122
Cost cutting, 233-234

Cram-downs, 155
Credit associations, 63
Creditors, 149
Creditor preferences, 71
Creditor-proof fortress, 139
Creditors' committee, 182
Customer channeling, 269
CVS, 31

D
Dalkon-Shield, 20
Dart Industries, 94
Debt restructuring, 155, 175
Debt shield, 143
Debt workouts, 155
De-market, 132
Distressed companies, 132
Distributorship rights, 270
Diversification, 27
Divorce, 9
Downsizing, 228
Drucker, Peter, 28, 136
Dump-buybacks, 211

E
Economic changes, 25
Edsel, 12
Embezzlement, 71
Emergency stage, 86
Empirebuilding, 254
Employee leasing, 116
Employee-stock ownership plans, 273
Employment contract, 3
Employment tax, 102
Errors, 23
Excess overhead, 33
Exemption laws, 290
Expanding, 230
Expense Reduction Analysts, 122

F
Fact finding, 92
Factoring, 245
Factoring fee, 106
Fadeouts, 221-222

Failure to change, 24
Family-owned business, 80
Faulty data, 47
Filene's, 59
Finance charges, 120
Financial controls, 29
Financial failure, 20
First Chicago Corporation, 129
Fixer-uppers, 63
Ford, 12
Foreclosure, 159-161, 196
Franchise rights, 270
Fraud, 71
Fraud claims, 289
Friendly foreclosure, 218
Friendly mortgages, 143
Future Shock, 25

G
Garment industry, 25
Garrett Group, 62
General creditors, 181
General Electric (GE), 84
George Orwell's 1984, 32
Getty Oil, 20
Goals, 1-2
Goodwill, 145
Government red tape, 32
Government regulations, 24
Grant, W.T., 132
Great Depression, 52
Growth power, 259-262

H
Harvard, 62
Hidden assets, 109

I
Iacocca, 40, 56
Idle space, 111
Implement change, 87
In Search of Excellence, 23
Initial Public Offerings (IPO), 247
Insolvency attorney, 65
Insurance waste, 119
Invested equity, 27

IRS, 37, 102, 191-193, 197-198, 286-288
ITT's Harold Geneen, 34

J
Jamestown venture, 19

K
Kissinger, Henry, 56
Knights of Columbus, 3
Kroc, Ray, 34

L
Labor unions, 127, 288
Laws of perpetual success, 262-264
Lawyers, 68
Leases, 199, 219, 269
Legal failure, 20
Legal fees, 68
Lender-liability lawsuit, 170
Levitt, Harold, 136
Liggett Drug, 31
Liquidation value, 162-164, 179
Limited liability company, 141
London, 53

M
Maber, Barry, 121
Macy's, 59
Management mentality, 8
Managerial failure, 20
Managerial snafu, 23
Manville corporation, 20
Marginal companies, 26
Market changes, 25
Marketing, 121
Mastercard, 107
McDonald's, 34
Meal tax, 102
Medicaid, 32
Medicare, 7
Middle East, 30
Money machine, 225-227
Multiple corporations, 142
Multi-pronged solutions, 22
Murphy's Law, 86

N
Napoleon, 86
Niche marketing, 230-231
Nieman Marcus, 59
Nonsense loan, 157-158
Nursing homes, 7

O
Objectives, 2
One-creditor settlements, 188-189
Organizational survey, 98
Out-of-court workout, 177, 198
Overdependence, 29
Override dollar, 149

P
Pareto's Law, 133-135
Partnership, 141, 247, 284
Partnerships, 9
Patton, George, 50
Penn Central, 39, 94, 132
Penny-ante management, 113
Pennzoil, 20
Pension plans, 110
Perks, 117
Personal liability, 2
Personally guaranteed corporate debt, 283
Peters, Tom, 23
Pipe-stack industries, 25
Pollution control, 32
Poor controls, 29
Poor location, 30
Price hikes, 232
Printing industry, 25
Product safety, 32
Professional fees, 120
Profit goals, 226, 236-238
Profit-planning tips, 235
Proprietorship, 141

R
Raw material, 24
RCA, 84
Real estate, 142
Red ink, 21

Reebok, 26
Refinance, 109
Rent concessions, 118
Rent-a-boss, 50
Revco, 31
Rite-Aid, 31
Robins, A.H., 20
Rogers, Will, 21, 56
Rolls Royce, 39, 46, 132
Room tax, 102
Roosevelt, Franklin, 52
Rose-colored glasses, 9
Rotary Club, 3

S
S corporation, 141
Sales tax, 102
San Bernandino, 15
Sears, 25
Second-chance financing, 239
Secured creditors/lenders, 156, 175
Secured obligations, 156
Security, 3
Self-confidence, 38
Self-delusion, 12
Service Corps of Retired Executives
    (SCORE), 64
Shrinkage, 114
Silicon Valley, 25, 109
Simmons Mattress, 135
Small Business Administration
    (SBA), 24, 249
Smother 'em marketing, 133
Society for the Advancement of
    Management, 63
Stanford, 62
Staying power, 93
Stifled management, 7
Stock-loan agreement, 273
Strategies, 85
Successful recoveries, 77
Sullivan, Barry, 128

T
Tactical, 23
Tax obligations, 156
Tax problems, 191-193, 286-288
Taxation, 32
Technological change, 25
Texaco, 20
Toffler, Alvin, 25
Trade credits, 27
Trade tariffs, 24
Travel and entertainment costs, 121
Tupperware, 94
Turnaround consultants, 61-62
Turnaround dealmaking, 243
Turnaround Loan Locator, 251
Turnaround Management
    Association, 63
Turnaround objectives, 83
Turnaround plans, 240
Turnaround strategies, 86
Turnaround targets, 84

U
Undercapitalization, 26
United Auto Workers, 56
Unpaid employees, 288
Unprofitable pricing, 31
Unsecured creditors, 156, 175
User-friendly company, 132

V
Variety stores, 6
Vein of gold, 93
Velcro, 25
Venture capitalists, 246, 251
Visa, 107
Vulture buyer, 274

W
Walkaways, 221-222
White knights, 62
Withholding tax, 102

Z
Zero-based management, 114

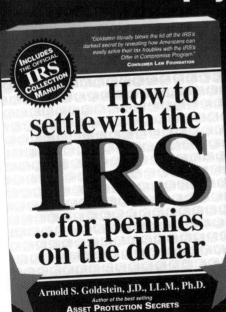